THE
WAY
OF THE
WAVES

MARTIN DOREY

THE
WAY
OF THE
WAVES

A cycling odyssey
to rediscover the soul
of European surfing

BLOOMSBURY

BLOOMSBURY SPORT
Bloomsbury Publishing Plc
50 Bedford Square, London, WC1B 3DP, UK
Bloomsbury Publishing Ireland Limited
29 Earlsfort Terrace, Dublin 2, D02 AY28, Ireland

BLOOMSBURY, BLOOMSBURY SPORT and the Diana logo are trademarks of Bloomsbury Publishing Plc

First published in Great Britain 2025

Copyright © Martin Dorey, 2025

Martin Dorey has asserted his right under the Copyright, Designs and Patents Act, 1988, to be identified as Author of this work

For legal purposes the Acknowledgements on p. 306 constitute an extension of this copyright page

All rights reserved. No part of this publication may be: i) reproduced or transmitted in any form, electronic or mechanical, including photocopying, recording or by means of any information storage or retrieval system without prior permission in writing from the publishers; or ii) used or reproduced in any way for the training, development or operation of artificial intelligence (AI) technologies, including generative AI technologies. The rights holders expressly reserve this publication from the text and data mining exception as per Article 4(3) of the Digital Single Market Directive (EU) 2019/790

Bloomsbury Publishing Plc does not have any control over, or responsibility for, any third-party websites referred to or in this book. All internet addresses given in this book were correct at the time of going to press. The author and publisher regret any inconvenience caused if addresses have changed or sites have ceased to exist, but can accept no responsibility for any such changes.

Every reasonable effort has been made to trace copyright holders of material reproduced in this book, but if any have been inadvertently overlooked the publishers would be glad to hear from them.

A catalogue record for this book is available from the British Library

Library of Congress Cataloguing-in-Publication data has been applied for

ISBN: HB: 978-1-3994-2026-6; eBook: 978-1-3994-2027-3; ePDF: 978-1-3994-2029-7

2 4 6 8 10 9 7 5 3 1

Maps by Dan Haylock Design

Typeset in Bembo Std by Deanta Global Publishing Services, Chennai, India
Printed and bound in Great Britain by Clays Ltd, Elcograf S.p.A.

To find out more about our authors and books visit www.bloomsbury.com and sign up for our newsletters

For product safety related questions contact productsafety@bloomsbury.com

For
Burt Lovejoy

&

Jeff Cherrington
Buen camino, mis amigos

With grateful thanks to the surfers who allowed me to interview them (or eluded me) for this book:

Paul Blacker, shaper, surfer, North Devon
Sam Bleakley, writer, academic, former European longboard champion, Cornwall
Jesús Busto, surfer, writer, historian, former director of the Pantín Classic, Galicia
Graeme Bunt, shaper and surfer, Cornwall
Tony Butt, big wave surfer and writer, Spain
Nick Chapman, surfer, Labenne-Océan, France
Kevin Cooke, trustee of North Devon World Surfing Reserve, Museum of British Surfing, Devon
Andrew Cotton, big wave surfer, Devon and Nazaré, Portugal
Rob Culley, first surfer to surf Tapia de Casariego, Spain
Emily Currie, Women's European longboard champion 2024, Cornwall
John Cutts, surfer and explorer, surfed Santa Marina Island in Portugal in 1968, and in Australia and Cornwall
Jesús Fiocchi, Spain's first surfer, Santander, Spain
Chris Hartop, shaper and eco-board maker, Cornwall
João Luís Moraes Rocha, one of Portugal's first surfers, Estoril, Portugal
Lee Newby, surfer and maker, Cornwall
Mike Raven, former European champion, Portugal
Neil Richardson, surfer, Australia
Craig Sage, owner of Mundaka Surf Shop, Spain
Dr Dave Sweet, surfer, Cornwall
Roger Tout, shaper and surfer, Cornwall
Pete Vickery, pioneer, Cornwall
Alex Williams, photographer, Devon
Martin Ward, surfer, Devon
Carwyn Williams, surfer, France

Contents

Prologue   x

Section 1 – France   1
Section 2 – Spain   127
Section 3 – Portugal   221

Epilogue   297
Surfing glossary   301
References   303
Resources   305
Acknowledgements   306

Prologue

4 November 2022
The Estrada Florestal, Figueira da Foz, Portugal

Lizzy climbed to the top of the observation tower. Sitting at the summit of a small, sandy ridge at the side of the road, it was the highest point for miles. Each of the tower's storeys, of which there were five, was linked to the next by a shaky aluminium ladder. The top level's metal hut had a walkway around it and reminded me of something you might expect to see above the walls of a prison camp.

The view from the top, Lizzy said, as she leaned against the guard rail and looked down at me, was amazing. On the third storey, where I was a little stuck due to my fear of heights, it was pretty good too. I leaned against the rail and looked up at Lizzy, and then out at the landscape we had found ourselves in the middle of.

As far as I could see, in every direction, was a sea of sand and scrub: undulating dunes that looked like a deep ocean swell with broad, kilometres-wide peaks and troughs. The scrub was broken up in places by a vivid green covering of semi-established strawberry bushes or the shocking greens of young pines. Where grasses and ground cover had taken hold, they swayed in the salty breeze that blew from the Atlantic we knew was somewhere to the west but couldn't see. The remains of tall burnt pines stood out like eerie black sculptures. Butterflies flitted from plant to plant.

Below us, the van sat at the side of the road, a strip of half-finished tarmac that ran almost completely straight for more than 20km and vanished either side of us. Aside from the tower and the van the landscape was empty of man-made structures. The sky was deep blue, fading to a hazy white at the edges, without a single cloud. The shadow from the tower, short and sharp in the midday sun, and the only shade for miles, wasn't much to hide in. I took pictures of the van, hoping that somehow the shots might be suitable for the cover of the book I was researching, *Take the Slow Road: Spain and Portugal*. If ever there was an image to emphasise the amount of space to be found on the west coast of Portugal, this would be it, even if otherwise the landscape might be considered barren and devoid of life.

The road, we could see (although there were no workmen anywhere), was in the process of being re-laid with tarmac, its edges frayed like a scruffy, inky-black ribbon laid on the sandy scrub. A heat haze rose from the surface, glowing and shimmering in the sunshine.

I looked to the south and noticed two figures moving slowly and smoothly towards us through the shifting light: a ghostly pair floating through an unearthly landscape. We waited to see what they would become as they approached. Lizzy climbed down from the lookout and joined me on the third storey.

The figures disappeared for a few minutes behind a trough and then reappeared at the crest of the next wave in the sandy sea. We could see that they were touring cyclists, side by side, loaded with panniers front and back, moving steadily towards us, their pedals turning in time. As they approached, we could see it was a woman and a man, possibly in their late 20s. Their tanned legs and faces, and dusty bikes and kit, gave me the impression that they had been riding for some time: weeks maybe. The watch tower might have been the first structure they had seen since they set out on the Estrada Florestal. They had probably been travelling its length for over an hour. They waved to us as they got closer, looking happy, a vision of freedom and peace. I felt envious. Travelling by van had been making me feel detached and claustrophobic of late.

We waved back.

'*Hola!*' I said as they drew level.

'Hello,' they replied together, beaming.

They put their heads down and passed us without stopping, continuing up the road and into the haze at the top of a rise to the north, setting like the sun behind a distant horizon.

'Wow,' I said to Lizzy. 'This would be a great place to cycle.'

'It would,' she replied.

'I wonder how far it is from here to Sagres.'

'No idea.'

'Would you like to do something like that?'

'Of course.'

Even though it had been many years ago, Lizzy had already cycled the length of Argentina and Norway, with extensive trips around Spain and France too, so she could and would do it. I knew that. She had cycled to Madrid to get her flight to Buenos Aires, while I, on the other hand, had, to date, only cycled the Devon Coast to Coast, overnighting on Dartmoor. Even though the idea of cycling so far terrified and excited me, I could see the appeal. The couple looked so happy; they made cycling seem simple, brave and romantic. As a hazy idea began to form, my stomach pulsed with adrenaline, as if I was about to paddle out on my surfboard into a big day of waves. I hoped my nerve would hold.

'Where would you start? Santander?' I asked Lizzy.

'Unless you flew to Porto,' she replied.

'How about Roscoff? Then you could cycle down the west coast of France too. And across northern Spain. Oh my god! Think of all the surf spots you'd pass!'

'I suppose you'd be fit by the time you got to Spain.'

'But what if you got to some remote beach break and the surf was pumping and you didn't have a board?'

'You'd rent one.'

'But there wouldn't be anyone there to rent from.'

'OK, so you'd have to find a rental place.'

'Yeah, but you're on a bike!'

'Then you wouldn't be able to surf.'

'What would be the point of cycling all that way and not being able to surf? Could you imagine getting to Mundaka and not being able to surf?'

'The point would be cycling.'

'I'm not sure I could do that.'

PROLOGUE

Lizzy knew this would be the sticking point. Cycling, or going anywhere, without the prospect of surfing, would be a problem for me. Taking time out, for me, meant surfing. Ever since I had discovered the so-called sport of kings in the 1970s, and then fallen hook, line and sinker in the mid-1980s, I had been a single-minded and selfish surfer. I had tied all holidays, and even work, to riding waves and being close to bodies of water with waves, such was its impact on my life.

I mean, let's face it, it was why we were in a van, on the west coast of Portugal, researching a book that would just happen to take us to some of Europe's surfing beaches. As it was, we were on the way to Nazaré to watch the giant waves we were sure would be breaking there in a few days' time (and calling it work).

We were following a section of the route taken by surfers since the 1970s. It was nothing new, of course, to travel Europe's Atlantic seaboard looking for surf, especially when the weather turned sour at home in the autumn: head south through France to Biarritz, across the north coast of Spain and down the west coast of Portugal to overwinter in the Canaries or Morocco. I knew lots of surfers who had done it in a van or car but wondered if anyone had done it by bike.

I considered whether or not I was capable. After 40 years of surfing, I now found myself a middle-aged surfer, and it frightened me that I might not be as able as I used to be. Injury had kept me out of the water. Fear, too, had kept me away from the kind of waves I used to relish.

But I wasn't ready to hang up my wetsuit quite yet: maybe chasing waves across Europe would help me prove to myself that my best days were not yet over.

The idea shimmered for a moment and then appeared, almost fully formed, out of the haze.

I turned to face Lizzy. She was still leaning on the handrail, her chin cupped in her hand, looking away from me, to the south, scanning the horizon.

'So we do it *with* surfboards. We set off from home and we cycle to Sagres, surfing as we go,' I suggested. 'You know, chase the waves south. We could surf whenever we liked.'

She turned and looked at me.

'How?'
'I don't know. On trailers?'
'Seriously?'
'Yes.'
'Do you know how far it is?'
'No.'
'I think you might be insane.'

Section 1
FRANCE

1
Designs and daydreams

'It was 1963. Burt Lovejoy decided he wanted to go to Biarritz. That was the place to go. He wanted someone to go with him, and I said I'd go. It was quite an adventure back then; it took us four days to get down there.'

PETE VICKERY, 2024

The idea settled in and wouldn't go away. The more I tried to forget about it, or dismiss it as a terrible, deeply flawed plan, for all kinds of reasons, the more compelling it became. Each time I took it to pieces I found I was able to put it back together again, and each time it rebuilt itself a little stronger.

We would cycle from home (Bude in Cornwall) to Cape Saint Vincent, Europe's most south-westerly point, with surfboards (somehow), to visit (and revisit) as many of Europe's surf breaks as possible. I would get my surfing mojo back* and prove that my age was no barrier to surfing and that injury was no reason to write me off. When we couldn't surf, at least we would be able to swim.

France's Atlantic coast would take us south as far as Hendaye, where we would turn to the west and cycle along the north coast of Spain, around the province of Galicia in Spain's north western corner and into Portugal. Once in Portugal we'd cycle due south

---

* I had had a crisis of confidence after paddling out into surf that was too big and on a day when I was alone. The only way back to the beach – the current was too strong – was to allow myself to get washed in. I held on to the tail of my board for floatation and endured an underwater rodeo that left me gasping for breath when I surfaced briefly between waves. I crawled up the steep stony beach, ready to kiss solid ground like the Pope landing back in Rome.

along the coast to Europe's most south-westerly point at Cape Saint Vincent and its nearby town, Sagres, Europe's last surfing enclave.

Getting home posed another problem we had to resolve. We would only have 90 days in the Schengen area so it seemed unlikely that we'd have time (or the legs) to cycle another 3000km back. Taking a train with bikes, trailers and surfboards didn't seem viable and we didn't want to fly. The only sensible solution we could think of – aside from abandoning the bikes – was beautifully simple: we persuaded our friends to take our van and drive it to meet us, wherever we ended up, hopefully Sagres. They would make their way home and we would load up the bikes, trailers and boards on to the van and drive to Santander to get the ferry home.

Cycling to Sagres would mean passing through Bilbao, Gijón, Porto and Lisbon and visiting surf breaks like Mundaka, Zarautz and Salinas. Each time I thought of it my stomach pulsed with fear and excitement.

We would also pass through the World Surfing Reserve at Ericeira, and visit Nazaré, the beach where a crew of elite surfers are continuing to push the Guinness World Record for the biggest wave ever surfed and – the mad fuckers – are actively seeking out 'the 100ft wave'.

As a surfer of 57 I knew my best days of surfing might be behind me. I could see it in the eyes of the groms (young surfers) as they paddled past me and in the way I had to work hard not to feel like a kook (a newbie who is bad at surfing). But I wasn't about to give up just yet. I had spent my life trying to live near the surf and make a living that enabled me to do so, and I couldn't imagine a time when I would stop surfing or stop wanting to surf. After 40 years of living and breathing surf, seawater ran through my veins.

Breaking my anterior cruciate ligament (ACL) 16 months before we were due to set off was a huge blow and made me fear that the worst outcome – that I wouldn't surf again – might come sooner than I imagined.

My knee was a mess. As well as breaking my ACL I had also torn my medial collateral ligament (MCL) and posterior cruciate ligament (PCL) and had damaged some of the cartilage. It happened while I was training with Bude Surf Life Saving Club on the beach and had been racing someone (who I should have been able to beat) when an unhelpful shove side-swiped me. With all my power going through my knee, it buckled at an angle it shouldn't have. I was left lying on the beach, looking up at a blue sky, in a wetsuit, howling in agony.

Luckily, I didn't have to get cut out of the wetsuit (no way was I letting that happen – it was almost new). But I was on crutches for weeks, in a knee brace for longer, and had a lot of time on ice, on the sofa, in pain and feeling very sorry for myself.

When I called the NHS consultant to ask about getting the ACL repaired, I was told by his secretary that, because of my age, they would favour 'conservative' treatment and wouldn't operate. I was furious. Screw that. How dare they write me off? Yes, I was 56, but I wasn't some overweight, middle-aged sofa surfer.

Even then, if they had agreed to fix it, the consultant told me, when I finally caught up with him, I would be on the waiting list for up to a year, with a recovery time of six to nine months at least. He shuffled me out, saying they would assess me again in three months' time.

I felt, if I wanted to surf again, that I had no choice but to pay for surgery. That was in March 2023. It was painful and difficult to deal with (and expensive) and came with lots of complications and problems: a bad back from being immobile for so long, worries about infection and deep vein thrombosis,* and not being able to do my job. I could barely walk for three months after the surgery and didn't surf for six. Recovery seemed to take forever, with lots of setbacks and visits to the physio and osteopath, although the surgeon threw me a life ring when he said that cycling was excellent for recovery. I took him at his word and doubled down on my determination. I started doing yoga, went for a few rides and made plans. The swimming pool became my psychoanalyst and personal trainer, easing my buzzing mind, calming my spasming spine and pointing the way back to surf-fitness.

In September 2023, after a summer of watching from the beach, I took a soft top† surfboard out for a paddle on a day when the surf

---

* The day we spent at Treliske A&E in Truro was fun. I had a couple of injections in my stomach, having waited for four hours, two days after the surgery.
† A surfboard that's made of soft material so it can't hurt if you fall on it. It's also very easy to use.

was clean and perfect. A wave came, I caught it and, when I was dropping down the face on my stomach, I thought, 'Fuck it, give it a go,' so scrambled to my feet. I whizzed along, in the pocket,* as if it was my first time on a green wave.† After that I was the cat that got the cream, the surfer who could glide again.

When I thought my surfing days were over (never mind the cycle to Portugal) it felt like my life had lost its purpose. Now, I thought, good sense be damned: we *would* cycle to Sagres!

As well as enabling me to put two fingers up at those who had written me off, the trip would also be a personal pilgrimage, the surfer's version of the Camino de Santiago, except we would visit beaches instead of churches, and lie prostrate on our surfboards in front of Mother Ocean rather than genuflect in front of a deity (not Rob Machado‡) in white robes and a long beard.

To British surfers the beaches of Europe have long been surfing's sanctum sanctorums. We go there to surf in warm water, on waves that are often beyond our ability, in sunny places that hum with good vibrations, cheap red wine, fun and freedom.

For me, crossing the Channel meant an escape from work and the often dreary summer weather in Cornwall. After a few disappointing summers at home I hoped, at least, that I might be able to spend some time outdoors without needing a coat.

Pilgrims have been travelling the Way of Saint James (the Camino de Santiago) to Santiago de Compostela from all over Europe for centuries. The first pilgrims travelled on the Camino Primitivo – the stretch of the Camino de Santiago that takes pilgrims from Oviedo in the north of Spain westwards to Santiago de Compostela in Galicia – in the 9th century. This was a journey of only 311km compared with the 800km distance for today's Camino del Norte – the stretch of the Camino de Santiago that goes from Hendaye in south-western France to Santiago de Compostela, largely along Spain's north coast. I reckoned our own version of the journey – a fusion of the route

---

* The point at which the wave peaks and breaks: the most powerful part of it.
† A green wave is an unbroken wave: before it breaks and turns to whitewater.
‡ Rob Machado is the nearest thing surfing has to God. He surfs like one and looks a bit like Him too, except he's white.

surfers have taken along the coasts of France, Spain and Portugal for decades with sections of the Camino del Norte and the Camino Portugués – would be at least 3000km. Oddly enough, the distance wasn't the thing that kept me awake at night.

Surfers, unlike the pilgrims of old, while enjoying the benefits of motorised transport, only began travelling down the Atlantic coast of Europe in the last half of the last century. They were more pioneer than pilgrim. As they explored the coastlines of France, Spain and Portugal throughout the 1960s and 1970s (many of them inspired by *The Endless Summer*, a popular 1966 surf documentary film about chasing the sun and surf around the planet, whose loose narrative style was the blueprint for every surfing film that came after) they discovered more and more places suitable for riding waves. Some of them, it turned out, were world-class, with waves of such perfection and power that they matched those found in Australia, California and, dare it be said, Hawaii. These became the holy of holies for surfers travelling from Britain, as well as those visiting the old continent from Australia or draft dodging from the USA, looking for space, peace and warmer water. In the beginning these breaks were whispered secrets on a new surfing frontier: travelling in Europe meant following an invisible line down the coast to Biarritz, Mundaka and beyond, guided only by word of mouth and the most meagre of intel.

It was a well-worn path by the time I finally got to Europe, in the summer of 1985, but it still had possibilities. I was a teenager and had just bought my first proper stand-up surfboard. I found an article in a surf magazine about four friends travelling in a Ford Fiesta to somewhere on the coast of Aquitaine that showed beautiful, empty, cylindrical waves, the likes of which I would doodle in class but be unable to ride.

'Why not?' I thought.

Three of us left the UK in my shagged-out VW Beetle, rescued a friend in Brittany who had been working in his uncle's pastis-at-dawn, horror-squat-toilet bar, and had the time of our lives.

When we surfed, we had no idea, going out in all kinds of conditions without any knowledge of waves or currents or how to deal with big and dangerous surf. That we didn't have to be rescued was a miracle.

I managed to stand up on my surfboard a few times but mostly ended up on my back, or on my hands and knees, in the shallows, my shorts full of sand, washed in among topless bathers. It was humiliating and demoralising, but the few moments of brilliance, when I stood tall and rode waves to the shore like a god – or so I thought – were enough. We drove back to the campsite in the evenings, after long days on the beach, transitioning slowly from kooks to cool kids as the freckles began to merge on our faces, being dragged along behind the car on skateboards, T-shirts off, gliding along the smooth, straight roads through the pine forest.

We smoked French fags, laughed a lot and got beaten up by the waves for day after glorious day. By night we partied, or hung about at the campsite, glowing with sunburn and pissed on flagons of cheap red wine. We played guitar as the cicadas sang in the pines and the waves crashed in the distance, booming like heavy traffic.

It was hot, hedonistic and, for the first time in my life, I felt truly free. When I realised that I could be someone I chose to be – instead of the person I was expected to be – I felt a rising tide of change. This introduction to the 'way of the waves' was intoxicating, delivering a dazzling promise. Everything else – college, work, life – would forever play second fiddle to surfing on my list of priorities.

By this time, I was a part of the second generation of surfers to make the trip across the Channel and down the west coast. Many of the generation before me – my surfing elders – belonged to a cohort that set off to explore the uncharted waters of Europe in the 1960s and 1970s. In North Wales, where I surfed while at polytechnic in Manchester, the guys I considered old but who were only in their 30s and 40s told us stories of waves, breakdowns and angry locals around the campfire. I listened as they repeated the names of the breaks that would become my stopping points on future adventures. In the telling, these tales took on a mythical quality.

As the idea for a long cycling and surfing trip formed and reformed, I thought back to those nostalgia-laden stories. Did a long-forgotten, golden age of surfing really exist or was it just wishful thinking? Is it still possible to find unridden waves in Europe? How does surfing now compare with then?

Would my trip ever live up to their surfing sagas or had those stories all been a load of bullshit to widen our young eyes?

I went to find the heroes of the old stories, and those like them.

Some were dead. Others, like my friends Pete Vickery, Graeme Bunt, John Cutts and Roger Tout, were very much alive. They had grown old but their memories still shone brightly in their eyes. Their tales took me back to a time in surfing when you could turn a corner and find unridden perfection. You could break bread with the locals and even settle down to a brand-new life. Their experiences, I decided, would guide me as I travelled south.

Travelling by bike would mean that we could only travel on old roads or quiet back roads, like the first generation, especially in northern Spain, where motorways have since made crossing the country a matter of a few hours instead of days.

Taking boards would mean that we would always have our essential equipment with us. And that would mean we would never miss a surf session, if there was one to have. While we could have travelled without them and hired boards at selected beaches, there was no guarantee that this would always be possible. I could not bear the thought of watching good surf without getting in the water on a board I trusted.

I also wanted to cut my carbon footprint. My preferred form of transport, which I had been espousing as at least better than flying, from a carbon point of view, I realised, was part of the problem. Being a surfer, travelling by van to find waves, wasn't helping, and didn't sit very well with my 'eco credentials'.* I had to pull up my big boy eco-trousers and admit it, then try something else.

Would a prolonged surf trip be possible by bike? I knew some people had done short trips on stretches of the French coast and in northern Spain carrying surfboards on bikes, but I hadn't found any evidence of anyone putting it all together and travelling from the UK to southern Portugal. I hoped that, if successful, our trip

---

* As a result of spending so much time at the beach and seeing plastic wash up with every tide, I became an eco-warrior, organising beach cleans, starting a global online campaign and setting up a beach-cleaning charity. Surfing, inevitably, led me to environmentalism.

might inspire others to ditch their vans or cars and try this way of surf travel.

I read an article that said, according to research published by Tobias Schultz in 2009 as part of the Surfboard Cradle-to-Grave Project, that surfers have a 50 per cent bigger carbon footprint than the average person. This is mainly due to driving (75 per cent) and flying (23 per cent), with the actual surfboard creating just 2 per cent of emissions. This is deeply ironic because it is always the surfboard and its petrochemical production that is used as the weapon to silence surfers who dare wave the green flag. The travel, however, is almost always forgotten.

The surf media published a piece about Tobias's work – how your footprint is 50 per cent bigger than the average person's – and then gave tips on how to reduce it. Some of these ideas, which included using eco surf wax or buying from companies that are using greener methods of production, were great, when part of holistic activism, but were just chipping at the edges if taken in isolation. Unless you tackle the real issue – surf travel – you can't ever hope to make enough of a difference or any meaningful change. Fiddling about with an eco-board or wearing a Yulex wetsuit is not going to counterbalance the carbon used flying to Australia. But could we bear to be confined to our local breaks, even if it might be for the greater good?

Should we simply acknowledge that giving up travelling is the one thing you cannot ask of a surfer?

Travel, after all, is one of the foundations of surfing.

Perhaps unsurprisingly, in an article about the research from his alma mater, University of California, Berkeley, Schultz later back-pedalled gently, as if he had dared to stare down the last taboo of surfing and blinked first. He is quoted as believing that 'the environmental costs of surfing might be outweighed by its social and environmental benefits' because it brought him to environmentalism. I get that – it happened to me too – but was it enough? Surfing often brings economic development but how often does that also translate into environmental protection and sustainable development?

It is interesting to note that, out of all the surfers I spoke with during this project, only one mentioned staying put. Doc Sweet, who has surfed in Tahiti, Hawaii, France and Australia, lives in

Widemouth Bay in Cornwall, so he doesn't need to get in the car to surf. As he said to me, 'We all need to be more conscious of our travel, so I stay at home and surf when it's good.'

The trouble with surfers, when it comes to environmentalism, and I include myself in this too, is that surfers can be incredibly selfish people. Waves take precedence: consequences be damned. It is spectacular cognitive dissonance. We can surf wooden boards made from sustainable materials, wear natural rubber wetsuits instead of neoprene made from cancer-causing chemicals, and invest in planet-positive clothing and accoutrements, but ask us to stay home or try travelling in a different way. Whoa?! Tough call.

Any of us can get on a plane. But just because we can, does it mean we should?

Prepping for the trip was fun. Choosing gear with as small an impact as possible, whether it was bought or made locally, made from environmentally responsible materials or just stuff we already owned was a challenge too. We bought a traditional Trangia meths-burning stove (no fossil fuels needed) and found wetsuits made from Yulex,[*] a natural rubber with a tiny impact when compared with neoprene. We avoided man-made materials wherever possible, favouring (responsibly sourced) merino for our 'technical' kit, which we had already (hence no Lycra – I am a MAMIM[†]). Panniers were bought from eBay. My friends at Rooted Ocean, a workshop in Bude, made us an insulated pannier liner out of surfboard bag material to help keep our food fresh. Plates and cutlery were from the camping box in the shed. My board, a 7-foot (2.1-metre) twin pin,[‡] was made locally by a friend out of recycled polystyrene wrapped in *Paulownia* wood, with cork rails and deck pads, and sealed with natural oil

---

[*] Yulex is a natural rubber product. It replaces neoprene, wetsuit material made using chloroprene and an oil derivative called butadiene. Neoprene usually ends up in landfill. Also, communities surrounding facilities that make chloroprene have been known to suffer very high risks of cancer.
[†] In case you didn't get the joke: middle-aged man in merino.
[‡] A twin pin is a twin-finned surfboard with a pintail. It is a modern take on the classic twin-finned boards that were standard in the late 1970s and early 1980s.

– so removing the harmful chemicals and processes from 'traditional' surfboard construction. Lizzy's board was a wooden production model, bought second-hand from a local surf shop. We chose 7ft boards to give us the best of both worlds: they were short enough to use in bigger waves and to transport on a bike and long enough to work in small or less than perfect waves.* Plus, they were good for surfers like us who aren't 64kg and 19 years old any more.

We would camp and cook as much as possible. However, I reserved the right to check into a hotel whenever we needed it, and wouldn't rule out hiring cabins or chalets if we pined for a proper bed (or needed space for a little cry) from time to time. We would have to carry everything with us that we needed, including camping kit, surfboards, wetsuits, cooking equipment, cameras, clothes, spares (spokes, brake pads, derailleur hangers and inner tubes) and any tech we might need along the way. How we would fit all of this in, exactly, I was still unsure about.

When we set off, I still had no idea if the trailers I had customised would withstand the load or the distance.

But it was also a nice puzzle to solve. I liked the idea of living with less, because I was sick of overpacking and overconsumption. Lizzy and I live in a small bungalow and don't have much compared with a lot of people, but we are still overrun with junk (some might call it possessions). Whether it's books, clothes, pictures, tools, surfboards, wetsuits, guitars or old children's toys, our house, at times, feels like it's being overrun. It was making me feel oppressed.

Travelling in a van for long periods felt the same. Just because we had the space didn't mean we had to fill it, and yet somehow everything always seemed to come with us, even though we never used it. We took snorkels, flippers, fishing rods, clothes and running shoes and rarely needed them. The flow of living easily and seamlessly seemed lost. Hence why the simplicity of surfing and cycling, without all the vapid trappings of a modern life, sounded like heaven. I wanted to find out if living with less would make me happier.

---

* In an ideal world I would have travelled with two boards: a longboard of around 9 feet (2.7 metres) for smaller waves and a shortboard of around 6 feet 4 inches (1.9 metres) for bigger waves. Taking just one 7-foot (2.1-metre) board was a compromise that I hoped would work well.

Maybe, too, cycling would give us some of the joy we had seen in the faces of those cyclists we'd encountered on the Estrada Florestal. If things went to plan, I hoped to be overwhelmed by happy chemicals: dopamine from cycling, serotonin from constant exercise and adrenaline from surfing the kind of waves that could give me a pounding.

They couldn't write me off just yet.

2

The pain and the pitfalls

'Some cyclists claim to eat hills for breakfast. I don't. I eat toast, preferably with Marmite. Or yogurt and granola if none is available, which is every day as we don't have a toaster or any Marmite.'

DIARY ENTRY: FRIDAY 24 MAY 2024

Stage 1: Day 1 | From: Tavistock | To: Roscoff | Distance: 36km

We set off from Tavistock, not our home in Bude. There was a very good reason for this. The roads between Bude and Tavistock are notoriously difficult for cyclists because there is little in the way of off-road cycling connecting them. We would have to choose between a very busy main road or tiny lanes with 3-metre-high hedgerows either side that are constantly patrolled by impatient, thundering milk lorries, fuckwit-operated* Range Rovers and teenagers in jazzed-up Citroën C1s doing 70mph. We figured this would end up being the most dangerous part of the whole trip. Tavistock, on the other hand, was the start of the Drake's Trail, a demure and very sensible, but still lovely, trail to Plymouth Hoe that crosses Dartmoor and follows the course of the Plym River through Plymbridge Woods and into Plymouth the safe way.

Our ferry, an overnight to Roscoff, left at 10 p.m. so we indulged in the fish and chippy delights of the Barbican, Plymouth's cobbled

---

* Range Rovers are just Fiat Pandas that haven't been to the gym in a while, at least in my view.

heart, before rolling past the red and white striped lighthouse on Plymouth Hoe to the port.

The crossing, aside from the fact that it was taking us over the Channel on the biggest adventure of our lives, was uneventful. We ate, slept and, in the morning, wound our way down the steps to the car deck when we were called, just like we had done many times before, except that we didn't have a van to hide in when we got there. Any lack of training or planning (of which there was plenty) would soon be revealed.

Our bikes were waiting for us, leaning up against a railing at the far end of the car deck. Packing what little we'd taken to our cabin back into the panniers, we faffed and fussed with nervous energy, as if these final moments of preparation could make it all an absolute breeze. Meanwhile, the cars, lorries and cycle tourers began to disembark.

My bike carried two rear panniers (one containing bike spares, tools, coats and waterproofs, the other containing the custom-made food bag), a two-person tent, a bar bag with my camera and cables, and two water bottles in cages on the frame. It was also towing a small trailer with a surfboard rack (a bit like a roof rack) on it. Strapped to the rack, with lockable straps, were our surfboards. Below that was a lockable aluminium strongbox (containing my laptop, a spare bike battery, sleeping bags and sleeping mats), on top of which sat a waterproof rucksack with two wetsuits and a pair of fins inside.

Lizzy's bike, which was identical to mine, carried two panniers containing her clothes and mine, plus wash kits, with a rucksack on top for bits and bobs, charging cables and cameras, a bar bag, a frame bag (for emergency sweets), water bottles and a trailer. Her trailer was the same as mine but had a bigger strongbox on it, containing our cooking equipment, bike chargers and extension leads, camping chairs, another bike battery, a spare D-lock and spare meths for cooking. Strapped to the side of the strongbox were two wooden bellyboards.

Yup. We had a lot of stuff.

As Lizzy tightened straps and checked buckles and locks, I took a selfie to mark the occasion. All smiles, a little nervous, about to set off. The articulated lorry next to us started up its engine, revved up and drove away. Its shadow gone, I realised we were alone.

Everyone else – cars, bikes, foot passengers and freight – had disembarked, so now it was only us.

'We've got to go.'

'I'm not ready,' Lizzy replied, looking down at her bags, agitated at being hurried but unaware that we were the last to disembark.

'Lizzy,' I implored.

She looked up as I flicked my kick-stand and began to swing my bike and its trailer in a big arc in the space left by the lorry.

'Oh, right!'

She buckled up her helmet, grabbed the handlebars and pushed her bike and trailer around in a semicircle to face the gaping mouth of the boat. The turn, to the right, had to be big and deliberate to avoid catching the back wheel on the trailers' towing arm.* We pushed our way across the vast, empty deck towards the bright light of the open bow, me slightly in front, smiling at the waiting crew.

I wanted to document this big moment with another picture but felt it might just have annoyed everybody. No matter how much we had tried to prepare – which wasn't much – we would never have been ready to disembark. There was just too much fretting to do. Before us lay a huge journey and the first step was to get off the ferry.

I pushed my bike into the sunshine, down the ramp and on to the quayside. I swung my leg over the saddle, stood astride the crossbar and waited for Lizzy to catch up. I could hardly believe that we were here. A year and a half ago, when we were up the observation tower, it was just a half-formed idea. Sixteen months ago, when I was having an MRI on my busted-up knee, it had seemed truly impossible. Even yesterday, when we were packing, it hadn't seemed real.

Now it was happening.

We had packed up all our stuff, crammed all our personal possessions into the loft, rented out our house, lent the car to my daughter Maggie and handed over the keys to our van to our friends Tim and Jo. We had got married just three weeks earlier with 150

---

* Left turns were OK but sharp right turns caused the back wheel to foul the trailer and could result in an instant, voluntary dismount. We soon learnt that all tight turns had to be made to the left.

family and friends, celebrating our good fortune at being surrounded by those we loved. Now we were effectively homeless and alone, in another country and about to set off on a journey, the likes of which I had never done before. Technically, it was our honeymoon too.

Fuck. Turning around and going home wasn't an option.

The next opportunity to get home would be by taking a ferry from Santander in northern Spain.

All we had to do for the next 90 days — our time allowed in Europe, thanks to Brexit — was pedal our bikes, follow the coast, pitch our tent, feed ourselves and go surfing. Would we experience the kind of freedom I had seen in the cyclists' faces in Portugal? Or would we feel weighed down by the kit we were dragging? Despite taking weeks to cut it down, I still worried we had too much.

'Shitting hell. This is really happening,' I said to myself.

We cycled down the quayside and joined a group of cyclists waiting to have their passports stamped. They all looked like bona fide riders to me, dressed in technical fabrics, lightweight high-viz jackets and cleated shoes that clicked and clacked as they shuffled forwards. I was wearing a pair of trainers, cargo shorts (my merino cycling shorts were underneath) and a puffer jacket. I felt a fraud. A middle-aged man pretending to be a cyclist. I could have been off for an afternoon spin or heading out to grab a pint of milk. The only giveaway was the caravan of stuff I was towing behind me.

I wheeled up to the booth. The customs officer looked at me, my bike, the trailer with the surfboards and asked, 'Where are you going to surf? La Torche?'*

'Portugal,' I replied.

'*Vraiment?* How long will you take?'

'Hopefully not more than 90 days.'

'Don't be more! You know the rules,† don't you?'

He looked at me over his glasses to make sure I had understood and handed me back my passport.

---

* La Torche is a famous beach in Brittany. It is the nearest reliable surf to Roscoff.
† Following Brexit, citizens of third countries — the UK — are allowed in Europe for 90 days out of 180. Overstaying risks a fine of up to €3000. Before Brexit, UK citizens had the right to work, live, love, retire and travel in Europe.

'*Oui, je sais. Merci.*'

'Have a nice trip.'

I pedalled off slowly, following some of the other cyclists up the ramp away from the port and towards a junction. Lizzy caught up with me and we dithered until I saw a sign for the Vélodyssée, the cycling route that would take us all the way to Spain, more or less, and that would be our lodestar. It would take us along the Nantes–Brest canal to Nantes, then out to the coast south of the Loire, across the Gironde estuary to Aquitaine and then through the pine forests to Lacanau, Hossegor and Biarritz.

We pedalled to the wrong side – the right side – fuck – confusing – of the road and headed south.

Less than 100 metres later, Lizzy stopped.

'We've missed a turn,' she shouted at me as I whizzed away down a cycle path that was heading somewhere I didn't want to go.

'Bloody hell.' I jammed on the brakes.

'It's this way,' Lizzy said, pointing to a tiny, overgrown lane off the main road. 'At least the Garmin says it is.'

'Really?'

We turned the bikes round and headed off down the rough path. Lizzy went first. The wheels of her trailer bumped and jumped as she dragged it down the path, panniers brushing the tall grasses on either side. Behind me the boards bucked and bounced as I followed.

I wondered what we had got ourselves into. And we were less than 500 metres from the ferry.

'Jesus, I hope it's not going to be like this all the way to Portugal.'

I tried to think about everything in the run-up to leaving, including navigation, but the only way of knowing if I had made good decisions would be to set off and see. Or at least to go on a fully laden trial run (which we didn't have time for, of course). Any weaknesses in our bodies, souls and equipment would soon show themselves.

The overgrown path widened, after a few hundred metres, into a lane, and then – joy of joys – a tarmacked back road. With no cars, it was quiet, except for the rumble of distant traffic and the chirruping of sparrows in the hedgerows, as we pedalled between granite houses and past fields of artichokes and cabbages. We arrived at a quayside with a shuttered pink granite cottage overlooking a slipway, and stopped to look across the water to a series of islands. The sea glowed petrol blue. It was the pause we needed to take stock, while scoffing our supply of emergency sweets.

The route, we could see, would take us along the coast, on to a muddy track and then into a wood of chestnut and oak. Looking at it, I figured we'd be OK. All we had to do was have faith in ourselves and the Vélodyssée.

'How's your knee?' asked Lizzy.

'Fine, I think,' I replied.

It was, although when it had grumbled a bit climbing the stairs on the ferry, I had chosen to ignore it. I didn't want to let the bad thoughts in.

We set off again, following the coast into the woods.

I didn't give much consideration to the fine art of wayfinding before setting out. I knew that we needed to follow the Vélodyssée in France, a 1300km-long waymarked route from the ferry port at Roscoff to Hendaye, a town on the Spanish border. It is a section of EuroVelo 1, the Atlantic Coast Route, a 10,000km cycle route that starts in the north of Norway and finishes in Porto in Portugal, having followed the coasts of Norway, Scotland, Ireland, Wales, Cornwall, France, Spain and Portugal.

I had downloaded all the GPX* files from the Vélodyssée website on to Komoot, a specialist cycling route-finding app, which would work on my phone and on a Garmin GPS bike computer I had bought. Working out how the Garmin, Komoot and my phone would talk to each other was a feat of navigation in itself, and I spent days downloading the files and working out if I could actually use them.

Lizzy had chosen to take the Garmin to read the Komoot files while I would use Komoot on my phone to double-check we were going the right way. It was a back-up that we had to rely on more than a few times – especially when the Garmin pointed the way 50 metres after we had already passed it.

---

* GPX files are electronic files that contain geographic location information for wayfinding.

The Vélodyssée was, as I had read, well signposted. This allowed me a certain nonchalance. But missing a sign for it less than a kilometre from the port shattered that confidence and made me realise that we would not be travelling on silky-smooth cycle paths with perfect signage. And that made me worry that it all might be a lot more difficult than we thought.

3
Preppers and picnics

'What a day of riding. Some beautiful stretches along the river into Morlaix and then a long, slow climb on the voie verte *to Scrignac, where we have conned our way into a youth hostel for the night. Just 57km today, which is not bad considering we've got the kitchen sink with us (and it's only the first day in France). Just 2943km to go.'*
INSTAGRAM POST: FRIDAY 24 MAY 2024

Stage 2: Days 2-3 | From: Roscoff | To: Rostrenen | Distance: 114km

The first proper tarmac we found after exiting the woods just outside Roscoff was a smooth, slightly downhill road that twisted and turned as it followed the course of a muddy estuary. It was divine and I prayed that there would be more like this along the way.

Until then my trailer had been grumbling and squeaking behind me, but on that silky stretch it rolled silently behind, happy enough with a steady 15–20km/h. Anything over 25km/h and it would zigzag around like a lorry about to jackknife. Remembering a video about how to pack a caravan to stop it weaving dangerously, I made a mental note to move the weight around so it sat more on the trailer arm than on the trailer wheels. Adding more 'nose weight' would allow me to go faster downhill.

I was on an absolute high as we pedalled easily along, getting to know the trailer, the bike and my new, rather expensive and highly recommended (by some) Brooks saddle. I ignored the person on

Instagram who tried to warn me off buying a Brooks, saying that riding the Coast to Coast on hers felt like being hit on the arse with a cricket bat for 225km. It was too early to tell at that point whether I would regret buying it – the only stock part I had changed on my bike – and it felt good beneath my backside, so far. I cycled along, excited, singing with happiness. I felt like nothing could stop me. Riding was magical. Everything would be OK. I was falling in love with this trip already.

The ramp leading up to the *voie verte*, a section of greenway on an old railway track that the Vélodyssée followed outside Morlaix, brought me right back down to earth. It was rough, muddy and suddenly very steep. I was in the wrong gear, which meant I ground to a halt very quickly before I could squeeze through a narrow wooden gate a few metres up the slope. I dismounted, turned the bike around – a feat on a narrow path with a trailer – and had another go, this time in 'Granny Gear One' (GG1), the easiest of the gears on my bike. I also treated myself to a little of the bike's more powerful modes, 'Purple Mode' (e-MTB), to give me a little boost. At the top of the slope, once we had reached the old railway track bed, I changed down to 'Green Mode' (Eco) and immediately felt the heavy pull of the trailer behind me as gravity snatched at it and tried to drag me back down the hill.

Something to note here, dear cycling purists, is that we rode e-bikes.

We should clear that up now. I apologise if you feel it was cheating – as so many people gleefully pointed out during the trip while happily ignoring the fact that we had still covered thousands of kilometres – but I am sure, if you decide to continue reading, you will agree it was a good decision. It certainly meant I always had something left in the tank. As it turns out, on a couple of mountains in northern Spain, I needed it. But that story of GG1 and 'Red Mode' (Turbo) will come later.

Lizzy would have preferred to set off on a traditional bike, with a stoic and unflappable countenance to take her up and over the mountains of northern Spain. I, on the other hand, veteran of multiple on-the-first-hairpin flaps and hissy fits, couldn't bear the thought of cycling that particularly hilly section of our journey without assistance (or a broom wagon,* which we'd left at home).

We went on a trial trip, from Bodmin to Penzance (no trailers, just bikes and panniers) in the autumn before we set off, to see how we got on with the e-bikes we already owned and to test my knee. My bike, a Focus 29er e-MTB I had bought in lockdown, had a 625Wh (Watt-hour) battery and a range of about 100km. Lizzy's Cannondale had a smaller battery and consequently a shorter range of about 65km. We figured that it wouldn't make a huge amount of difference because Lizzy liked to ride in Green Mode (Eco), the setting that delivers the least amount of assistance, because, being a purist, she can't bring herself to enact Red Mode (Turbo), even on the steepest hills, whereas I am of the belief that if I am given something, I should use it. Turbo (Red Mode)† was the gift that would enable me to cycle up the steepest hills as if they were mere foothills (and would allow me to ascend those terrible Spanish mountains to come).

Of course, Red Mode has a cost, which is to greatly reduce range. Still, I figured I could sneak a few miles of extra assist and still have the same battery capacity as Lizzy. Naturally I assumed my bike would die first, but it was hers that conked out on that training ride, at the bottom of a very long and steep hill leading to our campsite in Hayle. The decision to get bikes with better range was easy after that. Lizzy sold her old bike. She never liked it anyway.

On the bright side though, and ignoring the inevitable cost, it meant we could go shopping. We set about the long and difficult process of looking for e-bikes with a bigger battery capacity and longer range. That's when it started to get complicated. Lizzy's between-sizes-body also made it difficult as, on some large bikes, she couldn't put her feet on the ground when stopped, while she dwarfed some medium-sized frames. Geometry then added an extra layer of complication to the process.

---

* The Broom Wagon, or, in French *voiture balai*, is a car that follows the peloton of a cycle race and sweeps up slow riders who are unable to finish a stage within the time limit.

† Red Mode is Red Mode because it is the colour of the LED display on the handlebar when it is enacted. I liked that. Red made it feel like it was for emergency use only, and that made my sense of failure easier to bear whenever I used it.

Flipping heck, there was a dizzying choice of e-bikes, with each manufacturer offering varying ranges, battery sizes and carrying capacity. We spoke to people in all kinds of bike shops, all of whom seemed to recommend something different, and sat on a lot of bikes.

At times I thought we'd never find the answer. In the end it appeared close to home.

Leigh at our local bike shop, Ride It Cycles, rang me to say that their suppliers were doing a special offer. He suggested that instead of going for mountain bikes we should maybe consider a 750Wh touring version of the bike I already owned, but with lights, racks and mudguards already fitted. Its carrying capacity was 150kg, which was at least 15kg more than most other bikes (and would give me around 45kg for my luggage and trailer) and it was just £150 more expensive than the MTB version. It would also save having to retrofit lights, racks and mudguards.

We gritted our teeth, paid up, took delivery of the bikes in January and fell in love. Despite how I saw myself as a cyclist, I particularly liked the stand. Whatever I was, I was definitely not a bike stand kind of a chap, but after a few days of using it, I realised that it was actually a game-changer because fully laden bikes won't lean against anything without falling over, but they will stand up with a kick-stand.

With a motor to help me along, mudguards to keep my back mud-free, integrated lights to see by and a stand that meant I could leave the bike anywhere, my transformation was almost complete. The Brooks saddle – a classic that has battered the arses of generations of crusty cycling adventurers – would complete the look. Suddenly, with the help of a kick-stand, panniers and a motor, I was a sensibly attired cycle tourist. I drew the line at Lycra, however, both on fashion and environmental grounds.

Once we hit the gravel of the greenway (*voie verte*) I did my best to trundle along in Green Mode (Eco) to preserve the battery and extend the range (it delivers the minimum amount of assistance and, so they tell me, makes a heavy e-bike ride like a 'normal' bike). We had no idea what kind of distance we could expect when pulling the trailers (a result of not having conducted proper trials before we left), so we wanted to at least have the discipline to avoid using up power if we didn't need to. The first part of the trip, which we knew would be reasonably level, would also be our chance to build our fitness.

The section of the *voie verte* we were cycling began at 29 metres above sea level. Over 16km it climbed to 250 metres, at an incline of 1 per cent. While that might sound like a breeze, and it was, it was enough of a constant gradient to test my legs and ability to keep my thumb away from the power button. My joyful smile turned to gritted teeth as we slogged it out and arrived, rather pooped, at the Gîte d'étape at the Gare de Scrignac, a disused station that was now a cafe and hostel, after 57km of cycling.

The rain began to fall. We pushed the bikes to a picnic bench with a roof (a very welcome addition to the picnic experience) and put a pot of water on the stove to make tea. A quick google revealed the gite, a youth hostel, as the only place to stay within any easy cycling distance so we opted to wait until it opened after lunch (about 5 p.m. – a typically long French lunch) to find out what it entailed. I lay back on the bench, watched a green woodpecker for a few moments as it looped between trees at the side of the path, and fell asleep.

Following her luxuriously long lunch hour, the woman who ran the hostel turned up some time after the deadline. She tutted through our registration, booked us into a double room, sold us some cassoulet in a glass jar, showed us the kitchen, pointed to where we could store the bikes safely, gave us a set of keys and left for the night. Our first night under canvas could wait.

I spent the next morning worrying about my right leg, and knee, having noticed a few popping veins in the shower. For the first few miles I fixated on my new-found varicose veins (if that's what they were), my breathing and the chances of dying from a blood clot before we got to lunch. It was understandable, even if it seems laughable now. It didn't help that I am prone to bouts of health-related anxiety that one might reasonably call hypochondria.

The *voie verte* from Scrignac took us to Carhaix and then on to the Nantes–Brest canal, our home for the next 200km. The surface of the towpath was rough and, at times, badly pitted, lumpy from tree roots or just unmade and with grass growing down the middle. The canal itself was beautiful, with yellow iris marking the banks between the lush green grasses, cow parsley and meadowsweet. Every few kilometres we passed locks that raised us up like narrowboats another 3 metres higher. We passed fishermen watching floats between huge fallen trees that made the waterway un-navigable. Lock keepers' cottages, some empty, some occupied, watched over the waters. A stag party on kayaks shot down chutes into a basin below one lock.

My trailer, which had been enjoying the tarmac of the back roads, didn't like the towpath at all and rattled and bucked and leapt about like a petulant child behind me. I hoped that it would last the journey. If we had to abandon it – and the boards – it would leave us completely screwed.

Finding trailers to carry the surfboards was a conundrum that I had tried to solve more than six months before we left. I had discounted bike-mounted side racks that carry the boards along the length of the bike (like a window cleaner might carry a ladder on a Vespa) because they can be dangerous in side winds. That led me to trailers and the mind-boggling array of types available. I ordered a couple that were very cheap – and sent them straight back – settling for a slightly more expensive make that would break down easily for the journey home.

The lightweight aluminium strongboxes we lashed to the trailers were waterproof and could be locked while we surfed. This would mean we could leave the bikes unattended, knowing that at least our valuables – passports, cameras and irreplaceable bits and bobs – would be safe. The bikes could be locked to the trailers and the boxes, so creating a bloody awkward object to steal. Using lockable surfboard straps also meant that any would-be bike thief would have to grind their way through at least four locks, and padlocks on the strongboxes, to rob us. They would die of boredom before they got any loot.

The bikes were rated with a range of around 129km for a rider of my weight and height in Eco mode, which sounded like a fair amount but would mean we'd probably have to recharge our batteries every day. To give us the option of wild camping we decided it might save a lot of hassle to take spare batteries. Unfortunately, e-bike batteries are both expensive and heavy: they weighed in at a whopping 4.3kg each, making them easily the heaviest item in our luggage after the surfboards. However, having them would give us around 260km of range if we needed it. More than enough.

As we cycled along the never-ending kilometres of the towpath it seemed as if the summer was stretching out in front of us into infinity. I felt like I had skipped school and was joyfully playing truant.

We estimated we'd need to cycle around 40km a day to make it to Cape Saint Vincent, allowing for stops to surf. But there was still a nagging doubt we'd underestimated the distance. We cycled on happily, hoping for the best. All we could do was point the bike south and pedal.

At the end of the day we camped at a small campsite* run by a couple on their smallholding. We pitched our tent in a clearing at the back of their house with views over a wooded valley. Needing food, we cycled to the local town to find a restaurant. I had washed my padded cycling shorts (that I wore under my normal shorts) in the shower at the campsite so rode without them, in just my normal shorts. As I rattled down the hill into Rostrenen I discovered how hard the saddle was and how good the padded shorts were. My sitting bones felt like they had been kicked with a hobnail boot. It was an effort to sit comfortably in the crêperie, where we got tipsy and overordered.

I started to wonder which would give up first: my knee, the trailers or my backside.

---

* Camping Cyclododo: a tiny campsite on a smallholding for cyclists and walkers. Nice people, great spot, with access to showers in the owner's house. Pay as much as you feel like paying. Lovely.

4

Lone wolves and solitary saints

> '*I stand on my pedals to relieve my aching backside and rotate my neck to avoid stiffness. My legs keep turning. Every pedal gets us closer to the Atlantic. Closer to surf. Closer to the story of surfing.*'
>
> Diary entry: Monday 27 May 2024

Stage 3: Days 4–5 | From: Rostrenen | To: Roc'han | Distance: 91km

Sebastian was desperate to chat, I could tell. He tried when we arrived at the campsite at Guerlédan, a municipal site at the east end of the Lac de Guerlédan, a reservoir on the waterway, and had begun to set up. I was putting the bikes on charge at the electric point that sat between our two tents when he approached me.

'I have a five-metre cable,' Sebastian said, showing me the cable that snaked off from the socket to his tent. 'I can keep all my stuff dry when I charge it.'

'Yes,' I replied, not sure what to say, although I guess I should have recognised the signs: Sebastian was on his own.

Lizzy and I had cycled another long day, at the end of which it had started to piss down. We were wet and cold and I just wanted to set up, get warm and eat. The last 63km of the towpath had been rough but quiet. We passed a few cyclists as we pedalled, offering a jolly '*Bonjour*' to everyone. Not all of them reciprocated, which I found odd.

We failed to find anything to eat in the quiet but pretty village of Gouarec, as it was Sunday and everything was closed, so pushed on towards Mûr-de-Bretagne. Outside Gouarec, the towpath ended abruptly at a basin and a set of locks where the canal opened out on to the Lac de Guerlédan.

Traffic was backed up trying to cross the single-track bridge that led to the Abbey de Bon-Repos, a blank-windowed ruin in creamy grey stone at the side of the lake. A re-enactment day was taking place, with horsedrawn carts pulled by clip-clopping ponies not helping the traffic situation. A monk and a maiden walked past us, holding hands and, rather incongruously, an umbrella. We sheltered under a tree at the side of the road and watched. After not seeing anything other than towpath and the odd cyclist for the last few hours this was a strange spectacle to be plunged into.

We waited until the rain eased and then forced our way into the traffic to cross the bridge. I stopped at a signpost for the Vélodyssée that pointed to our destination, Sagres, 2470km away. This, I knew, was the short way, as the EuroVelo 1, of which the Vélodyssée is a part, heads south across Spain to Pamplona and then Salamanca after crossing the border at Irun. We would be going along the coast the whole way (we hoped), which would add a lot more distance. If ever there was a moment of realisation, this was it.

The route took us over the bridge, away from the abbey and on to a quiet, muddy track through woods and around the lake to Mûr-de-Bretagne, where we checked into Camping Le Point De Vue. We were assigned a space in the cyclists' area rather than a pitch, which was what brought us into contact with Sebastian. Despite being the only tented campers on the huge site, we had no choice but to pitch near enough to the electricity point, and Sebastian.

Once the tent was up the rain eased and the sun began to pierce the thin, pink evening clouds, so we wandered down to the lake for the first swim of the trip. Lizzy slipped into the cold, whisky-coloured water like a selkie returning home. I was more hesitant, as always, about diving into a large body of water, because I was without a crutch – a surfboard and wetsuit – to keep my mind above the waterline. Having been gaslit by public information films of the 1970s, it has taken a long time for me to be able to swim comfortably in deep water.

Lizzy swam far out into the lake, confident in her ability to self-rescue.* I crawled out 50 metres, trod water for a few moments and then sprinted back to shore as if my toes had been tickled by unknown forces.

'I hope you don't mind drum and bass,' Sebastian said once we had started cooking our dinner back at the site.

'Oh no, it's fine. Music is good,' I lied, craving peace and quiet.

That was the cue Sebastian needed to begin a conversation that would go on for some time.

He was tall and quite stocky, with wild dark hair and a beard, wearing jogging bottoms and a sweatshirt in black. He looked a bit feral, like he'd been on the road for a while. We found out very quickly that he was German, had given up his job in IT a few months earlier and was intending to cycle for a couple of years. He was three months into it.

Getting out from behind his desk, he said, was making him feel so much better: after a month his back ache had gone away. He was feeling much fitter and more positive as a result. This was good news to me and made me think that cycling might well be able to help me as much as it had helped him. I too had been struggling with a bad back, a product of sitting at a desk and on the sofa recovering from my operation. Sebastian's miracle cycling cure – obvious though it may sound – gave me a great deal of hope.

Everything, I thought, will be better when I get back on the bike.

Sebastian was cycling alone, although at this time he wasn't cycling because his bike, a bespoke build, with a Rohloff gearing hub, had broken. To fix it he needed a specialist part to be sent from Germany, so he had no choice but to stay on this campsite until it arrived. It had been five days so far and he wasn't sure how much longer it would be. He seemed upbeat. I didn't want to imagine being in the same position, with the Brexit clock ticking away for us. It made no difference to Sebastian. Time had taken on a new meaning, it seemed, since he had given up his high-pressure desk job. He spent

---

* When it comes to cold water immersion, in my experience it is always the men who stand at the side of the sea pool or on the beach, holding towels and offering unwanted advice while the women just get on with it.

his days editing content for his YouTube channel, playing about with Insta360 cameras and GoPros and listening to drum and bass.

I liked him. He was both cheerful and sombre but had a nice way about him, a kind of jolly, stoic countenance you might associate with tubby, to-the-point Germans, if you were allowing clichés to describe people. Getting talking was awkward, but once he started, he had plenty to say. His observations about his own travels and what it was doing for him would stay with me. Whenever my back hurt, I thought of Sebastian.

The Nantes–Brest canal would prove to be a gathering place for lone wolves. Placed in proximity by campsite owners hoping for better-paying campers and motorhomes to occupy the choice pitches, we often opened our hearts and ears as strangers let the tide of experience flood out of them. Even though we had been on the road for just 240km, and had a long way to go, we already felt a part of this community.

We pitched up at the municipal campsite in Roc'han (the Breton spelling for Rohan) the following day (49km – a short day of rain and cloud) and were given a spot right by the canal, adjacent to a guy travelling on his own with a trailer but just a little too far away to strike up a conversation. We said hello and got on with our evening prep. Another chap arrived and set himself up between us. He introduced himself as John. He was American. He reminded me of the nerdy character, Eugene, in the film *Grease*, who is well-meaning but constantly bullied. He was aged about 60, polite, a little overexuberant and very friendly and open, as all Americans can be, but, once he got talking, wouldn't stop. His accent, a nasal East Coast whine, together with a nervous tic that would see him lifting one shoulder constantly while bobbing his head towards it, made me think he'd spent his entire life being the underdog.

Eugene had almost completed the Vélodyssée, travelling from south to north from the Spanish border. He had also completed the Camino del Norte backwards from Santiago, and the Camino Portugués from Porto. He had lots of information to impart to us. Some of it was a bit suspect, like 'northern Spain is flat', but it was, overall, useful. His atrocious pronunciation of French and Spanish place names made us think of him when we reached them in the following days and months and his pronunciation of Vélodyssée – *Vay-low-dee-say* – stayed with us for the rest of the journey. Nantes, which is pronounced *Nont* in France, was butchered by Eugene, coming out as *Nan-tez*.

But I came to realise that Eugene was a saint, sent to share his gentle tips of the route ahead. He was, undeniably, neurodiverse. We suspected Sebastian was too. I wondered if there was something about cycling that quietens the busy mind, providing enough stimulation to soothe the mind without overwhelming. You could be invisible but still out in the world, with no past or future, just the road in front of you, living in the moment. Lizzy, who also has ADHD tendencies, could relate. Cycling, she says, gives her enough to look at, listen to and think about to be engaged without being overloaded, while the exercise gives her a steady supply of dopamine.

We listened as Eugene talked while we put up the tent, unpacked, cooked our dinner and sat down to eat it. He seemed oblivious to what we were doing while he talked, and didn't offer to leave us be or let us get on without interruption. We didn't mind. He was fun to chat with.

When we told Eugene about our plans he was wildly excited.

'Oh wow!' he said. 'Maybe I should play some Beach Boys music for you, like the soundtrack of your trip.'

I smiled, allowing the cliché to wash over me. As a surfer I was used to this. Non-surfers (and the media in general) find it easy to understand surfing if it has the 'California sound' of Jan and Dean, Dick Dale and The Beach Boys, playing over it.

'I have met a lot of people doing crazy stuff,' he continued. 'You guys are included in that. Cycling through France, surfing your way down the coast. That is cool!' he whined.

I appreciated Eugene's words. In fact they meant the world to me. I grew up in a stuffy town in the Stockbroker Belt and surfing had provided me with a neat way to be different, giving me a niche – and one that was beyond reproach – when all I saw around me was acquiescence to money and status. Surfing offered a kind of anti-status.

And speaking to first-generation surfers had made me realise my story wasn't so different. Surfing often offered a way out of a miserable existence.

Despite my landlocked upbringing, surfing hit me like a board in the face when I first saw it in real life. I was about seven. Watching someone surfing – I can still see it now – moved me in such a way that I gave up my holiday money in one go, therefore forsaking a week's worth of Fabs and Zooms, to buy a cheap polystyrene bodyboard.

My parents took our family on holiday to Bantham in the South Hams of Devon regularly in the 1970s. We often went with family friends because they provided my mother with a line of defence against my father: in company he was a riot; behind closed doors he was more of a rampage. With its tall hedges of pulsating glowworms, thatched cobb cottages and golf courses, the South Hams was the kind of genteel, peaceful place Mum aspired to.

My dad was a salesman and travelled a lot, often spending six months at a time in Africa, making him estranged and distant. He was booted out eventually but, for this trip, in 1974, he was still the big dog of the family: deeply conservative, with ethics to match and a temper to back it up. He was rugby, the forces, tennis club. Fun to the outside world. Always smart. Regularly disappointed by the shortcomings of his children.

One afternoon at the beginning of the holiday, as the tide was on the way in, I was building drippy sandcastles after a swim. I was sunburnt and my skin prickled as it tightened from the drying salt. My curly hair, usually tamed by the unrelenting comb of suffocating orthodoxy, had taken a rare opportunity to go wild. That day my hair was more smash and grab than Stockbroker Belt. The beach made it irrepressible, even though I was, as always, keeping a low profile, my exuberance in check. A slap could never be too far away.

The dropping sun had cast a golden light on the beach, making the shadows long and the dunes glow as if on fire. The sea sparkled like a sequined flag. Across the curve of the bay, Burgh Island's art deco hotel sat on its green hillock, marooned by the incoming tide, a white box with a pointed copper turret facing inland towards the bay.

I looked up from my sandcastle building and gazed across the water. Between me and the Island, waves were breaking out to sea, arriving at the beach in neat, convex lines. A figure sat on a surfboard beyond the broken waves, looking outwards towards the sun and the horizon. A wave, bigger than the others, approached. The surfer spun the board round and started to paddle for the shore. The wave rose from the depths, picking up the surfer and throwing him forwards. In a split-second he stood up on the board and began to ride the wave as it broke behind him.

I watched, open-mouthed, as the surfer, black against the golden sea, rode the wave towards me, his gilded board, gliding across the wave face, sending arcs of glittering spray into the air. I was spellbound. This was easily the greatest thing I had ever seen. It seemed so otherworldly and strange, so exotic and unattainable, and so far removed from the stuffy world I knew where I had to watch my step and do what I was told. It was, I was sure, better than tearing around the bomb craters in the wood near my house on my bike. Better than showing off to get attention. Better than home.

There, on the beach, where it was sunny and warm, where my hair could be wild without reproach and my skin could prickle with the salt and the sun, that golden surfer, riding a golden swell, looked like freedom and happiness.

At the end of the day I saw a polystyrene bodyboard for sale outside a shop. I whined and begged and, finally, persuaded my mother that I would be perfectly able to go without ice creams and drinks for the week if I spent all my holiday money – £5 – on the surfboard. In the morning, I gladly handed over my fiver and walked away from the shop with the board under my arm, down to the beach, to catch my first waves. I was hooked.

In those moments, like most moments while surfing, nothing else mattered. No amount of 99s could give me the same buzz that riding my surfboard could, despite the cold water, the cut feet, the wrinkled fingers and the sunburnt shoulders.

I was a surfer now. Everything else in my life – sensible shoes, uniforms, following in my father's footsteps – could fuck off. My life would never be the same again.

These days I am not a great surfer, and probably never was. I am average: not a beginner by a long way, and probably not even an intermediate any more, although sometimes I feel that way when things don't go right or when I get scared (something that has happened more as I have got older). That's surfing. You can't ever hope for any more than nature's compliance and its occasional mellow willingness to allow you to ride its shock waves. To think that you will conquer it is foolish. You might feel that you are able to equal nature's wildest swells because some days you can ride them, but nature will always win.

I am a surfer, like the majority of surfers who have been surfing for a reasonable amount of time (50 years if you count 1974 as the start), with average natural ability, who is competent enough in the ocean when the conditions are right. I can catch waves. I can trim.[*] I can do a bottom turn[†] and hit the lip.[‡] I can cut back.[§]

As you can see, I can also use surf lingo.

Don't be put off. Surfing jargon is an important part of the surfing experience, as it is in any sport. It can seem like a whole new language – and it is – but it's only there to describe equipment, sensations, situations and conditions associated with the act of wave riding. It's a bit like Inuits having lots of words for snow.

Surf jargon, in short, allows surfers to describe their sport and culture quickly and easily. It isn't designed to keep outsiders away, although it can be used, like all jargon, as a weapon against those who don't belong. Surf jargon can sound ridiculous – because of the way it has been used, and sometimes mocked, by the media – but, and this is important, there is truth to it.

My surfing ability, if I was pushed, and if I was surfing the kind of waves that would give me the chance, might allow me to manage a passable tube ride,[¶] or at least a cover up.[**] However, I can still talk myself out of a good surf because of the fear of getting worked[††] on the paddle out even though, with 50 years of experience, I should be able to manage it, apart from at the most serious beaches.

Even though I might never reach the peak of surfing the world's most difficult waves without drowning, and lack the ambition to do

---

[*] Trimming is riding along the unbroken part of a wave perpendicular to the shore.
[†] A bottom turn is a turn done at the bottom of a wave in order to change direction and move up it again. It is one of the most fundamental moves in surfing.
[‡] Hitting the lip is the act of allowing the bottom of a surfboard to hit the cresting part of a wave to use its intense power to bring the board around and to 'drop in' to the wave again.
[§] Cutting back is a manoeuvre to turn back towards the 'pocket' of a wave (the breaking part) to stop the surfer from outrunning the most powerful part of the wave.
[¶] Surfing in the hollowest part of the wave that creates a tube.
[**] Where the tubing part of the wave breaks over a surfer for a brief second.
[††] Beaten up by the force of the waves.

so, I have still devoted most of my adult life to surfing, living near the surf, or finding places to go surfing. Since I found it (or it found me) every decision I have made has been skewed by surf, except for the few times when I had to put it aside, temporarily, because I was injured, or so skint I could think of nothing but getting myself out of a hole. Even then I would look for slivers of silvery salvation between the dark clouds – a swim, bodysurf or bellyboard – to brighten my existence. Water always helped.

While I have never resorted to scams or drug running that some surfers have become famous for, everything has been about being able to live the life I want and the way I want it. Sure, there have been compromises, and I have had to chase my living in ways I might not have hoped for, but at least I have remained true. Many others do the same. They might not be ready to hollow out a board and stuff it full of heroin* to make enough to live in the tropics for six months, but they are prepared to accept that living by the sea will cost them money, opportunities and the kind of trappings many others think are what life is about.

That's the power of this thing. It's more than just a pastime, sport or even a manufactured lifestyle. It's a way of thinking that, once it grips you, will not let go. It becomes a purpose, with everything else secondary. And it doesn't take a brilliant or elite surfer to follow that star.

The polystyrene bodyboard I had spent all my money on in Bantham in the early 1970s languished in the utility room and was, inevitably, replaced in my affection by a skateboard in 1976. That was the year that 'The Craze' came to Britain after its difficult birth in California as 'sidewalk surfing'. The skateboard was surfing's bastard offspring,† but had grown up and now had polyurethane wheels that rolled smoothly, unlike the steel rattlers from skateboarding's first iteration, stolen from a pair of roller skates.

---

* This is not a cliché. It did happen and it happened a lot. Some of the biggest deals in the surfing industry have been financed by drug running. And yet, in some kind of dissonant logic, stuffing surfboards with drugs has become romanticised to the point where surfers who did this have become folk heroes when really all they were doing was dealing in drugs.
† Surfing has produced many offspring: skateboarding, windsurfing, kitesurfing, wakeboarding, snowboarding, stand-up paddleboarding and foil surfing. They all originate from surfing waves.

My parents, in typical reactionary middle-class fashion, had refused to buy me a skateboard because they had been radicalised by the hysterical fearmongering that accompanied the craze. They said it was because I might get hurt, but I think it was because my dad, a terrible snob, believed skateboarding was common.

I paid £8 for my first skateboard and rode it up and down my road – a landlocked surfer – until the local council passed a bylaw banning skateboarding from the streets. Skateboards were loud, brash and fun, something Amersham appeared to have an issue with. With the streets off limits, I had to join a local skateboard club if I wanted to skate, although I found it deeply intimidating. Its classlessness made going feel eclectic and edgy. I put my head down and practised until I could ride the tiny plywood quarter pipe.

Sadly, as with all good crazes, mainstream interest in skateboarding fizzled out, and by 1980 it was dead. Whenever I went skateboarding after that it was purposefully ironic, although, deep down, it wasn't. I still loved it and didn't care that I was spectacularly off-trend. Standing on a board and flying down a hill, especially a smooth one, was nothing short of heavenly. I guess you would call it the glide in surfing terms – a state of perfect trim and balance.

Skateboarding enjoyed a renaissance in the USA in the early 1980s as the Ollie, a move invented in the late 1970s, turned every piece of street furniture into a skatepark and enabled vertical skateboarding – on ramps and half-pipes – to take to the air.

VHS videos – the new media of the day – of this new style of skating drifted over from the USA. One I watched included a section about surfing. Having moved on, surfing had become the domain of hardcore locals, off-the-map travellers, outsiders and mavericks, and caught my attention again. I could see a direct line between the thrills I experienced while rushing down long, smooth hills on my skateboard and the freedom I had felt while riding waves on my belly at Bantham. Surfing had everything: it was classic counterculture, providing a neat way to stick two fingers up at authority. Plus, it was, compared with my home counties upbringing, cool as fuck.

I obsessed over learning to surf. If only I didn't live 370km from the waves.

THE WAY OF THE WAVES

In the summer of 1985, straight after the last of my A-level exams, a group of us rented a house a short drive from Bantham.* Still convinced that surfing would save me from mediocrity and cement my status as a maverick and glorious dreamer, I bought a proper, stand-up surfboard, a 6ft (1.8 metre) popout† from Windjammer in Braunton in north Devon (it was the only one I could afford).

I borrowed a wetsuit, drove to the beach and set about learning to surf. Of course, I had had no lessons and had no idea what I was doing. I foundered in the shallows, unable to progress past the whitewater, unable to judge the conditions or to determine my place in the pecking order of the beach.

I was a disaster, a kook of the highest order. In the way, out of my depth. I was the kind of person that real surfers would have dreaded seeing walking down the beach. I was JOJ, FOB. Just off the jet. Fresh off the boat. But what did I care? I was blissfully ignorant.

There were moments when I stood up. They didn't last long but they were enough to stop me from giving up. I felt, for the briefest time, a flash of joy, the weightlessness, the thrill of riding a wave of energy that was created far out in the Atlantic. I looked down at the water in front of my board as the wave pushed me towards the beach. It was like looking down at my skateboard as I cruised down a hill of smooth, flowing tarmac. The white lines flashing past, weightless, floating, soaring. The glide.

This was my first, brief taste of something surfers call stoke, an emotional and physical high from riding waves. Senses, overloaded with stimuli, are screaming with intensity. The sounds of the booming waves and rushing water. The taste of the salt on the wind. The concentrated, narrowed vision, the sunlight, the reflections. The feel of the water in my hair and eyes, the board under my feet and the way I was cruising over the sea, flying towards the shore. The smell of the beach, seaweed, ozone, sun cream, algae, the ocean. It was a heady, intoxicating mixture, a linctus for my soul. I was truly in the moment, tipsy on wave riding, in love.

---

* Yes, I know. This reeks of privilege.
† Popouts were mould-made boards with plastic skins. They were cheaper than 'custom-made' surfboards, as they could be mass produced. They were lumpy and not very refined shapes.

Dopamine stacked and exhausted, I came in and collapsed on the sand. I was buzzing. They call the benefits of being by the ocean 'blue therapy' these days, but I knew nothing of that. I just thought it was fucking amazing. My feet hurt and my arms ached and my eyes were stinging with salt. I was breathless and cold. But screw that. I was a surfer, taking my first baby steps towards the 'way of the waves'. Nothing could compare and nothing else mattered.

Back at the campsite, I said thank you to Eugene for what I saw as a great compliment, especially coming from someone I saw as a fearless traveller. He had seen me (or a version of me I would like people to see) and I was grateful for it.

He eventually disappeared into a tiny bivvy bag at about 9 p.m. when he had run out of chat, but not until he had gifted us an introduction to Buen Camino de Santiago, an app for people travelling the Camino that would save us a lot of bother once we got to Spain.

The next morning he was gone by the time we had woken. We missed him.

I thought of him often in the months to follow, but mostly, to my shame, recalling his terrible pronunciation of European place names as we cycled through them. Wheeling past difficult-to-pronounce places I would mimic his accent and imagine how he might pronounce it. All to an imaginary soundtrack of The Beach Boys classics.

Destination *Beee-ar-ayetz*.

5

Wood is good

'There is nothing like a tarte aux fraises to keep me motivated. We bought one in Josselin, a place I had been dreaming about reaching. I imagined riding past the pointed turrets of the castle. Today it was wet and grey and the only colour was the tarts in the window of the boulangerie. So we had them.'

INSTAGRAM POST: TUESDAY 28 MAY 2024

Stage 4: Days 6-8 | From: Roc'han | To: Nantes | Distance: 198km

The seats in Paul and Jackie's motorhome were plush and soft, the nearest things to armchairs we had sat in since disembarking at Roscoff.

Paul and Jackie were on their way home from a tour of the Loire when they messaged. Would we like to meet up at a campsite near the canal? Of course we would! It had rained on us all night at Rostrenen, it was raining when we pulled into Josselin looking for a cup of coffee under the Disney-turreted castle (it was lunchtime, no coffee, only a *boulangerie*), and it spotted with rain during our picnic lunch on a bench at the side of the canal in Redon. It was still raining when we strolled across the sodden grass at the campsite to Paul and Jackie's van too. Despite having been away for just over a week I was ready for pampering, even though I wasn't unhappy. I knew the rain would stop at some point; it was just a question of how wet everything would be when it did.

The soothing comfort of the van's captain seats, swivelled around to make space for four people at the table, made my backside feel like it had won some kind of heavenly lottery. I had been diligent with the chamois cream* since day one, applying it liberally each morning, so I wasn't sore or chafed, just a bit bruised. It was a delight to sit on something other than a hard leather saddle and be offered nibbles – equally as welcome as I imagine a night in a hostel or even just a clean set of clothes might have been to those setting off for Santiago in the 8th century.

We'd had a few good days and seeing our friends, so far from home, was absolutely wonderful, helped enormously by the comfy seats and a cupboard full of the kind of snacks we just couldn't carry. We had covered 358km since leaving Tavistock for Plymouth to catch the ferry.

The food that Paul and Jackie served us, and the shelter they offered, were most welcome. They pretended not to notice our greed when we stuffed our faces with olives and crisps before the main course. It was as close to saintliness as it was possible to get without a halo.

Back on the canal the next day, like all the other days on the canal, our bikes and trailers – and their unlikely cargo – didn't go unnoticed. Whenever we stopped, people would ask us about the surfboards or the trailers or where we were going. Sometimes we heard people exclaim '*Mon Dieu!*' as we rode by. A surprised '*Ooh la la!*' was my favourite, coming from an old lady sitting on a bench with her partner as we gave them a cheery '*bonjour!*' when we passed. I enjoyed being a novelty and soon came to think of the boards and trailer as an extension of my personality. When I was off the bike, for some reason, I felt like a part of me was missing. When I was with the bike, I felt I cut an easily recognisable figure: I was every inch the international long-distance surf cyclist, an imaginary niche I had carved for myself.

While we were waiting for a swing bridge to open to let a boat go by in Rostrenen, a portly bespectacled man in his 60s got out of his car and approached me. He had black wavy hair that looked

---

* Cream for the chamois, or the inside part of the cycling shorts, often made from chamois, where festering sores can attack the unprepared cyclist. Also known as 'udder cream' or 'arse cream'.

like it had been plonked on his head in a hurry and wore a holey Breton sweater. He rapped on the boards with his knuckles and declared '*C'est du bois!*' He then asked me if I was going to use the board on the canal, or perhaps on the tidal bore that rumbles up the Gironde estuary on big spring tides. 'Ha ha,' I said. He was, he told me, a restorer of antique wooden boats with a boatyard in the town. I explained how the board was made and he nodded in approval.

I was pleased that he had noticed. I wanted to ride a wooden board because of its environmental credentials. Unlike the 'traditional' materials used to make surfboards since the late 1950s, such as foam, fibreglass and polyester resin, wood has little or no environmental impact other than its transport and working. The *Paulownia* trees, like those used to make my board, can grow up to 1.8 metres (6ft) in a year and mature in just 10 years. They, like the cork used for the deck pad and rails, are a renewable resource. *Paulownia*, in particular, has a great strength-to-weight ratio, which makes it good for surfboard making.

Chris Hartop of Bandwagon Surfboards, a mad, bare-footed hippy-punk-scientist and maker of dreamy and experimental shapes, finished the board using natural oils, which means there were no harmful chemicals or fossil fuels used in its construction other than to make the electricity used to plane and sand it.

He had explained to me:

> The traditional surfboard industry is incredibly toxic and it really did my health in. I ended up with lung problems, respiratory problems. I developed oxy sensitisation, which is relatively common, but it means as soon as I'm near the dust, my neck swells up, I have a rash everywhere, I can't breathe. When the bottle says 'Can cause long-term genetic defects', you sort of know you're on to a wrong 'un. Whereas this [he tapped the deck of my board] is just wood shavings.

The benefits were twofold. First, I got to have a wooden surfboard that surfed brilliantly, turned heads and helped us to spread our message. Second, it meant that Chris wouldn't suffer from the long-term effects of using resin and glass.* It was question of survival: if he continued to use 'traditional' materials, he said, it could kill him. Fair enough. I was happy enough to support him in his death-avoidance business model.

While this 'eco' technology – using natural materials – might appear to be new to surfing, it isn't. If anything, using sustainable materials is going right back to surfing's roots with Hawaiian kings and Peruvian fishermen.

Surfing, every surf historian will tell you,† originated in Polynesia, with its spiritual home being Hawaii. Surfing was an important part of Hawaiian culture and society: a reflection of their mastery of navigation. They had, after all, migrated from South East Asia to the islands of the Pacific, from Hawaii in the north to New Zealand in the south, using the kind of ocean-going knowledge European sailors like Captain Cook could only dream of.

Everyone surfed in Hawaii, from children and commoners to kings and queens, making it a thread of egalitarianism that coursed through the veins of the whole community. However, as with all hierarchical societies, some were more equal than others and had access to all the better stuff, including wood and surf spots. If you were king then you got the best boards and surfed the best waves. This was part of the laws of Hawaii, the *kapu*, that governed all of society, including surfing.

The nobility got to ride on the biggest boards, known as *olos*, that were made from the lightweight wood of the wiliwili tree, the Hawaiian coral tree, and could be as long as 20 feet (6 metres). Wiliwili, an indigenous hardwood, grows at elevations over 460 metres (1500ft) in dry forest. It was also used to make canoes, while the flowers were used to make leis and in medicine.

The paipo board, at the other end of the scale, was the smallest type of surfboard, anywhere between 3 and 6 feet (0.9 and 1.8 metres)

---

* Polyester resin can cause burns, skin irritations, allergic reactions and has been suspected of affecting unborn children.
† If you are going to read about surf history, read Matt Warshaw's columns or his book, *The History of Surfing*. Matt is a former pro surfer and editor at *Surfer* magazine.

long. It could be made from koa, Hawaii's largest indigenous tree, often found in mesic (damp) forests, or ulu (the breadfruit tree), and were ridden, often prone, by children.

The alaia was your average and everyman board. It had a rounded nose, a square tail and was anywhere between 6 and 12 feet (1.8 and 3.6 metres) long. These too were made from the wood of the koa tree, although they could also be made from ulu. Koa wood was also used to make canoes, spears and ukeleles. Today, it is one of the world's most valuable hardwoods and is heavily protected.

Boards were made from entire trunks, ritually cut down (with sacrifices made to the tree) and carved then treated with oil. They were venerated by those who made them and blessed before being taken to the waves.

Surfing in Hawaii was important in a society that had transcended mere survival. It was ritual, competition and rite of passage, and may also have played a part in matchmaking and romance. While its origins were a part of industry – catching waves in canoes to get back to shore after fishing trips – there was no functional purpose to it (other than deciding who you might need to fight or fuck), unlike in Peru, where it was intrinsically linked with survival.

Peruvian fishermen rode 'tups' or *caballito de totora*,* as the Spanish called them, which were rafts made from bullrushes (*totora*) with turned-up noses. They were designed to be used in surf (sometimes with a paddle), prone or kneeling, to allow the fishermen to reach the calm zone beyond the breakers. The 'tups' then allowed the fishermen to catch waves and ride them to shore safely, with the turned-up noses stopping them from pearling (when the nose of a board sinks below the surface of the water and throws the rider off like a bucking horse). *Caballitos* are still in use today in parts of Peru, meaning they may have been used continuously for as many as 3000 years, maybe longer, although, under normal use, the boards themselves disintegrated in a few weeks.

Some academics have argued that native South Americans had been capable of migrating to Polynesia but DNA testing has proven that the Hawaiians (and Polynesians who arrived in Hawaii) came from South

---

* This roughly translates as 'little horses made from rushes'.

East Asia. This means the Peruvians were isolated in their surfing, making Hawaii the cradle of modern surfboard riding. It was certainly Hawaii that inspired the Americans and Australians, spreading the word around the world, but not before the pursed lips of the 19th-century missionaries did their best to wipe it out completely.

White Europeans crashed headlong into surfing in the 18th century, with Captain Cook witnessing board surfing and surfing in canoes in Hawaii and Tahiti in the 1770s. Later, a wave of European and American missionaries, who had a problem with the promiscuity and nudity associated with surfing, made it their business to convert the 'Godless' islanders to Christianity, seeing surfing as part of Hawaiian culture that should be repressed in favour of 'proper' worship.

So surfing all but died out in Hawaii – at least in the areas where the missionaries were active – until the late 19th century when locals started to ride the waves at Waikiki, mainly for pleasure but also for tourists who had discovered Hawaii as a holiday destination.

George Freeth, an Irish Hawaiian, was one of those who began surfing in 1900 on a wooden board that was gifted to him by his uncle. He was invited to the USA in 1907 to demonstrate surfing at the opening of a railroad from Los Angeles to Redondo Beach, staying on to work as a lifeguard and being much lauded and decorated for his bravery. He was the one who kicked off California's love of surfing.

Back in Waikiki, a group of young watermen and surfers, including a local family, the Kahanamoku brothers, were employed by hotel owners to entertain tourists by taking them surfing, paddling them in outrigger canoes or playing ukeleles around beach fires at night. These 'beach boys' embodied the 'spirit of Aloha' in Hawaii and, to some extent, as musicians, watermen and ambassadors, gave us the blueprint for surf culture: a hedonistic lifestyle under the sun, surfing, swimming, having fun.

The eldest of the Kahanamoku brothers, Duke, became an excellent surfer and swimmer and, in 1912 was selected to swim for the USA at the Olympics in Sweden. He won gold in the 100 metres freestyle and, in doing so, became a national hero. He toured the USA, surfing in California and introducing surfing to the East Coast. In 1915 he visited Australia for a swimming demo and toured Sydney's beaches before deciding to give another demo – this time surfboard riding – at Freshwater, a beach suburb. Duke made himself a board from local sugar pine for the demonstration, wowing the crowd and leaving the board with a local boy, Claude West, who went on to make more boards himself and helped to push the development of surfing in Oz.

The next important stage in the development of surfboards – and one that would make surfing more accessible – was the development of the hollow wooden surfboard.

This was down to a lonesome wanderer by the name of Tom Blake. He travelled to Hawaii in 1924, aged 22, and fell in love with surfing. Back home in California he set about trying to make a board that was lighter than the solid slabs of wood he had been riding. He drilled hundreds of holes in a 16-foot (4.9-metre) lump of redwood and then laminated it with a thin veneer. This board was substantially lighter than any other board available at the time and enabled him to win paddle races and surfing competitions. From there, Blake started making hollow boards using a skin of veneer over a frame like an aircraft wing. These 'toothpick'-shaped boards* could be paddled even faster than the solid boards and enabled the paddler to get out beyond the breakers quickly. The design was adopted by lifeguards in the USA because it was the fastest way they could get to drowning patients in surf. The design also found its way to Australia and became the board of choice for a generation of surfers.

Tom Blake's other contribution to surfing design was the fin. Until then, surfboards were finless and so lacked the ability to track or turn on steeper waves. By adding a fin, Blake was able to outperform any other surfer, traversing steep waves and making turns.

Balsa, a native tree to Central and South America, was the next wood to make its mark on surfing history. As an extremely lightweight and fast-growing material, it had a multitude of uses and was incredibly sustainable. Initially, when used for surfboards, it was varnished but would tend to crack and take on water, so, when fibreglass and polyester resins were refined as part of the American war machine during the Second World War, surfboard makers

---

* Pointed at both ends.

WOOD IS GOOD

jumped at the chance to laminate their balsa with a hard-wearing, tough and waterproof fibreglass finish.

After that came the ability to make blanks (a blank is the basic, rough surfboard shape, whether made out of foam or wood before it has its refinements shaped and before any finishing is applied) using chemical processes to create lightweight foam from plastics and fossil fuels. This was attributed to Bob Simmons, a Californian surfer, in around 1949. Simmons had spent the Second World War working in the aerospace industry and brought his expertise to the surfboard arena.

Give or take a few years, and the reluctance of surfers to change what they already knew, this is the point at which wood ceased to be a major element in surfboard design, apart from to create nose and tail blocks, stringers* and fins.

Wood's modern renaissance as a surfboard material was helped along by the closure of Clark Foam, the world's largest supplier of foam blanks, in 2005.† The news that Clark was closing its doors and that the company would be destroying all its moulds and equipment, to stop anyone else from continuing the business, sent the industry into a freefall, then a frenzy to find another way. Some shapers turned back to wood out of necessity while others fought over the limited supply available from other manufacturers. Others turned to wood for ecological reasons, wanting to break the grip of the fossil fuel industry on something so noble as surfing. The sport was supposed to be about nature and the environment and yet most surfers rode lumps of plastic, coughed up tonnes of carbon dioxide from their travels and wore wetsuits made of cancer-causing chemicals.

Today, it seems odd that the term 'traditional surfboard construction' is now used to refer to fibreglass and foam made from petrochemicals rather than to the original material, wood.

---

* A stringer is a length of wood that runs down the centre of a surfboard blank to give the foam extra strength.

† Clark Foam supplied 90 per cent of surfboard blanks to the USA and 60 per cent worldwide when Grubby Clark closed the company in 2005. It was a shock to the industry that had relied on it for decades. The reason? Possibly problems with environmental standards or lawsuits from former employees. In 2015, *Surfer* magazine said of Clark's closure: 'It was the best thing that's happened to the surf industry since the invention of the polyurethane blank.'

The return to traditional-traditional methods can only be a good thing, if only for the health of the people handling toxic materials. Sometimes we need to look backwards to look forwards.

I am sure the boatbuilder would have agreed with me, had I had the chance to sit down with a glass of red wine and discuss it with him. I was proud to be towing a board that looked to the past and the future at the same time and it made me happy that people were seeing and appreciating it. Making the board visible would be our way of making it acceptable — or at least a possibility — for surfers who believed that there is only one way to make surfboards.

He moved on, however, and was now admiring another traditional part of my set-up: my leather bum cracker, the Brooks saddle. He pointed to it and said, 'Ah! Brooks! *C'est bon!*' with a tone of further approval. I didn't tell him that some evenings Lizzy and I could hardly walk after several hours in the saddle, but it was, slowly and surely, getting easier. How long before they would be properly broken in?

As the swing bridge moved back into position, he skipped back to his car and nipped in front of us before we could cross. I guess he didn't want us to hold him up.

The canal offered great, if samey, cycling, but after a few days we were ready to leave its safety for something different. I got bored with the long straight sections where nothing happened except loveliness and a calm, rural beauty. I wanted waves and the coast and to start looking for surf.

In the meantime, while we pedalled in the intermittent rain, I looked up to see swifts soaring above my head in a blue sky swirling with black, thundery clouds. A frantic splash in the water revealed a black duck surfacing with an enormous eel wriggling in its beak. It dived again, losing the glistening eel for a moment before resurfacing with it, triumphant. An otter cruised along in the muddy water, oblivious until it noticed us cycling along beside it and ducked into its holt. Jays rose from the branches above our heads and moorhens and coots swam away as we disturbed the sublime peace of the iris, red campion and ragged robin-lined banks we passed, kilometre after gorgeous kilometre. Herons stood their ground, still and ever watchful, unless we stopped to take pictures, when they would take off and land a few hundred metres further up the canal, graceful in effortless flight.

Lizzy had always told me she enjoyed the pace of cycling. It is, she said, fast enough to never be boring and to give a constant stream of stimuli, but slow enough to give you time to see and identify plants in the hedgerows and verges. She was right. We often stopped to take pictures of plants or to identify something unusual, but we rarely needed to stop to appreciate those we knew. The pace allowed us to feel fully immersed. We were never, at any point, separated from the environment, as we would be if we were driving. Our senses were being bombarded: we could smell the fragrances of the river and its banks, hear the noises of the wind in the trees or of birds calling, and could taste the mustiness in the air after rain.

I loved the way that dragonflies and butterflies flitted in front of me, as if they were checking me out. Their presence, whenever they buzzed along, was always a source of wonder. I watched them, open-mouthed, like a baby watching bubbles float by.

I did my best to recall the names of the plants as we passed them, calling them out to Lizzy if I could identify them and asking her what they were if I couldn't. This was normal for us. Lizzy is a gardener and botanist and can identify most plants, so it's a game for me to try to spot things she doesn't know or to try to impress her with my own plant knowledge.

'Oooh! What's that?' I would call out while pointing to something in the verge as I whizzed by.

'Interesting!' Lizzy, riding behind me, would reply. 'You should know this. It's pea family!'

When I met Lizzy I could identify a few plants, but not many. Since we had started to travel together I had come to realise they are the keys to unlocking landscapes. I can now name a lot more than just the yellow iris that used to grow in the springtime at my favourite surf break.

For some reason, though, I can never remember bird's-foot trefoil. I remember the rhythm of the words – there is something very satisfying about it – but can rarely get them in the right order or even remember what they are. I always know what it is when I spot its orangey-yellow flowers in verges, in meadows or even in dunes, but just can't nail its common name. I didn't let this failure hold me back. I made up my own names for it. I adopted this same technique for certain other experiences along the way, using expletives to reflect how I might be feeling at that moment.

'Wet foot arse flap,' I shouted as I ploughed through a puddle.

'Dog's bum shit cakes,' I called when my front wheel parted a dog turd on the path.

'Wet wank sad face,' I moaned as the rain dribbled down my neck from off my helmet.

The more we pushed on, the better, and faster, we got. Apart from the rain it was easy going and largely flat. I felt myself getting fitter each day and was enjoying every moment, even if I was momentarily miserable when I was wet and cold or hungry. We were averaging around 55km a day, riding anywhere between three and five hours each day. I slept well and was the most comfortable I had ever been in a tent. Our insulated inflatable sleeping mats fitted together perfectly in our tiny tent to make a comfy, albeit temporary, double bed (as long as they were pumped up to the same pressure).

It took us nine days of arse-breaking pedalling (I guess we could have ridden it quicker if we had chosen to, been better cyclists or had not been towing trailers but I dread to think about the state of my arse if we had) to complete the Nantes–Brest canal from Roscoff. Considering we could have done the whole thing in less than a day's drive it seemed like a very long time. But it was a great ride. And we hadn't even got to the good bit yet.

Our last day on the canal was the longest so far. Having eaten their snacks, we said goodbye to Paul and Jackie and took to the towpath, with our sights set on reaching Nantes by the evening. I estimated the distance to be around 60km, thanks to Komoot and Google Maps, but was quietly worried it might be more.

At Nort-sur-Erdre, where the canal flows into the Erdre River, we left the towpath and headed cross-country towards the city. We cruised down quiet country lanes, between farmhouses with barking dogs in the yards and along the edges of fields of young maize. At Sucé-sur-Erdre we followed the signs for the Vélodyssée down narrow, overgrown footpaths into the town. Cobbled lanes led us to the riverside and then through the one-way system. People sitting outside cafes and restaurants gawped at us as we rattled by.

We waved and said a cheery *'Bonjour!'*, loving the attention. The contours changed as we approached Nantes and, for the first time, had to cycle up a hill. Looking back at the stats on my bike computer I can see that they were really nothing to moan about, but at the time I feared the good times of the flatlands might be over.

The countryside turned into suburbs and the path into a cycle lane alongside a busy dual carriageway. The rain stopped and it was beautifully warm: steam rising from the pavements. We comingled with other cyclists, commuters on electric scooters and dudes on fixies as we approached the city. We were overtaken often and felt like bumpkins after days on the towpath.

We had already hit the 60km mark somewhere out in the fields outside Nantes. The 70km mark passed by on the outskirts and then, with my knee starting to grumble, just before we arrived at the campsite in the city centre, we hit 80km. I was exhausted. I had just completed the longest ride since I was a teenager and could barely walk after dismounting.

I limped into the campsite's reception and tried to string together a coherent enough French sentence to ask for a pitch for the night.

'Je suis désolée, monsieur. Nous sommes complets ce soir!' the woman at reception told me.

We are full tonight. What? Fuck.

'No pitches?'

'Oui.'

'Nothing?'

'Non.'

'Really?' I thought that maybe it was because I was a sweaty, knackered mess, with shit French.

'There is a conference tomorrow. We are full.'

'Is there anywhere nearby we could try?' I asked.

'There is a campsite 15km to the east.'

'Fuck. That's the wrong way. I just cycled 80km.'

'I am sorry.'

'OK, no problem.'

I hobbled out of the reception to where Lizzy was waiting with the bikes.

'Erm. They are full.'

'Eh? Shit.'

'I know. The nearest campsite is 15k in the wrong direction. I don't think I could do that.'

'Me neither.'

We looked at the map and started to google local hotels. There was nothing. I had no idea what to do. My knee was starting to swell up and my back was aching. I needed to stop and I needed to stop NOW!

Lizzy, never one to let the world get in the way of what she needs, sent me back in. I sheepishly returned to reception and immediately apologised for hassling them.

'Er, *rebonjour. Désolé.* If you have no camping, do you have *any* accommodation? A chalet maybe? Or glamping?'

'Maybe. I will look.' She looked at her PC.

'Thank you.'

'Monsieur, we have a chalet but it is €90 for the night, plus a deposit of €200 for security.'

She looked at me as if I would start counting out cents on the desk in front of her.

'Why didn't you say? Here's my credit card.'

It was the best news: a victory snatched from the jaws of defeat, our fortunes changing in a moment. All we needed to do was ask the right questions.

In less than 10 minutes we were in. The chalet had two bedrooms, a lounge-cum-kitchen and diner, and a shower room. Outside, separated from the other chalets, was a grassy yard and a deck with table and chairs. In less than 20 minutes we had turned it into a jumble sale of wet kit. All our clothes were strung out on the deck's railings and our tent was stretched over our bikes, drying off in the last of the sunshine. Our batteries, phones, satnav, cameras and my laptop were on charge on the kitchen table in a tangle of cables and adaptors.

In under an hour we were showered, had changed into our spare, going-out clothes and were heading for the restaurant. A Caesar salad, a crème brûlée and a couple of local beers later and I was ready for bed. We had completed the first section. The coast was within a day's cycle.

Shit yeah, surf calls.

6

How much is too much?

'I like the idea of paring stuff down to the essentials to move freely. Cycling makes it impossible to ignore. You have all you need and nothing more: food, water and perambulation. Of course, though, some of our kit is about pleasure and that is non-negotiable: surfboards, wetsuits, fins, bellyboards.'
                    DIARY ENTRY: SUNDAY 2 JUNE 2024

Stage 5: Days 9–12 | From: Nantes | To: Sandaya La Grande Côte, Fromentine | Distance: 163km

Following directions for the Vélodyssée from the campsite, we nosed out into the Nantes traffic and headed towards the Erdre River. Cycle paths took us through an industrial estate and the university campus before bringing us to the riverside, then across the river and into the city centre. The cycling was exciting and exhilarating: we were able to follow cycle lanes down the middle of busy roads, be the first to cross junctions and have priority over cars, all while feeling safe. With a lot of other people cycling too, it felt like a good place for it. Nantes is, in fact, considered to be one of the world's most bike-friendly cities, with almost 500km of cycle lanes. It takes a brave urban planner to put bike lanes down the middle of a busy road, with priority given to bikes when the most powerful lobbies want business as usual in the form of car culture because they are making a tidy profit from it.

It was our turn to gawp at a courier on a cargo bike pulling a huge, pallet-sized load and we smiled as commuters on slick city bikes overtook us. We were among our own people and it felt a little like the future, if the future came to its senses and put people first.

'Hey, man! We are cycling through Nan-tez!' I imagined Eugene would have said. 'Neat!'

Crossing the Loire was a bit of a mess though, due to having to pull off a roundabout suddenly to find a footbridge over the river. It was a big moment for me, because I had only ever crossed it on the Saint-Nazaire Bridge, a 3.3km-long monster that rises to 61 metres (200ft) above the river and is scary enough in a van. I couldn't imagine riding over it and, if we had followed the coast instead of the canal, couldn't see a way around it other than cycling upstream to cross the river in the city. Taking the canal had circumvented the problem.

South of the Loire, the Vélodyssée took us on a weaving route through small villages at the river's marshy margins until we reached the Canal Maritime de la Basse-Loire and followed its tedious, hot, windy banks for 10 straight kilometres to Paimboeuf, a tiny village a few kilometres short of the estuary, where we pitched up with a view of the river in a marram-fringed campsite among tall pines.

The terrain had become more familiar: the west coast of France is famous for its sandy pine forests and getting here was a watershed moment. Being among the pines for the first time, smelling their scent and feeling their cushioning needles under our feet, confirmed that we were on the Atlantic Coast at last. It brought back a lot of good memories but also some regrets that I hadn't been in the forest – and with friends who dwelled there – for a few years.

The smell of pine always meant that the adventure was beginning. After my first trip to France in 1985 I went again in September 1986, camping in the forest in Lacanau and surfing among the crowds gathered for the Lacanau Pro. I crawled out of the whitewater early one perfect morning after getting swept down the beach and beaten in the impact zone. It was humbling in the extreme.

I went, reluctantly, to film school in Manchester in 1986, because I had failed to get into the film school in Bournemouth (probably a good thing, since the latter is a short drive from Kimmeridge and its distracting beach and surf). At Manchester, I met a group of friends:

HOW MUCH IS TOO MUCH?

Nick, Spout (who now runs West Coast Surf Shop in Abersoch), Jez and the old boys of the North West Surf Club, a great crowd with their own place in the history of British surfing. We surfed in North Wales and on the east coast of England, at Sandsend, Staithes and Scarborough.

In 1987, a brief cover up from a wave that kicked up unexpectedly, as well as some dodgy judging, handed me the win at the North West Open, a competition that morphed out of Bez Newton's Sol y Mar Surf Club events of the late 1960s. I had surfed on the inside while all the serious surfers waited out the back for waves that never came. It was the pinnacle of my very short competitive career.

After film school I went to London to find my way as a tea boy in the film industry, a moment when I believed a career might be useful. I resigned from my first permanent job,* as a runner in Soho, after breaking my leg skateboarding at a derelict 1970s bowl in Kentish Town in 1990. It was a perfect excuse to run away to Cornwall, to St Ives, where I worked at WindanSea surf shop† and cleaned caravans at Ayr Holiday Park on Saturdays. I rented a cottage on Teetotal Street near Porthmeor Beach so I could walk to check the surf every morning, usually at first light. Come the autumn, after turning down an opportunity to run the shop over the winter, I returned to London and told myself I would freelance as an assistant director in the film business and then travel rather than settling in Cornwall. I spent the summer of 1991 sleeping in the back of my Citroën 2CV on the east coast, in North Wales and in Cornwall. I visited Nick in Barbados in 1992, returned to France in the summer of 1993, surfed in Ireland in 1994, travelled to Sri Lanka and Bali in 1995 and bought my first proper camper van in 1994. In between times I went back to France to visit my university friend Nick, who was now living in Tarnos in south-western France.

---

* I've only had two: that one and the one where I was a copywriter.
† I lied and told my bosses that the break was so bad that I wouldn't be able to do my job, even after the plaster came off. While working my notice, I used crutches to keep up the pretence. Unfortunately, that meant I couldn't do my job and so was put on reception while the receptionist, a really lovely woman called Holly, did my job, which she hated with a passion. Meanwhile, in the evenings, I would throw away the crutches and play football in Regent's Park. Sorry, Holly.

In 1996, after spending a lot of time in Devon and Cornwall, I decided to buy a home in Devon rather than a flat in London. For the next five years I travelled between London and Devon, surfing while at home and working on films in London or abroad. Meanwhile, I travelled to surf in France, Spain, California, Bali, Lombok and Panama. Eventually I quit the film industry and started an internet cafe in Barnstaple with my now ex-wife, which enabled me to surf more regularly but almost bankrupted us.

In 2002 I started work at Bray Leino, an advertising agency, as a junior copywriter. My writing partner and I, Dean Sampson, surfed Lynmouth, Croyde and the breaks around Westward Ho! while supposedly 'brainstorming' ideas for big campaigns. Somehow we always managed to come up with the goods, despite surfing a lot. It was a great ruse that pulled the wool over no one's eyes.

I spent my 40s surfing in north Devon and Cornwall, exploring out-of-the-way waves with Simon Cooper, Justin Seedhouse and others, and visiting France regularly to surf with Nick or staying with my now ex-wife's family in Ireland (exploring surf possibilities on the Copper Coast and further west). In 2012, while the UK was going mad for the London Olympics, we took the kids out of school and travelled through France and Spain in an old VW camper van, staying with Nick and his new wife Abi, a friend of my then wife, for weeks on end. We moved to Bude in 2013, to a house that was close enough to Crooklets Beach to be able to walk in a wetsuit to surf. I was writing for a living, and loving it, and surfed a lot, but my life was falling apart.

As I transitioned from my 40s to my 50s everything changed. I spent a lot of time at the Surf Club, qualified as a coach and requalified as a lifeguard, cleaned the local beaches (a great therapy for an unhappy marriage) and started the #2minutebeachclean project.

One day in April 2013 I lost my board while surfing big Widemouth Bay on my own and endured a long, cold swim back to the beach. With severe chest pains I was taken to hospital and spent 10 days waiting for an angiogram, after which they found nothing wrong with my heart, so concluded that I had had peri-myocarditis, an infection of the heart that causes heart attack-like symptoms. That threw me and caused me to have panic attacks (be still my rampaging hypochondria!) but also helped me to re-evaluate what was important. I was desperately unhappy in my marriage, needed to shake things up, and in 2016, during another trip to France, the truth came out – the day, by coincidence, that they announced the results of the Brexit referendum.

Divorce meant I lost the house but managed to stay close to my children, even though I desperately missed the day-to-day of trying to be a good parent. Then I met Lizzy and my life changed for the better: I had found someone I could truly love, with the same ambitions, who wanted to be fit and capable and make the most of every moment, like me. She surfed too: an extra bonus. We talked a lot about travel and made plans. She had cycled in France and Spain with her ex-husband and loved the freedom and carefree life it gave her. What she remembered most about the French pine forests was, naturally, their cleansing, memory-making smell.

Lizzy and I delayed leaving the campsite at Paimboeuf because we wanted to visit a cycling festival that had been advertised on posters around the village. They seemed to promise a big event with lots going on, so we took our time packing down, enjoying a warm morning padding about on the pine needles. The festival was advertised as starting at 10 a.m. but when we got there at 11 a.m., it didn't seem like much was happening. We wandered around the meagre stalls that were still setting up on a green between the Loire and the village, excited and looking forward to sharing details of our journeying with anyone who would listen. I felt that we should, at the very least, be welcomed by our own sort, if not as travelling dignitaries. Failing that, in a flight of egotistical fantasy, as cycling royalty: we were carrying an important message and travelling, against the odds from a faraway land, with an unusual and difficult cargo.

We received no acknowledgement whatsoever. Not even a nod, even though we didn't utter a word to anyone to give away our crap French accents. We noted that one of the stalls was devoted to e-bikes so figured we weren't being ostracised for that, even though we had been on the rough end of e-bike snobbery more than once. Perhaps we didn't look right. I was disappointed, but in the land of the Tour, where

Lycra-trousered legends are born astride the saddle, we were, after all, just a couple of scruffy tourists passing through on the Vélodyssée.

By this time – we were nine days into our ride – we had experienced enough to feel like proper international surfing cyclists. By rights we should have been a curiosity: our clothes were grubby, our faces were starting to get a ruddy complexion from spending all day outside and our kit was filthy. Perhaps, I thought, we had passed the 'romantic cyclist' phase and moved straight on to 'fruitcakes on bikes'. We had reached the coast but were still a way from any surf. Perhaps the boards marked us as absolute nutters who should be avoided at all costs.

We didn't help ourselves when we stopped for lunch in the middle of Pornic, a swish port town on an inlet just south of the Loire estuary, and became more an irritant than a curiosity. We parked our bikes in front of a bench overlooking the quayside and, taking up half the pavement, with several posh restaurants overlooking us, using Lizzy's strongbox as a table, set out a full picnic of French bread, ham, cheese, mayonnaise, cucumber and tomatoes. I didn't care that people in boating shoes and with sweaters over their shoulders, or wearing nautical Breton tops and slacks, turned their noses up as I munched on my half of the baguette. We had earned our place at France's picnic table.

La Bernerie-en-Retz, our overnight stop, came quickly afterwards, even though we had covered 52km since leaving the cycling festival. It was a decent day's cycling and brought us to the northern edges of the Marais Breton, a vast area of salt pans and swamp. We had become used to the Vélodyssée taking us on back roads and down seemingly impossible alleyways and understood that it was linking up the cycle paths. Sometimes it was a little convoluted but it always resolved the same way: on a stretch of pleasant off-road cycle path along the coast, through the centre of a village or into lovely open country. We had been on the road for 10 days and had begun to trust the Vélodyssée and its efficient waymarking: everything would be all right in the end.

While Lizzy went off to the showers I put up the tent and made camp. I put on some water for a brew and looked around at our kit. I still felt we were carrying too much and that it was beginning to weigh us down: our panniers were stuffed full. The strongboxes were full too, which meant we had to go through a time-consuming

HOW MUCH IS TOO MUCH?

packing process each day, with everything needing to be put away in a set order. It was not conducive to being light-footed.

We took a rest day in La Bernerie-en-Retz – our first since we had left home – taking time to re-evaluate everything, from the spices we were carrying to the clothes we had packed. Some of it we really needed, like the tent and sleeping mats, but other things we didn't. We had a range of spices that took up space and weight, as well as a bike cover, spare tarps and electrical equipment. If we could lose a few kilograms it might help to make our journey easier.

Lizzy was less inclined to agree. Her reaction was to feel deprived, criticised or being accused of failure, and this resulted in a stalemate. I argued that we could easily send home simple things like curry powder or spare socks, hoping that marginal gains might add up to make a significant difference. In the end it was me who sent home the most stuff, on the basis that I shouldn't ask of someone what I wouldn't do myself. I packed up a box with my spare merino, a pen knife, the bicycle cover, two pairs of socks, shampoo and conditioner bars (Lizzy kept hold of hers for me to use), shaving brush and shaving soap, all my underpants except three pairs, a spare pair of cycling shorts and my favourite bottle opener. That saved us 5kg, most of which was being carried by Lizzy in her panniers anyway. It didn't really tackle the biggest single issue: the spare batteries. They alone weighed 5kg each. That's an awful lot of curry powder.

We spent the rest day lazing around the campsite pool and swimming at the beach near the campsite, a sandy bay with estuarine water. A tidal pool with a sandy beach allowed us to swim at low tide when the beach became acres of silty mud flats. A day off the bikes, for the first time since we left home, gave my knee time to settle down, even though I missed cycling. When we did remount the bikes I felt like I was back where I belonged. Everything was OK when we were cycling.

The cycle path along the coast south of La Bernerie-en-Retz ended abruptly with a sharp turn and deep sand. Until then we'd been cruising beside the water enjoying an early start on a beautiful sunny day, admiring the fishing huts on stilts close to the shore. They were connected to the coast path by planked walkways. At the seaward end, huge square nets hung off long counterbalanced poles. Some of the huts were dilapidated while others were brightly painted, jolly icons of the region. We passed scores of them but never saw any in use.

I was going at quite a pace when I hit the sand. My bike bogged and stopped very quickly and I had to make an emergency exit, leaping off to avoid going over the handlebars. The bike fell over. Lizzy followed me into the sand and stopped just as abruptly, although she managed to keep upright. I picked up my bike and tried to push it. I couldn't move it, even with walk assist (where the bike's motor turns over to help push the weight up hills), as the trailer's wheels had also bogged. A family of walkers, who we had just passed, came to our rescue, helping to push us through the sand and on to the asphalt beyond.

We definitely needed to lose some weight.

The Marais, a huge area of wetlands, creeks and pools, was a relatively easy ride, although the route took us on some rough and dusty tracks that ran in big squares around the salt pans and pools, along the top of dykes and through the maze of waterways. When we headed south we enjoyed the constant north wind at our backs but, as soon as we had to change direction – to navigate a creek or go around a salt pan – it slammed into us, making riding a slog.

Navigating inlets with boats moored up on rickety wooden jetties and drop-net fishing huts casting their lattice squares into the blue sky, we watched a pair of coypu swim in a canalised section of waterway while egrets and avocets waded in the shallow pools beyond. A marsh harrier flew towards us and dived away at the last minute.

We camped adjacent to the arched road bridge to the island of Noirmoutier and swam at the beach overlooking it. I got sunburned on the back of my head and my ears. That evening I noticed, despite putting sun cream on each day, that I was beginning to get a cyclist's tan: my face was very brown but my body was lily white. My legs had taken on a lovely golden colour too, although my feet looked like marble.

I was every inch the international surfing cyclist: squinting at the sun, ruddy, windblown cheeks, peeling ear lobes and tired knees. We had covered 600km since leaving home.

And still hadn't done any actual surfing.

7

Everything, connected

'We were having a beer and Burt said, "I want to go to Biarritz." I said, "I'll go with you!" So we arranged it and off we went. It was a big step for me. He'd travelled over from Australia, obviously, and other places. But I hadn't been many places at all.'

PETE 'VICKO' VICKERY, 2024

Stage 6: Day 13 | From: Fromentine | To: La Sauzaie | Distance: 50km

I checked Surfline, a surf forecasting website, for any signs that I might find some surf soon. It wasn't looking good. With a northerly airstream failing to produce any swell out in the Atlantic, it seemed that it would be a while before there were any surfable waves.

Surf forecasting is an important part of life for all surfers. Since the 2000s anyone can log on to Surfline (or Magic Seaweed as it was previously called in the UK) and get an accurate forecast for the surf near their home, or anywhere they are going, so taking a lot of the guesswork out of finding good waves. With detailed information about swell height, direction, local winds, storms and weather, it has become possible to get a very good idea about what is going to happen in the next few hours, days or even weeks.

This has been good and bad.

On one hand it allows surfers to make better decisions. On the other it allows them to become lazy and disconnected. Forecasting enables surfers to make travel plans well ahead of time, whether it is booking an afternoon off or a flight. It makes the 'strike mission', where surfers from around the globe congregate based on the forecast, possible. This can result in overcrowding and undoubtedly contributes to some surfers' above-average carbon footprint.

Things haven't always been like that. Before online surf forecasting, decisions had to be based on guesswork, learning to understand the shipping forecast or to read the weather charts in the newspapers (or on the TV) or calling the local surf shop. Some say it was part of the reason why the 'golden days of surfing', if that's what you want to call them, in the 1960s, 1970s and even the 1980s, were what they were. Those in the know got the best waves. You might get it wrong – I did many times – but there were also times when you could get it right – and have the surf to yourself.

Travelling through Europe to find good surf in the autumn, at the end of the summer season at home, would put any travelling surfers in the line of fire to surf the waves when they were likely to be at their best. As the weather worsened at home in the UK, visiting Aussie lifeguards and British surfers packed up and left, travelling south to where the water was still warm and where brewing storms in the north Atlantic would create surf on coastlines that enjoyed better weather and remained calmer than at home. There was never any question of jumping on an easyJet flight to catch a swell. You simply had to go and see. It was all part of the magic.

I amazed myself by not minding too much that there was little prospect of surfing in the next few days: I was having the time of my life, despite the lack of waves, and had already declared this 'The Best Surf Trip I Have Ever Been On' even though I hadn't surfed one wave.

It also seemed pretty pointless fretting about the forecast and wondering if we should be somewhere else or wait for surf to arrive. We couldn't travel any more quickly than we were and wouldn't have the time to wait for days on end at a spot we wanted to surf. In some ways it was liberating and we had become slaves to the road more than we were slaves to the waves.

The first famous surf spot on our route, the reef break* at La Sauzaie, was just a day's ride away, but the best surf, on the long

---

* A reef break is a wave that breaks over a rock or coral reef.

beaches of Aquitaine, was still a week or so to the south. We would still get to visit La Sauzaie but, sadly, without any waves that would enable us to see it at its best. Even so, I figured, we could still walk on the beach and get a feel for it.

Cycling was giving me enough to keep me happy. We developed a morning routine that was comforting but took a couple of hours: put the kettle on, eat breakfast, pack away the bed and tent, load up the bikes, apply a few centimetres of Chamois cream, slap on the sun cream, pull on our cycling gloves and hit the trail. With the weather improving, yesterday's cycling shorts, washed in the shower the previous day, like grapes being trodden to make wine, were looped under the surfboard straps to dry in the sun. Later, when we started to swim regularly, our towels added to the mess, flapping about in the breeze like a mobile laundry.

I had to admit that I never thought I would be happy without surf, but I was. Nothing, I would have insisted previously, would ever come close. However, this trip was different. I was content and knew that once I did get to surf it would make me feel great, whatever the waves were like. In years gone by I would have been impatient to drive as quickly as possible to the surf. Now I had no choice but to travel slowly.

As we were riding along its Atlantic fringe, France was about to prove, beyond all doubt, that it was a fully-fledged and serious surfing nation. In August, having debuted at the Olympics in 2020, surfing would grip the world at the 2024 games, providing an incredible image of Gabriel Medina taken by French photographer Jerome Brouillet, during the surfing competition held at one of the world's heaviest waves, Teahupo'o in French Polynesia (Why not in France? The waves in France are great, but can be unreliable in the high summer, whereas Teahupo'o would benefit from southern Pacific storms at that time of the year). Kauli Vaast took gold for the host nation in the men's event, while Frenchwoman Johanne Defay took bronze in the women's event.

If ever there was a moment for France to ride the wave, this was it. Teahupo'o is the kind of wave that most surfers marvel at but could never ride. It rises out of the deep Pacific and creates huge cylindrical tubes over a very shallow reef. It breaks quickly, although predictably, making it an impossible dream for anyone of below brilliant ability. Those who surf it well, dancing the fine line between glory and disaster, are heroes of the sport.

Surfing is hard enough without surfing waves that break quickly and heavily. To catch a wave and slide down its face, then stand up and surf without falling off or being drilled[*] into the bottom requires exquisite timing with a combination of physical ability, intimate knowledge and mental fortitude. It cannot be bought off the internet or learnt in a few lessons, and can often take years of learning and practice to perfect. Surfing, and surfing to any kind of professional level, is hard.

As well as having an Olympic champion, France also has lots of other excellent surfers. In fact, many of them are world-leading: Justine Dupont, a big wave surfer who learnt to surf in Lacanau, won the Nazaré tow challenge[†] in 2020 and has won multiple world titles in different disciplines. Michel Bourez, from French Polynesia, has won the Billabong Pro Pipeline Masters at Pipeline in Hawaii.[‡] Jérémy Florès, from Reunion Island, is the most successful European surfer of all time, with two Billabong Pro Pipeline Masters wins as well as a win at Teahupo'o.

France has been a surfing nation since 1956, when Richard Zanuck, son of the movie mogul Darryl Zanuck, hid two Malibu boards[§] in a container heading for the set of Hemingway's *The Sun Also Rises*, but it could be argued that the love affair with riding waves started many years before.

Prior to 1956 the French had been taking to the waves on *planckys*, wooden surf craft similar in design to the British

---

[*] 'Being drilled' is a phrase surfers use to explain being pummelled by tonnes of whitewater after falling off while surfing critical waves.

[†] A big wave surfing competition where surfers are towed into waves by jet skis. These waves are usually too big for surfers to paddle into.

[‡] Pipeline is a dangerous reef break in Hawaii. Generally, the Pro is regarded as the highlight of the surfing calendar and winning it is the pinnacle of a pro surfer's career.

[§] Malibu surfboards are generally considered today to be over 9 feet (2.7 metres) in length. They are named after the style of board developed at Malibu in the 1950s.

bellyboard. These plywood boards were sometimes used with fins and were surfed all along the coast of Aquitaine. A French inventor and later surfing pioneer and member of France's first surf gang, Georges Hennebutte, is credited with creating the *plancky* in the 1920s from recycled plywood steam-bent to create a nose rocker.*

Today, *planckys* are a rare sight on France's beaches, perhaps because of the meteoric rise of Malibu surfing in the late 1950s or the availability of cheap polystyrene alternatives and boogie boards. Early surfers, many of whom had been *plancky* riders, abandoned their plywood craft in favour of the Malibu board.

Planckys, or bellyboards, have become an integral part of my surfing experience and I travel with them whenever possible, which is always. It was unthinkable that we might do this journey without them and there was no question of sending them home when we discussed jettisoning some weight.

I even had an inkling that on this journey I would find, in the humble wooden bellyboard, the true soul of surfing in Europe. There is something about riding a bellyboard that cannot be matched by a stand-up surfboard or even by a bodyboard (boogie board), which are made of floaty plastic foam or polystyrene. You travel – almost – within the wave so feel more a part of it. It feels faster, more precarious and without ego. No one can claim a wave as their own and showboating isn't possible. Almost anyone can bellyboard without spending years learning. It is a shared, cross-generational experience and that makes it special.

Despite these humble early roots, which are not dissimilar to the roots of surfing in England, Spain and Portugal, stand-up surfing arrived in France with all the bang of a Hollywood blockbuster in 1956.† Peter Viertel, a screenwriter, had written the script of *The Sun Also Rises*, which was being filmed in Paris, Pamplona and Biarritz.

---

*A nose rocker is an upwards curve on the front (nose) of a board to stop the board from bogging or pearling).
† There are all kinds of versions of this story. I took mine from an interview with Peter Viertel himself in 2021, plus Joël de Rosnay's version from *The Surfer* in 1962 and 1964, and other versions online.

Viertel was invited along to watch the filming – so he visited the set and stayed on for a holiday in Biarritz.

Meanwhile, Darryl F. Zanuck, 20th Century Fox movie mogul and the film's producer, was having trouble with his son Richard, who was spending too much time in Malibu, the cradle of Californian surf culture in the 1950s. To straighten him out, Darryl decided to send Richard to France and give him a break in the family movie business. Viertel, who knew Richard was a passionate surfer, sent news that the waves he had seen in Biarritz were perfect, and urged him to bring a board or two. Richard duly stashed a couple of boards in a container full of costumes* destined for the wardrobe department in France, which then ended up with Viertel. But when Zanuck Senior found out about his son's plans to surf in France he demanded he head back home in disgrace, leaving the boards behind.

Intrigued, Viertel took one of the boards to the beach, La Côte des Basques, in Biarritz in the summer of 1956 and began to try to surf. He lost the board and it got smashed on the rocks. Georges Hennebutte, the inventor of the *plancky*, was asked to repair it. One witness was Joël de Rosnay, a rich young Parisian who spent his summers swimming and bellyboarding in Biarritz. He befriended Viertel and started surfing with him and others every day, sharing the boards. When Viertel went home, the boards stayed, although he returned the next year, according to some sources, with three more. A local engineer and keen surfer, Michel Barland joined forces with local craftsman and surfer Jacky Rott to make the first home-grown balsa boards in 1958.

De Rosnay, along with others, went on to form the Waikiki Surf Club at La Côte des Basques in 1962. Viertel's wife, Deborah Kerr, became the absentee 'godmother' of the club. De Rosnay had also become the 'French correspondent' for the fledgling surf magazine, *The Surfer*, and had written an article exposing Biarritz as a bona fide surfing destination. The article was the first time France had been

---

* Again, this story has many versions. At the heart of it lies the truth that boards (or a board) were brought over from Malibu. Some reports say the board(s) was/were Velzy Pigs, a design innovation from 1955 that was at the cutting edge of board design and allowed greater turning ability in more critical parts of the wave.

given any kind of attention in any surf magazine and included a map of Biarritz and its breaks.

The Surfer, which was started in 1960 in California, was important because it was the first time that surfing had its own voice in any kind of mainstream media. Until then it had been represented, largely, by onlookers rather than the protagonists. The founder of The Surfer, John Severson, was different because he was an insider. His magazine was, and remains, the authentic voice of surfing's early years.

As part of my research for the trip I tracked down the spring edition from 1962, Volume 3 No. 1, which mentioned 'Le Surf – France' on the cover. Inside was Joël de Rosnay's article, the first mention of Europe in any surf publication.

The article told of France's roots as a surfing nation and how the current scene had developed since 1956. Also included was a map of Biarritz showing the waves at La Côte des Basques, Grande Plage and Chambre d'Amour and even the Waikiki Surf Club HQ, which was, by 1962, the HQ of surfing in France. Maps are rare in surf magazines because they can give away secrets, so this was a surprise.

I continued to turn the pages until I came to a small ad for 'The Newest Idea on Wheels', Rick's Ric-Shaw. The image showed a surfer on a bike pulling a two-wheeled trailer behind him, on top of which was strapped a Malibu board. Rick's Ric-Shaw was a strange-looking contraption that attached to the bike's rear pannier rack, so allowing a surfer to cycle while pulling a surfboard behind. It looked more like the landing gear from a Sopwith Camel than a bike trailer, with two small, fat wheels beneath a skinny frame.

I could hardly believe it. Rick's Ric-Shaw wasn't so very different from my set-up. I felt as if I was living in and repeating history all over again. Travelling by bike with a surfboard was nothing new. In fact, it was as old as surfing itself. Well, almost.

Somehow, though, the bicycle surf rack didn't enjoy the same trajectory as other surf wagons – like the Ford Woodie Station Wagon (as immortalised by Jan and Dean in their hit song 'Surf City') or the VW Microbus (as immortalised by a bunch of hippies and just about every other surfer this side of 1970). For a start, a bike couldn't provide you with shelter, a place to change, a rudimentary kitchen and the ability to move locations quickly and easily. The bicycle never became a symbol for 1970s' counterculture either, unlike the humble camper van.

Then e-bikes happened. They caught the attention of the surfing masses when they realised that the addition of a motor to a bicycle could allow them to easily reach places that were previously unwalkable and out of bounds to other motorised vehicles.

Some people didn't like them, thinking they invited the rabble to previously quiet, exclusive spots, or were somehow cheating, but I didn't think that way. When my neighbour whined past me on his e-bike, board under his arm, on the way back from surfing at Northcott Mouth during the long, work-free days of Covid-19, I was sold. Pedalling my longboard on my 'analogue' bike up the mile-long hill to my house on the way back from epic surfs, sweating and swearing like a navvy, was exhausting. I cursed him under my breath as his electric motor cruised him past me effortlessly for the duration of lockdown.

To the purists who believe that bikes should remain motorless, I say, 'whatever'. Seeing that advert for Rick's Ric-Shaw made me feel as if I was carrying on a proud tradition of work-dodging through low-impact transportation. In riding our bikes, Lizzy and I would be representing the beginning and the end. And, when everyone finally caught up with us and realised that fossil fuels were so yesterday, we would be the answer for the future too.

Back to Joël de Rosnay, *The Surfer*'s brand-new 'French correspondent'. His article inspired many surfers to travel to Biarritz in search of waves, including Peter Vickery (Vicko), who travelled to Biarritz in 1963 with Australian lifeguard Burt Lovejoy and, in doing so, was one of the first surfers from Cornwall to travel to France. Lovejoy, also inspired by the article from de Rosnay, made up his mind to travel to Biarritz after his lifeguarding work finished for the season.

Vicko is a constant presence at the beach near my house so when I interviewed him, I was excited to hear about his adventures in France. For young Cornish surfers like him, travelling was a big thing in the 1960s. He got into surfing through Bude Surf Life Saving Club, the first surfing club in the northern hemisphere. He made his first surfboard – a slender, hollow 16-foot (4.9-metre)-long 'toothpick' board – himself from plans in Australia's *Blue Book*,* brought over by Cliff Welsh, an Australian lifeguard who had travelled to Bude to work as a lifeguard.

Vicko's story isn't that dissimilar to that of lots of surfers today. He wasn't born into money and had to work on his father's farm to earn a living:

'My father used to say to me: "You've got to choose if you're going to be a farmer or a surfer." It was awful. I'd be working up there on the coast and check the surf and all I wanted to do was get down here and go surfing,' he told me during the interview.

Vicko is an important part of British surfing history, although he's rarely mentioned in dispatches because he never won any contests or made a big noise. He was, and still is, a great pioneer.

Australian lifeguards, visiting the old country and working for local councils across Devon and Cornwall, took off to explore Europe after the season finished, with money saved from their seasonal work. Their influence cannot be underestimated in the story of British surfing and European surf travel. As well as world-beating lifesaving know-how, they brought plans, surfboards and a fearlessness that might not have been found elsewhere in post-war Britain. Travel wasn't such a big thing for them. After all, they had travelled from Australia to work, so the matter of a few hundred miles to surf in France would have been nothing.

'If anyone flew in, they flew into London,' Alex Williams, surf photographer, explained to me when I interviewed him.

We met on Alex's farm at Bantham in South Devon. He has been travelling and shooting surfing in Europe since the 1970s. In the hallway next to where we were sitting, I spied a board that was at least 70 years old.

Alex, who collects vintage surfboards and stories, continued: 'All the big names from back then would come into London and you know, they'd come down to Newquay and Cornwall and have a look around and then go over to the Continent. So, a lot of those

---

* The *Blue Book* was an almanac that was produced between 1946 and 1950 and contained details of all Australian life, including hobbies, farming and 'women's interests'.

early, really good surfers, they'd all fly into here. Like *The Endless Summer* film crew flew into London and then travelled from there.'

Exploration in Europe had already begun in earnest, with surfers from Jersey making the trip to Biarritz in 1962, a year before Vicko. Peter Gould, a surfer from Jersey and one of the first Brits to travel to surf in France, describes the moment they made first contact with Joël de Rosnay and other French surfers in Roger Mansfield's book about the history of surfing in Britain, *The Surfing Tribe*: 'After surfing at Chambre D'Amour, where we were the only ones in the water, we drove towards Biarritz town. We drove around a corner, with all the boards on top of the van, and saw a French car with boards on it coming the other way. What a moment. We all stopped in the middle of the road and got out to meet each other like spacemen meeting another lifeform on Mars.'

Despite the explosion in surf culture that was taking place globally in the early 1960s – we're back to Eugene and The Beach Boys providing the soundtrack here – surfing was still a very small world, especially in Europe, so it stands to reason that different tribes would come into contact sooner or later. All their stories are interwoven. The story of European surfing is also the story of surfing in the USA, is also the story of surfing in Australia, is also the story of surfing in Britain.

My story, as a surfer and member of Bude Surf Life Saving Club, is connected to everyone else's story by the simple act of riding waves and by the people I have met on my surfing journey. Just as I began by riding prone, so did the surfers of Europe. Our roots are the same.

Everything is connected.

Even in my home town in Bude, a town of fewer than 10,000 people on the Atlantic coast of England, we are connected to surfing's big stories in unexpected ways. A series of European and British champions[*] were brought up on Bude's beaches but none of them has had as much influence over the sport as a super-fit, energetic and impetuous Australian called Allan Kennedy, who visited Bude in the

---

[*] Bude has produced European and British surfing champions in Mike Raven, Joss and Reubyn Ash, Jobe Harriss, Miles Lee-Hargreaves, Stan Norman and Emily Currie. In 2024 Betsie Reay became girls under-12 European champion in Tenerife.

early 1950s. He was a big noise in the Australian lifesaving movement before and during the Second World War (when he trained troops on lifesaving) and was convinced that Australian lifesaving techniques could be transformational elsewhere. Frustrated that things weren't moving quickly enough, he requested a transfer to London and began working as a dairy assessor for the Australian High Commission in London. In the wake of an epidemic of drownings in Cornwall in the late 1940s and early 1950s due to the boom in tourism, Kennedy was desperate to import Australian Surf Life Saving techniques to Britain. He found Bude, thanks, in part, to Australian airmen who had been recceing the coast after the War. They had declared Bude as 'Britain's Bondi' because of the waves they saw. Kennedy visited Bude, went bodysurfing and then set about finding a squad of 11 local men to train in surf lifesaving techniques. In August 1953 one of the recruits, Alan 'Chuckles' Brock,* by virtue of his name beginning with B, became Britain's Lifeguard Number 1, and Bude Surf Life Saving Club was born: the first of its type in the northern hemisphere. The influence has been profound. Today, surf lifesaving is part of the fabric of the town: the clubhouse is a focus for community, and the club trains future lifeguards, and offers a pathway for young people instead of working in hospitality.

Kennedy also played a small part in a profound change in surfing, particularly in Australia. Until 1956 – that year again – Australian beach culture was defined by the Surf Life Saving movement. Lifesavers at clubs all over Australia used regimented drills, using a reel and line,† to save swimmers from drowning. They also used hollow 16 feet– (4.9 metre) long 'toothpick' paddleboards, like those developed by Tom Blake, to surf and rescue patients. These kinds of boards went straight on waves, without the ability to do tight turns, as their primary use was getting from outside the surf break to the beach as fast as possible. At the time, in California, surfers had progressed to riding much shorter boards, often made of balsa, of

---

* Chuckles passed away in March 2024.
† Using a reel and line was a common lifesaving technique in the 1950s, requiring a six-man team to reel out a line with a swimming lifeguard then retrieving the swimmer and patient. A reel given to Bude Surf Life Saving Club by Surf Life Saving Australia in 1953 was brought back to the UK by SS *Gothic*, the ship that took the young Queen Elizabeth II on her tour of Australia.

around 9 feet (2.7 metres) in length that enabled them to surf in a 'hotdogging' style, using the steepest part of the wave (the 'curl', just before it broke) to gain speed, turn and execute moves the Australian boards were just not capable of.

In 1954, Kennedy, as part of his mission to bring Australian lifesaving techniques to the world, had travelled to the USA to develop contacts (he also travelled to Biarritz, interestingly). He noted that, 'In a Santa Monica beach shed there were quite a number of surfboards or as the Yanks call them paddle boards, these members journey to Malibu some distance north whenever the surf is running there.'

Kennedy was sure that bringing a team of lifesavers from the USA would be vitally important for the success of a surf carnival that was planned to showcase Australian lifesaving techniques as part of the Melbourne Olympics in 1956. A group of lifeguards from Malibu and Hawaii were duly invited to take part (the GB 'team' was made up of one lifesaver, from Bude: Michael Martin).

This invitation changed Australian surfing forever. Among those invited were Greg Noll and Mike Bright, two of Malibu's pioneers and rising stars. Noll would go on to be the first to surf huge waves at Waimea Bay in Hawaii and became a world-renowned surfboard shaper. These surfers brought their Malibu boards to Australia and, between official events, surfed. After one event, at Avalon, Perth, the Americans paddled out into the surf on Avalon Point and demonstrated what they could do in front of a large surf club crowd. The session has passed into surfing folklore as being the moment when Australian surfing changed forever.

These demonstrations sparked a revolution that split beach culture in two: on one side were the 'clubbies', who had their regimented surf lifesaving drills and techniques; on the other stood the free-thinking, free-wandering counterculture of the Malibu-riding surfers.

On visiting Biarritz, pre-1956, Allan Kennedy had said, 'Biarritz in the Bay of Biscay has two beautiful surfing beaches with lifesavers who patrol the beach and use flags. However, these members cannot surf. An [official] visit here [by a team of Australian Life Savers] would be sensational and our methods in surfing would be adopted overnight.'

Kennedy never got his wish. If he had, the story of French surfing might have been very different.

We continued to cycle south, always pushed along by the north-westerly wind that was still producing no swell but was helping us to get closer to Biarritz and the Basque Country. The nearest I got to riding anything was taking my sleeping mat into a campsite pool to try and find a puncture that had left me lying on hard ground in the night. It made me feel every inch the tourist: like I was traipsing down to the beach with a Lilo to float away on the tide.

At La Sauzaie we walked across the dunes at sunset. It was low tide and the reef was exposed. We hopped from rock to rock and paddled through the maze of deep channels full of rock pools. I was amazed at how alive it was. Crabs scuttled away from us as anemones retracted their tentacles and juvenile fish scattered. Hundreds of multicoloured starfish lay open-armed as if sunbathing on the rocks. In the dunes, which were protected from traffic and trampling, we found orchids among the waving grasses.

But no waves.

8

Bike shop saints

'French cyclists. The men wear Lycra, no matter the bike. The wife usually rides behind, often on an e-bike, never in team strip. His team shirt says it all: "I am usually on the Tour but today I am on holiday".'

DIARY ENTRY: WEDNESDAY 5 JUNE 2024

Stage 7: Days 14–19 | From: La Sauzaie | To: Saint-Palais-sur-Mer | Distance: 311km

With no surf to distract us, we cycled on, putting in some good days in the saddle and passing surf spots at Bud Bud (flat), Jard-sur-Mer (flat) and Les Sables-d'Olonne (flat) before slogging it down the long, rough roads of the Marais Poitevin wetlands. In some places the surface was so bad I feared for the bikes and trailers. As I weaved around water-filled potholes it was only ever a matter of time until the trailer's tiny 40cm wheels slammed into a rut like a dandy horse crashing into a milestone.

The northerly wind helped us, mostly, and in three days we had covered 173km. We cycled through beautiful coastal scenery: alongside dune systems full of grasses and orchids, beneath the canopies of pine forest and along straight and lonely roads with no tree cover, under big skies in the wetlands. Cycle lanes between beach towns took us around headlands with low cliffs and beside long sandy beaches filled with sunbathers and swimmers.

We passed other riders often. I found that the long-distance cyclists were more likely to say hello than those who were day-tripping. We recognised, in each other, I would like to think, the distance we had covered and the struggle we had been through. A couple with two small children, one in a trailer and one riding a tiny bike, looked at our surfboards with pity while we looked back at them with as much compassion as we could muster. I couldn't imagine camping and cycling with two small children. It was hard enough dragging surfboards.

Sadly, though, it always seemed to be amateur hour on the Vélodyssée, with people on rented bikes outnumbering the cycle tourers. They wobbled along, wearing their helmets on the backs of their heads – rendering them useless in the event of a crash – and rode flat-footed, straight at us, without a word.

The men, who were mostly older, wore cycling jerseys, no matter the bike they rode. Sitting astride a rental or a shopper, their paunches stretched the logos on their club jerseys, their knees splayed, looking every inch the club rider gone to seed. These men almost always rode out in front while their wives or partners rode behind on sit-up-and-beg e-bikes.

Lizzy often rode out front, not because she is a feminist and it's a feminist issue (she is and it isn't) but because she had the Garmin. When we couldn't ride side by side, it made sense for the sake of navigation. I pulled in behind her, happy to be drafted by her slipstream, the perfect place for a back-seat navigator.

'Left here. Left here.' And then a little more desperately, 'Left!'

'I know.'

I had offered up an almost universal '*Bonjour*' to cyclists we passed on the Nantes–Brest canal but had become a little more selective with my greetings, especially if I felt they wouldn't be reciprocated. The '*Bonjour*'s I received in reply were often truncated to a lazy '*B'jo*'. At times this became an almost imperceptible nod and faint pursing of the lips, as if signalling to a waiter that the wine was, in fact, OK and they could continue pouring.

Tree roots defined the Canal de Marans à La Rochelle when we reached it. They spread out across the towpath in unpredictable lumps and bumps, causing us to either ride them out with bangs and crashes or slam on the brakes and roll over them slowly. There was no right or wrong way to do it.

The canal brought us right into the heart of La Rochelle. It was hot and busy, with lots of people eating in outdoor restaurants around the old port, cycling on the cobbled streets and milling about, often right in the middle of the bike lanes. More last-minute braking.

We were about to leave the next day when I noticed that one of the spokes on Lizzy's back wheel had broken. I took the wheel off and strapped it to my trailer to take it to a bike shop a few blocks away from the campsite. While doing that I saw that my trailer also had broken spokes – four of them – two on each side. I took the wheels off and strapped all three wheels to the good trailer.

The mechanics set to work on Lizzy's spoke straight away. They didn't have the right-size spokes for the trailer wheels (we had brought spares for the bikes but not for the trailers), so sent me off to their sister shop to see if they could help. Sadly, they couldn't, so I rang a couple of bike shops. By this time, I had picked up the French words for spokes and trailers and was getting quite good at explaining the problem, even if speaking on the phone in French wasn't easy.

One of the shops, a community bike workshop, said over the phone that they could look at the trailers but were closing for lunch soon. Realising that because it was Saturday we'd have to stay another two nights in La Rochelle if we didn't get the spokes fixed that day, I went into panicked action mode. I picked up Lizzy's now-complete wheel and raced back to the campsite to collect her and all our kit. With the clock ticking – and the stress levels rising significantly – we navigated the narrow lanes of the old city to find the shop just before it closed.

Six hours later, after a long lunch and a swim at one of La Rochelle's beaches, we returned to the bike shop. The mechanic had replaced the spokes on the trailer wheels, albeit with spokes that were not quite the same, and trued them up. We left with him giving us a warning that our trailers were, perhaps, too heavy.

It was a great relief to be rolling again although I now had 'bike anxiety', if that's a thing. The trailers were definitely the weakest part of our set-up, with wheels of an uncommon size and with replacement spokes not readily available. We could continue for now, but what if we broke more spokes? What would we do then?

I tried not to think about how we would deal with a wheel collapsing in the middle of a long, lonely stretch of traffic-free cycle path.

We rode 20km to a campsite on the coast at Châtelaillon and pitched up for the night. The next morning we went for a swim in the sea and then found a supermarket. While Lizzy was inside I gave our bikes the once-over: were her wheels still true? Check. Were the trailers still OK? Check. However, there were two broken spokes on my back wheel. Bollocks. I was so annoyed with myself. I could have had them fixed the day before, if only I had noticed. It was unlikely they had broken on the ride from La Rochelle. What a twat.

Not a lot happens in the cycling world on a Sunday in France, other than club rides in full kit (sponsored by a local pet groomer), so it was unlikely we'd get a fix straight away. A google search revealed a Decathlon with a bike workshop in Rochefort, 40km to the south. We couldn't go back to La Rochelle (partly out of embarrassment) so we voted to carry on, pitching for the night and setting out first thing to get the wheel fixed. Following the Vélodyssée, we took a wrong turn (for the Decathlon) and found ourselves at the beautiful transporter bridge – the last in France – connecting Rochefort with Les Chaumes on the south side of the Charente River.

The bridge was closed for lunch (can a bridge close for lunch?) but would open in an hour. We were lucky it was open at all: it had been replaced by a road bridge in 1991 but had recently reopened after four years of refurbishment. We plonked ourselves on a picnic bench with a view of the giant steel structure and ate our lunch, another French stick stuffed with ham and cheese. I googled bike shops: on the other side of the bridge there was a campsite and a bike repair shop that would open at 9 a.m. the next day. We changed the plan and when the bridge opened, wheeled our bikes on to the gondola – a platform that transports passengers on foot, in cars or on bikes from one side of the bridge to the other. On the south side of the river, a ride through some woods along a rutted and muddy path took us to a rural campsite with leaky showers built in an old outhouse and pitches alongside a murky river.

I was anxious to get to the bike repair man early – before some other stranded cyclist got there first and delayed us[*] – so we arrived

---

[*] Remember this bit when I talk about restaurants later.

at the shop before time. We waited while the opening hour drifted by and then rang the number displayed on a sign. After a brief conversation the owner arrived, smiling, and opened up the garage doors to reveal a tidy, well-kept and fully kitted-out workshop.

Half an hour later we were ready to get back on the road. The mechanic was a saint, of course, as all bike mechanics are. They never move with much urgency but always understand the importance of the mission. A bit like paramedics, you never see them running.

Onwards then, complete once more, but with the creeping feeling that we were still carrying too much weight. How many more spokes would we break? Which pothole would be the one to send us home?

We put in a good day of 60km through more wetland, along the Canal de la Charente à la Seudre, over the Viaduc de la Seudre, a 1km bridge that took us to the Côte Sauvage, a section of beach with surf on the right day (but not that day). We pottered along, spotting egrets, storks, black kites, ducks, swans and moorhen.

By now it was day 19 and we had covered almost 1000km since leaving home. I never thought I would be capable. Sadly, though, we still hadn't found any surf. By the end of the day we were just 29km from Royan and the ferry that would take us to the 200km-long beach of Landes.

The ferry would also bring us to Eric.

9

Ericycles of Soulac

'When everything is transient, the bike, and everything on it, becomes home. It means everything to be able to keep rolling, even if you are rolling from one temporary home to another. It's a fragile and precious freedom.'

DIARY ENTRY: TUESDAY 11 JUNE 2024

Stage 8: Day 20 | From: Saint-Palais-sur-Mer | To: Soulac-Sur-Mer | Distance: 29km

We could almost have been in Biarritz: the bike path followed the coast as it wound its way around a series of small horseshoe-shaped bays, watched over by grand detached villas with pointed finials, slate roofs and shutters in pastel shades. Each bay was every inch the genteel, well-heeled French resort we expected to see further south (or in a pretentious perfume advert). Between the bays were cafes and restaurants with views out to the Gironde estuary and Les Landes, the promised land of sand and surf, an area of 10,000 sq km of maritime pines planted by Napoleon in the late 19th century. In the bays, yellow buoys marked the swimming areas in the deep blue water. The air felt salty and thick with oxygen and ozone. A few people lay on the white sands in the early morning sun. Some, but not many, swam.

We reached the ferry at Royan just as it was about to leave, buying tickets hastily at the kiosk and pushing the bikes straight on, along with a few jostling, impatient cyclists.

This moment marked the end of one phase of the trip and the beginning of another. From here we would be riding at the back of the 200-kilometre-long beach of Landes, on cycle paths through the forest, always with the possibility of finding surf over the dunes.

As I sat on deck looking at the Pointe de Grave coming into view across the Gironde, I was transported back to the summer of 1985 and my first trip on the 'way of the waves': I had no idea what we would find on the other side of the river but hoped it would be every bit as good as the magazines had promised me: 3ft barrels with nobody else out riding them. If I closed my eyes I could be back there in a flash: getting drunk on red wine, playing guitar, being beaten up by the waves.

I wasn't the only one to discover France in my early surfing career. Almost every surfer I have ever met has sought sanctuary there at some point or other. Some competed while others spent months on end in camper vans, drifting, surfing, escaping.

Sam Bleakley, writer, commentator, filmmaker and multiple European longboard champion, has made the trip many times, often competing on the longboarding circuit. He told me:

> Once you got to Lacanau it was a new environment with the pine trees and the straight coast. I'd sleep in the car or rent a place. Maia Norman, Damien Hirst's ex-wife, was a passionate surfer and was particularly connected to the longboard crew. She and Damien used to rent a villa in Saint-Jean-de-Luz and hold these amazing parties when the Biarritz surf finals finished so all the longboarders who'd done the Biarritz Surf Festival would go. All the big names from Hawaii and Australia and America were there too. It felt like anything was possible.

My trailer clunked as I cycled up the metal gangway on to the quayside. It was a new kind of a noise and that worried me. I stopped outside the port, propped the trailer up on a pallet and took its wheels off to grease the bearings.

It was worse than a lubrication issue: another five spokes had broken on one wheel. We were in trouble and in need of drastic intervention.

Without much else to do right there and then we cycled into Soulac-sur-Mer, the nearest town, to find another bike mechanic. Thankfully, the wheel survived 15km on the bike path without disintegrating. I half expected to be dismounted by a collapse each time I hit a tree root or cycled over a lump or bump.

What were our options?

Find someone who had the right spokes? Unlikely. Send for some? I had already looked online for spares of that wheel size and had drawn a blank. Buy a new trailer? We might have to. Lose some weight? We had to consider this, even if we got the trailer fixed. What would we send home? The heaviest items were the spare batteries.

We caught the first bike shop just before lunch. The mechanic couldn't help but offered to order a new trailer. 'Buy it in the next 30 minutes and I'll have it by tomorrow,' he said.

I said I would think about it. It was €350. But there was no guarantee it would be suitable for our requirements. It was too much of a risk. Lunchtime came and we left the shop.

Another bike shop, on the other side of the town, would open in an hour's time. Meanwhile, I found a post office and checked if they would allow us to send bicycle batteries to the UK. Unsurprisingly, it was a no. We would have to come up with something better if we wanted to lose the extra weight.

Eric, the owner of Ericycles, was chatting away to a friend when we turned up. He was short, rotund and wore round tinted glasses with bright yellow frames. He had a tiny greying quiff on top of his oval head and reminded me of Timmy Mallett. He looked at the trailer, measured the spokes and disappeared into his workshop at the back of the disorganised shop. Several minutes later, he reappeared shaking his head: no spokes. But, he said, he did have an idea. He mounted an electric scooter-trike and headed down the road.

'I go to my storehouse!' he shouted over his shoulder, a mechanic with a mission.

He returned 20 minutes later with two rusty wheels: spares, he said, from an old trailer. He threaded them with the axles from the old wheels and offered them up to the trailer. It would have been too easy, I thought, as he pushed them on. They almost fitted but not quite. Eric disappeared into his workshop again.

We waited, hearing banging, whizzing and grinding and some compressed air being released. Eric returned and offered up the wheels again. They almost fitted now, but still not quite. He disappeared again, returned with a mini-grinder and started to hack away at the plastic inserts where the axles fitted. He shaved off a few millimetres and offered up the wheel again. No good. He took off another few millimetres and offered up the wheel. As he pushed the axle in, I heard the spring that holds the wheel click into place. Eric spun the wheel. It ran freely. We both squealed with delight. I almost hugged him.

'Wait here,' Eric said as he dragged the trailer and wheel into his workshop.

We retreated to the cafe next door. Thirty minutes later Eric appeared with the trailer. He had fitted both wheels and given them brand-new tyres. We hitched the trailer to the bike and I pedalled up the road. It worked! Eric had saved our trip. We couldn't thank him enough. He said proudly that he had been fixing up holidaymakers' bikes for 30 years.

'I can see you like a problem,' I said.

'We solve it or your holiday is over,' he replied.

Eric was the fifth bike shop owner we had met in the last four days and he was, just like the others, keen to help. He understood the urgency of our problem: we had no choice but to keep rolling. He knew, I was sure, how we must be feeling.

I found it unsettling to think that a broken bike or trailer could leave me feeling baseless, as if everything was about to be taken away. After three weeks on the road, to ride was everything. The bikes were our anchor and home. They carried everything. I realised that, if we were to avoid breaking more spokes, a lot of that everything had to go.

I called my friend Andy, who I knew would be taking August out in Cap Ferret, a swish resort on the Arcachon Basin, 110km to the south, to see if he could help.

Andy made some calls and sorted out a safe place in Cap Ferret where we could stash some stuff until he could pick it up later in the summer and then bring it home. It was a great relief. I started making mental notes of what we could leave.

The surf report for the next morning looked promising, with a small wave predicted and light winds first thing, so we got up early. We loaded up the boards and set off. As we were about to pull on to the road outside the campsite my trailer pulled me into the curb. One of the new tyres was flat. Bugger!

We went back to the pitch, fixed the puncture and headed back to the beach. The wind had come up and the surf looked awful. But at least there was surf, even if it was small and choppy.

There was no rush. The waves would come. All we had to do was make it to Cap Ferret.

After that it would be plain sailing.

10

Everything is lovely

> 'It's the culture, the food, the sun, the waves, everything compared to England. It's warmer. The food's better. The waves are better. Everything's like . . . lovely.'
>
> EMILY CURRIE, WOMEN'S EUROPEAN
> LONGBOARD CHAMPION, 2024

Stage 9: Day 21 | From: Soulac-sur-Mer | To: Maubuisson | Distance: 69km

I was the happiest I have ever been when we cycled out of Soulac-sur-Mer.

OK, slight exaggeration, but it was definitely in the Top 10 of Moments I Will Cherish Forever. Those included the moment I realised that everything was going to be OK while standing next to Lizzy at our wedding, the birth of my children, the day I got a job as a writer at an advertising agency, and catching waves at Izzy's* with my mate Simon. To be pipped by those was nothing to be ashamed of.

The cycle path wound its way through the forest, smooth and flowing. The pines were releasing their scent again, fresh and deep and full of memories. It transported me straight back to my past,

---

* Izzy's is a break in North Devon. Simon and I surfed it for the first time two hours after the birth of his daughter, Izzy, so we named it after her. It's a long walk and rarely worth it, but sometimes, when swell and wind align, it can be brilliant.

yet everything seemed to be brighter and more intense for seeing it from the saddle of a bike. I felt connected.

I remembered the good bits, naturally, and never the bad. Time had turned the disasters into beta male victories to laugh about around the campfire. Nostalgia, rose-tinted as it was, added to the emotion as I weaved between the trees on the buttery, frictionless tarmac.

My back, as Sebastian had predicted, felt good. My knee wasn't grumbling. My heart was pumping and my legs were pushing, one after the other, in an easy rhythm as the 29er wheels rolled over the smooth tarmac with a gentle hiss. There was no hardship or pain, just movement and joy.

I put aside any anxiety about breaking more spokes. For the moment we were rolling. It had stopped raining. Our bikes were humming happily. All we had to do was cycle 100km without breaking anything.

The land was low and flat, with the occasional easy climb up gentle dunes. It ran alongside the road from time to time, but mostly struck out on its own through the forest. The pines provided a dappled, cooling shade. Despite being a man-made forest, it still felt wild and deserted at times, like we really were cycling through an adventure all our own.

The cycle path crashed out of the forest and into the bright white light of day outside Montalivet-les-Bains. We joined a road that ran along the beach, just behind the dunes. There was a small onshore wave breaking on the sandbars. I didn't need any encouragement; the waves weren't perfect, but they were good enough for a bellyboard. We locked up the bikes, stashed our stuff in the strongboxes and wandered off to the swimming area, in the lee of a rocky groyne that sheltered the waves from the northerly winds, allowing them to clean up a little, and gave us protection while we changed.

I waded into the water and jumped a few lines of whitewater until I was out where the waves were just starting to break. As one approached, I turned, held my board in front of me and pushed off the sand towards the beach. The wave picked me up and drove me towards the shore, sloshing, splashing and hissing at my back as its power dissipated around me.

The waves were a bit crap, as surfing waves go, but I didn't mind. The joy from riding waves is the same, whether you ride waves that could kill you or tiny little runners like these. The happy chemicals pulsed through my body; I had caught a wave in France, on the Landes coast, and had got there under my own steam. Brilliant! It wasn't even that cold without a wetsuit. When I put on my T-shirt afterwards my skin prickled with the heat of the sun and the drying of the salt. It was a familiar feeling.

There was nothing but joy in the tiny waves, although there was no mistake who was in charge. Even those small swells had the power to knock us over if we weren't careful. We had enough experience to enjoy it as fun. I was glad. I didn't want fear – of drowning, the violence of the ocean or dealing with crowds – to get in the way.

As the journey continued, I hoped to be able to push my personal limits. The moments between glory and disaster – and the fear that goes with it – are the moments that make riding waves so intoxicating. Entering a stormy sea for pleasure is to fight an instinct that is screaming at you to head to safety. Surviving is to escape the watery clutches of death itself.

I wasn't hoping for any life-threatening experiences, it must be said, but I wanted to feel the frisson from close calls: waves my fear would tell me to avoid but that I paddle for anyway.

We continued south, through the commune of Hourtin, and on towards Carcans and Maubuisson, a village at the south end of the Lac d'Hourtin-Carcans on the Route des Lacs. We pulled into a campsite not far from the village. I recognised it immediately as the site I had stayed on in 1985 on my first trip to France. I remembered it being OK, but now there was an air of apathy and indifference about it, as if this was a last resort. But after cycling 70km we didn't have the energy to carry on to somewhere better. I don't usually mind less than amazing campsites but this site made me feel like I was admitting defeat.

Most of the park was taken up with caravans on neglected seasonal pitches and there appeared to be a lot of people living there permanently. Chairs and tables were green with algae, the electricity points looked hacked and dangerous and it all felt sad and forgotten. The few pitches for tents were adjacent to a muddy pond buzzing with clouds of insects.

After such an excellent day it was a huge disappointment. And to think that I had had such a good time there in the past. Of all the campsites I have stayed at, this was one of the worst. It was messy, decaying, uncared for. I couldn't wait to leave. But first we needed to charge the bikes, have a shower, eat and sleep.

We ate out that night.

11

Lacanau Pro, cycling amateurs

'On leaving Arcachon the rain was very heavy. We shared a tree with a couple and had a chat. Dashed from tree to tree. Then the wind really came up.'

DIARY ENTRY: FRIDAY 14 JUNE 2024

Stage 10: Days 22–23 | From: Maubuisson | To: Dune du Pilat | Distance: 93km

I wasn't expecting hills until northern Spain so it was a bit of a surprise to cycle through what felt like a mini mountain range in the dunes between Maubuisson and Lacanau-Océan. We peaked at 66 metres above sea level and by the time we pulled into Lacanau we had climbed around 300 metres. Not much really, but when you have just covered 1200km on mostly flat roads, it felt like a lot.

I wanted to stop at Lacanau, particularly, because it is the first significant surf town on the way south and somewhere I had visited in 1986. The town, which was founded in 1903 by railway builder Pierre Ortal, has a long history of surfing, with the first board arriving from Biarritz in 1962: alien craft sliding in the slices of ocean glimpsed between grand villas of the 'architecture balnéaire' style on the sea front. Today, many of the fine, turreted and shuttered villas have been lost to the developers, who replaced them with charmless, five-storey boxes made from breezeblocks.

At the north end of the esplanade, overlooking the beach, lay the well-appointed Lacanau Surf Club, a modest building with a reception and shop upstairs, and changing rooms and gear stores downstairs.

Inspired by surfing competitions in Australia, America and Hawaii, the club put on its own professional contest in 1979. Bar a few fallow years due to lack of sponsorship (and Covid-19) it has been taking place consistently ever since, making it the longest-running competition in France and Europe. The list of surfers who have won it reads like a rollcall of the greats: Wayne 'Rabbit' Bartholomew, Barton Lynch, Mark 'Occy' Occhilupo, Tom Curren, Tom Carroll, Martin Potter, Kelly Slater,[*] Rob Machado, Joel Parkinson, Jordy Smith, Gabriel Medina and Filipe Toledo have all made their mark on European surfing in Lacanau. The club runs training programmes and courses aimed at women, children and the disabled. Their Surf School has been in operation since 1978.

I watched the Pro on my second visit to France in 1986, the year Tom Curren[†] won it (he moved to the Basque Country in 1989). I remember thousands of people on the beach watching the heats from the sizzling sands. Today, the Lacanau Pro (now known as the France Pro) is a beach festival with music, skateboarding, food and beach cleans. Outside the competition, the Lacanau Pro gave everyday surfers the chance to surf with the greats. My friend Jez was very proud that Sunny Garcia, Hawaiian legend and one-time world champion, once paddled up to him and said, 'Hey, man. You are burning up.'

---

[*] Kelly Slater, 11 times world champion, won the Lacanau Pro in 1992, his first ever professional win. He would go on to win the World Championship for the first time that year, aged just 20 – the youngest ever winner.
[†] Tom Curren won the world titles in 1985, 1986 and 1990.

I wandered into the clubhouse – the first surfing clubhouse of its type in France* – to say hello, and was met by Fiona, a Scottish-born woman who has lived in France since she was a child. She showed me around the club and filled me in on a little of the history. I felt humbled to walk where so many famous and talented surfers had also trod.

On the beach, the surf was small and onshore and a few surf schools were taking clients out in the sunshine. The surf schools, we noticed, were ubiquitous. Every surfing beach we had been to, almost without exception, had a surf school. When I started surfing surf schools didn't exist in the UK in the way they do now. I don't want to be one of those embittered old men who says things like, 'We had to struggle in crap wetsuits, surfing crap waves, on crap boards and no one to tell us what to do' and pretend it was a good thing, because I can't. I wish someone had taught me how to surf. I might have spent less time at the school of deep wipeouts being a kook.

We hit the cycle path again and continued south through the forest to Cap Ferret on a mix of rough, broken tarmac and lovely smooth stretches. The tree roots always got me: *bang, bang-bang.* Ouch. Listen for that telltale sign of impending disaster: a sharp metallic crack followed by a rhythmic *thtwick thtwick* as the broken spoke clicked against the frame.

Andy texted us the address of the 'safe house', which lay in a leafy back street of Cap Ferret. We pulled open the sliding garden gate and pushed the bikes in, hoping that we wouldn't be challenged, as we had no idea who it belonged to.

The house, set in a large, shady plot of pines and strawberry trees, was ultra-modern with lots of glass and concrete – a world away from the flamboyant villas of Lacanau. I found the key safe, dialled in the code and flipped it open. Inside, as Andy had promised, was the key. I pulled on the up-and-over garage door to reveal a basement full of bikes and surfboards.

We emptied the contents of our panniers and strongboxes on to the front lawn of the house to work out what we could lose. After some

---

* Lacanau's 'Maison de la glisse' was built in 1990.

negotiation we packed up the batteries in a waterproof backpack along with a pair of fins, spare sunglasses, a lamp and one of my cameras, padded out and protected by our waterproof jackets. The jackets, while waterproof, took up a lot of space, I argued, therefore they had to go. We had down jackets to keep us warm at night and were now in southern France. Would we need them? Surely not!

I tied everything up into a neat package, wrote a note explaining that it was to be picked up in August, and closed and locked the garage door. We headed into Cap Ferret, past some of France's most expensive real estate, our sights set on sampling the oysters Cap Ferret is famous for, before taking the ferry to the posh town of Arcachon, across the Arcachon Basin – a trip that would save us a 50km cycle.

With clouding skies threatening, and a well-heeled clientele pursing their disapproving Gallic lips, we paid almost a tenner each to sit outside a swanky patisserie in Arcachon and scoff a celebratory *tarte aux framboises* with a cup of tea. We had cycled away from the house feeling lean and lithe, having lost around 25kg of stuff, and felt we deserved it. On top of that we had managed to get the bikes on the ferry. They felt like frisky gazelles beneath our arses as we scampered to the jetty to try our luck. The crew seemed in a good mood and didn't appear to mind at all lifting everything on to the tiny boat, although they did make a few noises about the trailers being heavy. Little did they know.

Fortified by tart, we set off to climb the Dune du Pilat, Europe's largest sand dune. Our route took us around the basin, right next to the water, with views back towards Cap Ferret. I didn't notice the wind picking up at first, but felt it hit us from the side when we rolled along a beachfront path. Then the rain came: light, annoying drizzle moistened things up a little before big, fat globules of heavy, condensed Atlantic splashed my face and ricocheted off my helmet. We stopped to shelter under the biggest trees we could find, looking longingly over the rain-lashed water to where, on a clear day, Cap Ferret – and now our coats – should have been. It was too late to turn back.

We dodged the cloudbursts until we ran out of trees to shelter under on the lower slopes of the dune. Unless we wanted to wait for the rest of the day under a tree, getting slowly wetter and wetter, heading out into the open was our only choice. Pilat suffered a major wildfire* in 2022 following weeks of unusually dry weather that destroyed 90 per cent of five campsites on the dune, including one of my favourites, Camping Dune du Pilat. The trees that had once covered the lower slopes were now nothing more than blackened stumps offering zero shelter to the sodden cyclist. I felt very sad that this beautiful landscape had been devastated but equally sad that the rain was running down the backs of my legs and into my shoes. My down jacket, now the only form of protection against the weather, and not a very good one at that, was stuck to my back. We stopped under a bush just before launching ourselves at the last section of the climb: miserable, soaked, in danger of getting very cold and grumpy.

'What shall we do?' I asked Lizzy, shouting over the storm.

'Dash for it. Find the first campsite. Check into a chalet.'

'Yeah. This is shite.'

We were glad of the shelter that night, although the chalet we were assigned at the first campsite we came to had a canvas roof and sides, the likes of which you'd expect to find on safari. At times, as the wind blew in from the sea over the dune, it felt more like an old wooden boat under sail, groaning and creaking as the storm raged outside. We draped our wet kit, tent, shoes, panniers and sleeping bags over the furniture, whacked the heating up and streamed a movie while sitting in our pants, steaming. As I was learning, misery never lasts long. You just have to bear it until things improve, which they will.

Outside, the dune loomed over us like a cliff face that could topple at any moment. Some of the site, much of which was newly rebuilt after the fire, had already been taken over by the sand. It felt precarious to stay there, at the mercy of nature and the weather.

And there was us with no waterproofs. What had we done?

---

* As the fire began to move, and the authorities decided it was threatening the campsites – it had been raging for several days already – 3000 people had to be evacuated at 3.00 a.m., within 30 minutes.

12

Wild in the woods

> '*I think that bit of south-west France, there is something really magical about it, and I don't know why. I just can't put my finger on it. I guess it's in my subconscious from those early days. It's like a magnet that's drawing you in.*'
>
> LEE NEWBY, SURFER AND MAKER, 2024

Stage 11: Days 24–27 | From: Biscarrosse | To: Labenne-Océan | Distance: 190km

The French Army owns a vast tract of the forest – the Camp de Naouas – south of the Dune du Pilat, between Biscarrosse Plage and Mimizan, so access to the coast is restricted. It meant making a big detour inland to the Étang (lake) de Cazaux et de Sanguinet (where we swam by the side of a noisy waterpark), around the Lac de Biscarrosse et de Parentis, into Biscarrosse town (the inland version, got a bit lost), along a long straight (and quite boring) stretch of old railway to Parentis-en-Born and then on to Gastes, where we found a fantastic campsite* with grassy pitches, a pool and pizzeria by the side of the lake. It also had a resident hoopoe. Here we encountered a family, consisting of a mum and her two teenage children, plus the mum's parents. The grandparents were the advanced party, travelling by camper van, while Mum and the girls, both of whom had spectacular long red hair (they were Scottish), travelled by bike.

---

* Municipal Le Camping du Lac in Sainte-Eulalie-en-Born is a municipal site that's well worth a stop.

We rode with them later and they explained they were travelling from Roscoff to Santander. They met up with the grandparents at the end of each day, camped together and then departed to do their own thing before meeting up again. It was, to us, an amazing, inspiring family adventure.

This stretch of the coast, when we could get to the coast, is home to places that many surfers will know. They are the breaks and stop-offs on the road south towards the Basque Country: Mimizan, Contis, Cap de l'Homy, Saint-Girons, Moliets-et-Maa, Messanges and Vieux-Boucau-les-Bains. For surfers heading to France's most famous breaks, these are the approaches: the foothills to the wild and woolly mountains to be conquered later at Hossegor or Biarritz.

After the storm that had rocked our chalet at Pilat, the surf was huge, distorted by onshore winds, so we gave it a miss – but at least it wasn't flat any more.

Things weren't so wild by the time we got to Le Penon, the nearest beach to Seignosse, a couple of days later. The surf was looking good and the sun had come out, making for a windless, hot day, so we locked up the bikes and hit the beach. There were a few too many surfers in the water on the peak nearest the path to the beach so we half walked, half trotted across the scorching sands a little way to the south, climbed over a groyne and set up camp in front of a left-handed wave that looked like it wasn't busy and was breaking nicely, about head high.

It seemed that I would get to surf, after all. However, Lizzy, after watching the waves for a few minutes, decided she would sit this session out.

While she shares my passion, Lizzy came late to surfing. She was 50 when, after years of an unhappy marriage, and having nursed Poppy, a severely disabled child, for five years until her death, she decided she should start to make an escape. Surfing was part of that. She surfed initially with Bude Surf Veterans and began the process of healing, with surfing, once again, providing the catalyst for freedom.

It is testament to Lizzy's spirit that she took up surfing at this age. She could have sat on the sofa and felt sorry for herself but instead, she threw herself into surf lifesaving, cycled the South Downs Way alone and took herself to the Scilly Isles to celebrate her 50th birthday.

When she was 54 she won gold in the Women's Board Rescue*
event at the Lifesaving World Championships in Holland. At ages
56 and 58 she gained, and retained, the title of British champion in
the Ocean Woman† event at the British National Surf Life Saving
Championships.

She is fearless in so many ways, and more than capable, but surfing
often takes her out of her comfort zone.

I watched the wave for a few minutes before committing to
paddling out through the shore break that was sloshing up and down
the steeply shelving beach and crashing on to the sand. The surf
wasn't huge but it was big enough for me to be anxious about going
out for the first time at a new spot, even though a current, running
along the side of the groyne, would help my paddle out. I watched
someone make it to the line-up without too much difficulty, so I
changed into my wetsuit and paddled into the green and silky water,
its surface ruffled by the gentle offshore breeze.

I sculled over a few waves, looking at them from the safety of
the rip. They looked great. 'I can do this,' I thought as my anxiety
subsided and I got myself into position for a set wave. As a peak
began to rise I turned and paddled for the shore. I was in a good
spot: not too deep, not too far out on the shoulder. The wave lifted
my board and, as soon as I felt it begin to slide down the face, I
pushed up on my hands and allowed myself to fall forwards, bringing
my legs between my arms and planting my feet on the deck of the
board. I stood taller as the board continued to slide down the face of
the wave: legs still a little compressed, arms bent, looking ahead of
me at the place I was planning to take the board next. The wave was
curling over, beginning to form the first part of a tube above me and
tapering away into the channel ahead. I was in the perfect position,
and I noticed another surfer paddle out, looking at me.

Then it all went wrong. The nose of my board skimmed the
surface, penetrating ever deeper in the fractions of a second it took

---

* An event whereby a board paddler has to pick up a swimmer/casualty and paddle them back to shore.
† The Ocean Woman event is the Big Mumma of all surf lifesaving events: an individual medley that comprises a swim, paddling a rescue board and paddling a surf ski, with runs in between. It is a hardcore event.

for the board to bog and fling me over the front of it, headfirst: a classic 'pearl'* sending me 'over the falls'.† Rookie mistake.

I surfaced in the shallows, pulled my board back to me with my leash and climbed aboard.

'You twat. You screwed that up,' I said to myself as a line of whitewater approached me. It was humiliating to be seen going over the falls. It was a sign that I was a potential kook. That would give me a low ranking in the invisible, imperceptible pecking order of the line-up.

I caught a few more waves – I could still surf! – until the tide ebbed and the waves stopped breaking on the sandbank. Despite the shaky start I was stoked to have surfed French waves again. It had been too long and I had forgotten how good it could be to slide down glassy waves, to sit in the water and watch the sets approach, under a hot sun and in water that was warm. I hadn't spent too long in the washing machine‡ either, and, when I had, it hadn't been too bad. I felt fit and happy and ready for more. I showered, changed and, feeling like I was almost worthy of talking with a surfing legend, sent a message to Carwyn Williams.

Carwyn, who has lived at Seignosse for many years, was a professional surfer in the 1980s. He was the 'Great Welsh Hope', the boyo done good, a miner's son from Mumbles who beat world champion Damien Hardman in a man-on-man heat in the 1988 Rip Curl Pro competition at Hossegor. He broke into the Top 30 in the world that year too, having spent the season living out of various cars, travelling the world on a shoestring. His dreams about to be realised – to compete in Hawaii that winter – he was involved in a horrific car crash on the way back from Mundaka that should have ended his career. Doctors told him he'd never surf again but his determination,

---

* Pearling is named after the act of 'pearl diving' – going straight to the bottom.
† Going 'over the falls' is to go over with the breaking lip of the wave.
‡ The 'washing machine': being tumbled about underwater by breaking waves, usually after falling off.

commitment and love for surfing meant that he did, and in style too, becoming European Number 2 two years later.

In a lot of ways Carwyn's story epitomises the spirit of surfing: a talented and determined young surfer heads off to Europe to find waves and glory. He spends years living on nothing and never gives up, even when injury threatens. He's a hero to surfers of that era, like me, and is well loved in the surfing community. Today, Carwyn runs a boarding house for surfers in Seignosse, Carwyn's Surf House.

Carwyn's fame, both for living out of cars and vans and surfing, particularly in France, is the result of a time when free campsites in the forest were all a part of the surfing experience. Alex Williams, surf photographer and surf archivist, told me: 'There was a free campsite in the forest in Hossegor. Carwyn based himself there for a year. Everybody heard about it and then it became music and drugs central, getting a bad reputation, so none of the surfers went there then.'

Sadly, real, lasting success in competition and on the professional circuit proved elusive for Carwyn.

He also proved elusive for me. I had been messaging with him for a few weeks to try and meet up. He had invited Lizzy and me to stay at the Surf House when we were passing Seignosse, so that was our plan, although things had gone quiet. I messaged to say we were on our way and would see him soon. Carwyn's place was 10km away so would take us a while. We had lunch, dodging sunbeams, and set off towards Seignosse town through the woods.

An hour later we found ourselves standing in front of a house with a leafy, banana tree-engulfed garden full of surfing junk and with doors wide open. No one appeared to be around, until a neighbour turned up and told us that Carwyn had gone to Bilbao for the weekend with his girlfriend.

What next? Our back-up plan was to head for Labenne-Océan, a little to the south, to stay with another Welsh import, my old friend Nick, an architect, and his wife Abi, a partially sighted artist. I was keen to see Nick because his story is as much a part of the 'way of the waves' as Carwyn's story is. He's spent large chunks of time living in his van in the forest and was here, when all's said and done, for one reason: surfing. Nick and Carwyn are friends: fellow Welshmen living the surfing dream.

I shared a flat at polytechnic with Nick but met him previously in North Wales, where he learnt to surf. During the summer he travelled to France with friends Jez and Spout.* His second trip, in 1989, with a friend who enjoyed the French lifestyle so much he drank all his cash and had to get the bus home, took him all the way to Portugal, following the route we were taking.

Back in France, Nick met a French woman, a local surfer from Tarnos. They travelled together and then went back to France when she became pregnant with their son, Nico. Nick and Vanessa split up in the mid-1990s, after which Nick and toddler Nico lived in their van on the beach in Tarnos.† When Nick met Abi, she moved to France and they bought the house in Labenne.

Nick and Abi's house had long been a safe space for me. Abi was a friend of my ex-wife (Nick and Abi met at our wedding in Ireland) so when we went there (when we were still married) it was like a family reunion where I could lose myself in the waves, the company, and the distance it allowed. Being around other people meant we could insulate ourselves from awful truths. At the time I couldn't face up to the fact that I was unhappy. Divorce, I knew, might mean losing my home and children. I wish I had spoken to Nick about it but I was afraid that talking might make it real. I regret the distance it caused and the shame I felt about it.‡ Since the divorce, we had become estranged.

The house is a small bungalow set in a large plot on the edge of the forest about 500 metres away from the beach at Labenne-Océan. There is a long veranda running along the front, leading to

---

* Before I went to Manchester Polytechnic I wrote to Colin Moore, of the North West Surf Club. He suggested I meet Spout and Jez, two surfers from Stockport. Meanwhile, I went to the Freshers' Ball, where a band called the Surfing Lungs were playing. I spotted two blokes wearing surfing T-shirts and accosted them. It turned out that they were Spout and Jez. Our surf gang – Spout, Jez, Nick and I – was tight for many years.

† This was at a time when it was easier to live in a van or car at the beach. Access was unrestricted and it was acceptable. Today, it is more difficult.

‡ My parents divorced when I was a teenager. At the time, the early 1980s, divorce was still stigmatised and I felt a deep shame about it.

the kitchen and main living area. This is where all the socialising, eating, drinking and living happens. In summer it's shaded and in winter it's dry. It's a 10-minute walk through the forest to the heaving, challenging peak that Nick and his family have been surfing for years.

When we arrived on our bikes it was, for me, like coming home. Going to Labenne, and sitting under the veranda, was important to me. Lizzy knew that, but it didn't make it any easier to go to the house of a friend of my ex-wife.

Nothing much had changed at the house except the kids had grown, two of them had moved away and Rosie, the youngest, had turned from a delightfully precocious, red-haired six-year-old into a shy, beautiful, dark-haired teenager. Nico, Nick's eldest, who I have known since he was a baby, had just got engaged and was living down the road in Bayonne. Alfie, Rosie's older brother, was full of life and optimism. Time had been good to them.

As I sat back into one of the wooden chairs under the veranda I travelled back 10 years. Labenne was always a stopping point. In 2012, when I travelled through northern Spain for three months with the kids in my old VW camper, Labenne was the place we always returned to. On other occasions, when we had time, Labenne called us. It was a sanctuary where the wine and good times flowed: days could pass in a blur.

'Right then,' Nick would say. 'What now? Who wants a brew?'

No one would move.

Like Hossegor, to the north, the surf at Labenne is heavy and difficult. The beach shelves steeply so the waves break in very shallow water, making them pitch violently. They break quickly too, which means you must get to your feet rapidly or else you go over the falls. In one surf session, many years ago, I broke a board, then, after I had run back to the house to fetch another board, broke a leash.

After the disappointment of not managing to meet up with Carwyn it was a great relief to be somewhere familiar. Nick sparked up the barbecue and we ate and drank the evening away under the veranda. While Abi and Lizzy got to know each other, Nick and I talked about life and surf here in Labenne.

Covid-19, he said, had brought great change. During lockdown the French authorities wouldn't let anyone surf or go on the beach. This was enforced with big fines and helicopters and officers with guns patrolling the coastline. When people were allowed on to the beach, it was only for exercise. It was bonkers, he said, authoritarianism gone mad. Since then, Nick felt, there had been a shift in attitude. There were more people surfing and more aggression in the water. Surfers were more likely to experience or commit acts of localism and dropping in.* The etiquette of surfing† had broken down.

Labenne is south of Capbreton and Soorts-Hossegor, a conurbation that surrounds the Canal d'Hossegor, a waterway that links the Lac d'Hossegor with the Atlantic. Capbreton sits to the south of the inlet with Hossegor to the north. Between them is the Port of Capbreton. The church at Soorts (the original settlement of Hossegor before 19th-century tourism) was built in the 14th century and was a stop-off for pilgrims following a coastal route towards Santiago de Compostela. Today, Soorts-Hossegor is the home of the French Surfing Federation, an organisation that was formed in 1964 by Guy Petit, mayor of Biarritz. The federation, its roots deep in the Biarritz sand, was created to unite the local surf tribes.

In 1987 the Federation created the State Surfing Certificate, authorising the taking of payment for teaching surfing and allowing surfers to make a living from their sport. This was a pivotal moment for surfing in France; now licensed, surf schools appeared up and down the coast.

Hossegor, or more precisely the beaches of La Nord and La Gravière, have become famous for handling huge surf because of a deep underwater canyon called the Gouf de Capbreton, which cuts through the continental shelf. The bathymetry of the canyon allows more swell to travel towards the coast and intensifies it, creating bigger surfable waves than anywhere else along this coast. Across the

---

* 'Dropping in' is when a surfer drops in on a surfer who is already surfing a wave, so ruining the ride for them. It is very bad manners.
† The etiquette of surfing is a set of rules concerned with dropping in, taking your turn in the line-up, paddling out so as not to interfere with people already riding, and respecting others.

channel from Hossegor, in Capbreton, the waves are usually smaller at Santocha and Océanides (more commonly called VVF after a nearby holiday centre, although I always knew it as 'Very Very Fast').

As the conurbation begins to fizzle out to the south of Capbreton there is an *aire de camping car* (an area reserved for camper vans and motorhomes to stay overnight) that's usually full of surfers' vans, and a campsite. On the ocean side of the dunes are the breaks at Santocha, VVF and La Piste, notable for the huge blockhouse that lies, shipwrecked, on the beach, known as 'the bunker'. It was just one of hundreds of structures that made up Hitler's Atlantic Wall, built between 1941 and 1944, that stretched from the Basque Country to Norway, to defend against invasion.

Labenne is the next town to the south. Thereafter the settlements of Ondres, Tarnos and Boucau sit on the north side of the Adour River with Bayonne, Anglet and Biarritz to the south. Beyond are Bidart, Saint-Jean-de-Luz, Guéthary and Hendaye. After that, the Bidasoa River and then, unbelievably, for me, because we had come that far already, Spain.

It's only about 60km from Soorts-Hossegor to Hendaye, but it's a stretch of coast that has had so much influence over European surfing it cannot be underestimated. It's no coincidence that many of the world's biggest surf brands have chosen to locate their European HQs here.

Before heading south to Biarritz, Lizzy and I surfed a small wave at Santocha among the surf schools and foamies. I took off my wetsuit and surfed in just a pair of shorts – the first time in a long while I had been able to enjoy such a luxury. It felt good to be able to surf in a crowd and I sensed my confidence grow a little.

That night, as we lay awake in our tent, a huge lightning storm rolled over Labenne. Hard rain thumped the tent and long rumbles of cracking and booming thunder exploded above us. A bolt of lightning landed somewhere in the forest behind the house, making us feel very small and vulnerable in our tiny nylon home.

13

The European pipeline

'There were a few guys that surfed. Mostly the French rich kids. Most of those who surfed were the Parisians that came down in August. We saw a lot of rich French kids surfing. I say kids, mid-teens, all with posh cars and beautiful girlfriends.'

MARTIN WARD, AKA 'MASHER', 2024

Stage 12: Day 28 | From: Labenne-Océan | To: Bidart | Distance: 42km

Staying with Nick and Abi gave us the opportunity to wash and dry our clothes and take a break from fending for ourselves. We had been on the road for four weeks and really appreciated small things like laundry and good food. Life under the veranda was easy, but although we were making good time, we had to keep going if we were to have any chance of making it to Portugal before our Schengen Area allowance ran out. We were a third of the way through the journey, both in time and distance, and had yet to explore the cradle of surfing in Europe: Biarritz, 30km to the south.

The lumpy bike path through the woods to Ondres and Tarnos was rough and tricky, with big muddy puddles. Once we reached Boucau the route ran alongside the railway line into Bayonne on a very narrow bike path, where we encountered a puss-faced sit-up-and-beg cyclist coming the other way who, apparently, couldn't wait for 10 seconds, and had to have priority. This sent us into margins of broken glass while our faces were brushed by a hedge of unrestrained privet. We missed a few signposts for the Vélodyssée too, found ourselves in narrow, one-way streets and made a mess of the whole thing.

As I trundled along a busy road I heard a sickening, hollow clatter. I turned around and realised that it was the boards, which were now lying in the road behind me, having slid off the rack. I jumped off the bike and rushed to them, as if they were patients in need of emergency care. I fully expected them to be knackered beyond repair, but was relieved to find that, bar a few scratches, they were, incredibly, OK and wouldn't need CPR. Had a vehicle been following me it would have been very different. Boards are fragile, despite being strong, and can be wrecked by a careless baggage handler, never mind a car or truck. It was my fault entirely as I hadn't checked the straps were tight enough before we set off.

Since having the new wheels fitted in Soulac by Saint Eric I had had to strap the boards on the bike in a different configuration because of the way the trailer sat on its bigger wheels. They rolled better over potholes but made the trailer lean forwards more, so the boards sat lower over my rear pannier rack. This meant the tent and wetsuits needed to be off the rack and the boards needed to be lashed in a very specific way so they didn't sit too far back and cause the trailer to weave or too far forward so they didn't poke me up the arse when I went down a kerb. If I ever got rear-ended I dread to think what might have happened.

We crossed the river in Bayonne and rewarded ourselves at a patisserie in the narrow streets of the old town, then followed the bike lanes along the Adour River out to the coast and the most lamented of all France's beaches, La Barre, the lost jewel in France's surfing crown (if I may use a cliché like that).

La Barre, the first beach south of the Ardour, was once considered to be the 'Pipeline of Europe',[*] attracting an international crowd

---

[*] Waves are often compared with Pipeline in Hawaii, one of the heaviest waves in the world, especially by those wanting validation for their local spot. 'It's like Pipeline on its day' is a common phrase you might hear at beaches all around the world. The response is, of course, 'No, it isn't.'

of travelling surfers. Fast, hollow and heavy, it was the wave that everyone wanted to surf because it would work at any size, at any tide, and was protected from the summer's daytime onshore winds.*

Kevin Cooke, chair of trustees of the Museum of British Surfing and one of the co-founders of North Devon World Surfing Reserve, who first travelled the 'way of the waves' in 1971, surfed La Barre before it was destroyed. He's in his 70s now but still has the surfer's glint in his eye. He told me, over a cup of tea at his home in Woolacombe:

> We were taking it quite far out on the shoulder but because of the steep beaches there, you knew that you only had a couple of strokes and you were on a wave. We weren't taking it as deep as many of the guys out there. But we all had our moment and all came out of the water grinning.

Doctor Dave Sweet, a pioneer surfer from Bude, who travelled to France in the autumn of 1968 with Pete Vickery and Bude surf shop owner Dick Willoughby, found La Barre by accident and, in doing so, happened upon a pivotal moment in France's surfing history:

> We got to Biarritz, headed towards the sea and found La Barre. It was big and one of the Lartigau brothers[†] was out surfing. There were three or four guys on the beach watching. And we said to them, 'Are you going in?' and they said, 'No, it's too big.' It was Ted Spencer, Wayne Lynch and Nat Young. I think Sumpter[‡] was there too. I think it was in one of his films.

---

[*] In summer the 'continental offshore effect' causes onshore winds during the day because the land heats up more quickly than the water. In the morning and evening, the wind often blows offshore.

[†] Arnaud and Jean-Marie Lartigau were stand-out surfers from Biarritz. Jean-Marie was French champion from 1962 to 1968.

[‡] Rod Sumpter features later but, for now: he was born in Watford but moved to Australia with his parents on a £10 ticket in the 1950s. He became a very good surfer, was featured in *The Endless Summer* and won numerous titles. He made a few surf films, with Simone Renvoize, the daughter of Newquay photography shop owner, in the 1970s and 1980s, after moving to Cornwall.

In 1968 the first European Championships were held at La Barre, adding to the hype, along with appearances in surf films of the day. Nat Young, who was the 1966 world champion, and Wayne Lynch, Australian junior champion at the time, surfed in the 1968 Championship, bringing with them the new, shorter boards that were in full transition in Australia and elsewhere in the world but had yet to reach France.

If you wanted to see the future of surfing in late 1960s Europe, La Barre was the place to go.

The wave was all but destroyed by dredging and the extending of the jetty at the mouth of the Adour River in the early 1970s. This has added to the mystique surrounding it, and perhaps amplified its importance. But there is little doubt it was a big draw for travelling surfers. Rare film footage of La Barre by British filmmakers like Bez Newton* and Rod Sumpter and his co-conspirator Simone Renvoize brought the first generation of surfers to La Barre – while it lasted.

Arriving at La Barre, for me, was underwhelming, if I am honest, although I knew the place resonated with history and soul. Perhaps it didn't help that the surf was flat, but maybe it was for the best: how depressing would it have been to see a small wave there and think of what it had once been? The wave was destroyed for reasons of commerce, but I wonder how much that commerce is worth to the region today compared with the surfing industry.

Neil Richardson, a surfer from Rochdale who travelled to Biarritz in 1978, had told me about a darker side to La Barre:

> A lot of people used to stay at what they called 'the desert' or 'the tip' at La Barre. There was a quite a heavy scene there in those

---

* Bez Newton was a British surfer and filmmaker who started the Sol y Mar surf club and was influential in British surfing, surf publishing and competition. He is perhaps most famous for writing two semi-pornographic novels about surfing, *The Natural* and *The Islander*. He also invented a board game based on surfing contests.

days, you used to get your stuff ripped off, so my missus wasn't keen; she wanted to stay in a proper campsite.

We stopped at Les Cavaliers, Plages d'Anglet, La Madrague and Chambre d'Amour — all famous surf breaks — before taking the steep cliffside path from the tasteless superyacht-like hotel Belambra Clubs' 'La Chambre d'Amour' to the clifftop road that runs into Biarritz. As we cycled across a pedestrian crossing with painted surfboard shapes instead of black-and-white stripes, I felt the weight of surfing's influence. This small, chic and hip town became, in the late 1950s, surfing's European fountainhead. Surfing, it seemed, ran through Biarritz like the letters in a stick of rock.

We passed stone-built villas, apartment blocks and turreted houses hiding behind the bushy purple-fronded tamarisks lining the walkways and esplanade above Plage Miramar. A right turn on to Avenue de Generale de Gaulle brought us to the municipal gardens behind Grande Plage and the first view of the beach and Casino Barrière, the building that dominates the Biarritz beachfront. It was every bit as swanky as I remembered and I felt like an imposter among the beautiful people in my sweaty merino and with my mud-splattered trailer.

We followed the road around the beach, to the harbour, by the side of Sainte-Eugénie Church of Biarritz and through the short tunnel leading to the Port Vieux, a tiny beach that was thronging with scantily-clad gadaboutery. Around the point and along the side of the cliff towards the huge beach at Côte des Basques, home of the Waikiki Surf Club, and the first surf shop and surf school in Europe, run by Joe Moraiz, one of France's first surf gang.

The Vélodyssée took us along the coast, past the surfing beaches of Milady, Marbella and Ilbarritz, the Cité de l'Océan museum and on to Le Pavillon Royal, a campsite at the southern fringes of Biarritz where we would make our home for the next three wet and windy nights. Sainthood goes to Ana of The Caravan and Motorhome Club for organising a one-roomed mini apartment for us that was boiling but overlooked the pool and was just a two-minute walk from the sand-covered reefs of Pavillon Royal, a popular choice for surfers like Neil Richardson, who didn't want to risk wild camping at 'the tip' in the free-to-camp-but-good-old-bad-old-days at La Barre.

We dragged the mattresses off the two single beds, whacked them together on the floor, unpacked our panniers, surprised ourselves how much we could fill a space with our crap, and hit the bar.

Joël de Rosnay had implied that Biarritz was ready for surfing when it arrived, even if it was in the form of a borrowed board that had been sent over from Malibu and left behind. The conditions, as it were, were perfect, as Joël explained in *Surfer* Magazine in 1962:

> For a long time a lot of locals have been fantastic bodysurfers. The bellyboard was introduced around the [19]30s and bodysurfing just after the war. Michel Barland, André Plumcoq, Robert Bergeruc, the Moraiz brothers began to progress very quickly.

Michel Barland, an engineer from Bayonne, became very influential in French surfing when he began to make boards, starting with balsa but eventually blowing his own foam, in the late 1950s. Together with Jacky Rott, a cabinetmaker who had started to make *planckys* in the early 1950s and who had tried to copy Viertel/Zanuck's board, Barland began to manufacture surfboards under the Barland Rott label, and became mainland Europe's first commercial board maker. In the 1970s, Barland invented a computer shaping machine that predated anything anywhere else in the world by more than a decade.

Joël de Rosnay, in his second article as the 'French correspondent' for *The Surfer*, said of surfing:

> It is a real passion. It means friendship, liberty, holidays. Surfing is a new field, almost a new way of life. I am not interested in making a profit from surfing; the sport will always remain a passion and an occasion to meet and talk with others, from far distant countries, about the same passion. Sometimes you meet someone who will talk to you about surf, a light shining in his eyes – that's enough, he will be a surfing friend.

I wondered if I would still find that spirit in Biarritz.

14

Back to the beginning

'When things got crowded at La Barre, we moved further down towards Biarritz itself. Côte des Basques became our place ....You could sit on the wall for sunset surf, watch it all go down and then go to the pub afterwards. Up to the Steakhouse.'

KEVIN COOKE, CHAIR OF TRUSTEES OF THE
MUSEUM OF BRITISH SURFING, 2024

Stage 13: Days 29–30 | From: Biarritz | To: Biarritz | Distance: 0km

The wind dropped in the mid-morning and turned light offshore so we suited up and walked down to the beach from the campsite. A set of stone steps, undercut by the waves at the bottom, led us directly on to the sand at the north end. We walked southwards, towards the dark, cheerless mountains of the Pyrenees, to where a couple of surfers were already in the water, surfing a peaky left breaking on the seaward side of a shallow lagoon. The waves were small – about 2–3ft – but breaking nicely. Lizzy walked a bit further down the beach to try her luck with a right-hander that was breaking away from the lagoon. The waves were punchy and powerful, even though they were small. I duck-dived a few – more than I thought I would have to – before breaking through the last one and reaching flat water beyond the impact zone.

The Spanish hills lay across the water to my left, some 20km away. I tried not to think about them as I sat on my board and waited for a set to approach. When the waves came – in peaks rather than in straight lines – the offshore wind held them up until they broke with a crack.

I surfed a few of the rights then decided to surf the left. It was bigger and was breaking more regularly, and more steeply, although the two surfers were taking a lot of the better ones. I paddled over and waited for a chance to surf one for myself. I didn't want to start competing with the French guys for waves. It never feels right to try and steal waves from under someone's nose when they were enjoying them. All it does is create an atmosphere.

I was in a perfect position when a wave came, the tallest part of it right in front of me. I turned for the beach, put in a few quick arm-strokes and dropped straight into a beautiful curling wave that was about head high, still unbroken to my left, tapering off into the channel. I reached the bottom and turned back upwards, hitting the steepest part of the lip as it curled over. I dropped again with the whitewater, pushing the board hard on to its rail to gain speed. I hit the lip again, straightened up and set up to trim in the steepest part of the wave, gliding, flowing. The wave died out in the shallows and I kicked out, turning back to paddle out again, smiling to myself.

When things go well, surfing feels effortless. Allowing the wave to do most of the work means you are surfing with it, rather than against it, using its pockets of power to pick up speed, turn and fall again. Most of the manoeuvres surfers perform are functional, allowing them to remain in the steepest and fastest part of the wave.

For me there is never any question of conquering the waves, only of being in harmony. If that takes me to the edges of my capabilities and out of my comfort zone, all the better: let the adrenaline flow.

Sadly, so much of the language around surfing is aggressive, focusing on surfers 'dominating' the waves. I see this as crass and toxic: a sign that machoism is still an unfortunate part of the sport. All you can ever hope to do, as a surfer, is dance the fine line between disaster and glory. The closer those things are to each other, the better the opportunity but also the greater possibility of failure.

BACK TO THE BEGINNING

If a pulse of swell (or wave) travels out of deep water into a very steeply shelving beach, or a very shallow rock or coral reef, it stops suddenly and violently, rising until it has no choice but to trip over itself. The top, still travelling at the same speed as it was in open ocean, sometimes creates a tube, sometimes a gentle cascade of whitewater, but mostly a curl. That's the steepest part of the wave where all the energy is being dissipated – the part where surfers want to be.

This is the principle that governs all surfing waves (other than those caused by tides)* and makes some waves better than others, even if the quality of the ocean swell is the same. It is the shape of the seabed that, mostly, makes the shape of the waves. The underwater channel at Hossegor, for example, allows the swell to travel unimpeded in deep water before it hits the shallow sandbars. This means the waves rise quickly and violently – usually in the same spot – and are bigger than anywhere else on the coast.

Winds that blow offshore (from the land to the sea) help to hold up the wave and make them steeper and more surfable. When the wind blows onshore (from the sea to the land) it blows the waves over, flattening them and making what might have been an organised sea into a frothing, confused mess.

Another factor that makes waves what they are when they reach landfall is the quality of the swell. Waves are formed by wind blowing across the surface of the ocean. The harder the wind blows and the longer it blows for, the bigger the chop, and then the waves, that will be created. As waves radiate out from a storm they organise themselves into ocean swell and the longer they travel in open ocean the better-organised that swell will be. The distance a swell travels is known as the fetch. Storms far out at sea create waves that are more organised and have a longer wave period (the time between waves) and may be easier to surf than those created locally, because they are more predictable. Local winds create short-period waves and are often harder to surf as they are less easy to read.

---

* Tidal waves, or bores, are waves created by tides travelling up a constantly narrowing river.

After surfing at Pavillon Royal I left the water feeling refreshed and happy, buzzing with adrenaline and the memory of a few nice rides, in warm water, on a trip that I was absolutely in love with.

My stoke was short-lived.

We walked into Biarritz via Cité de l'Océan et du Surf, a museum and attraction devoted to the ocean and surfing, which lies just behind Milady Beach, a little to the north of the campsite. Set within a huge white building that looks a bit like an enormous cobbled skate ramp, it is a state-of-the-art museum with exhibition spaces devoted to all aspects of the ocean, including surfing, naturally. As well as the big-hitting attractions – 3D and virtual reality – it houses a large collection of vintage surfboards from across the eras of surfing: my main reason for wanting to go.

I was reluctant to try the surf simulator, but stood in the queue anyway. Through the magic of virtual reality it promised me an unforgettable journey to surf the world's best waves, so who was I to argue? It would, at the very least, perhaps, give me an insight into how the modern world sees surfing.

Projected on to the VR headset were digital recreations of 'Seven Mythical Waves' around the world, including Pipeline in Hawaii, Mundaka in Spain, Nazaré in Portugal and Belharra in the Basque Country. All of them, in the real world, are terrifying monsters: giant, hollow waves, jacked up by shallow reefs or sandbars, heaving from deep ocean or, in the case of Nazaré, another deepwater canyon like at Hossegor.

I have surfed Mundaka (more of that later) but wouldn't dream of paddling out at Pipeline or Nazaré, so this would be my chance to virtually ride like the big boys and girls. I took my place on a surfboard-shaped pad on the floor, alongside four other 'surfers', and put on the headset. As the playback began I was transported to Hawaii to surf Pipeline (or at least a digital recreation of it). To 'surf' I had to lean forwards to go faster, lean back to slow down and wave my arms about to turn. It felt, to me, like a pastiche of what Hollywood might think people look like when they surf. Imagine Elvis surfing in the film *Blue Hawaii*, or, in the very worst cases, the Village People, in boardshorts, spelling out YMCA.

I thought of Eugene: where was my Beach Boys soundtrack when I needed it?

BACK TO THE BEGINNING

Pride, of course, got in the way and I tried to 'ride' the waves as authentically as possible, using the kind of body positions I would have used if I had to surf such terrifying waves (curled up in a ball in a hotel room most likely) instead of operating the machine as it wanted. I didn't want to look like a kook. The plan failed: I was 'hosed' by my own petard and the virtual me got the beating of his life.

Everything about it felt wrong: the sound of waves crashing and booming, the wind blowing offshore and swirling with the turbulence caused by the breaking waves, the weight of tonnes and tonnes of water, the sun, the salt, the smell. It was all missing.

When the 'ride' finished, a woman in high heels had won the most points. The man collecting headsets congratulated her and asked her if she was a surfer.

'I had a lesson last week,' she said.

Everything I knew was useless in this modern, virtual world! Today, it is the person who knows how to press the buttons who wins at this game, rather than the one who has spent a lifetime learning how to read and surf waves. The soul of surfing has moved on.

Lizzy queued up for another simulator, the 'Surf Sensation 5D'. With a VR headset giving her a view of the waves, she virtually surfed Teahupo'o while being drizzled with spray and wafted by an oscillating fan, standing on a board that moved beneath her feet, hanging on to a safety rail.

I sulked off to look at the vintage surfboards, which were hung on the walls, in search of something more. Each one of the boards represented a moment in surfing history. I stood beneath them and looked up to examine them as if looking up at statues in a church. Despite the history and soul that oozed from every inch of wood, faded yellow foam, fibreglass and cracked resin, I was the only one looking at them in any detail.

These surfboards – spanning more than 60 years of surfing history – were a Trojan horse in this house of modernity. They were ever-present but were not the main attraction because people wanted to be entertained. What better than a virtual surfing machine? You can master the world's biggest waves in five minutes without taking off your stilettoes.

The boards, however, were incredible, iconic* even. There was a hollow 'cigar box' from the 1940s of about 16ft long, and a solid wood 12ft paipo that was ridden by generations of Hawaiians. There were modern shortboards – thrusters, twin fins, bonzers and quads – as well as single fins from the beginning of the shortboard revolution in the late 1960s. There were two of Greg Noll's 'Da Cat' models signed by Miki Dora (the bestselling signature model in the history of surfing), some boards by local shapers Barland Rott and a signature Jo Moraiz. They were a tangible link to the past and to France's surf history: a solid reminder of the waves discovered and ridden before.

But these boards were museum pieces and would probably never see water again. Certainly never under my feet. They were priceless. Beautiful.

Barland Rott boards were the first boards to be commercially manufactured in France: there were a few on display. Michel Barland was among France's first group of surfers – the *tontons*† – and won the European Championships in 1962. Barland's boards were expensive and beautifully made but not everyone could afford them, which opened opportunities for British surfers looking to pay for their travels by selling surf stuff.

In the 1960s, and even into the 1970s, the surf industry had yet to take off in Europe but was thriving in the UK. British manufacturers like Tiki in North Devon, Bilbo in Newquay and Freedom in Jersey stepped in to fill the hungry, open mouths of the fledgling French wave sliders.

Martin 'Masher' Ward, who was working for Tiki, went over to France regularly to sell boards and gear. His first trip to France was in 1970. He told me:

---

* I don't use the word 'iconic' lightly. Its true meaning, having been partly lost by TV, the internet and influencers who call things 'iconic' when all they are is good, different or even passable. It annoys the shit out of me. Sorry not sorry.
† The uncles, or forefathers.

BACK TO THE BEGINNING

There was no French surf industry. Barland was making boards. They were good boards, but expensive, so the French surfers were always trying to buy ours. You could subsidise your trip by taking a spare board down and flogging it to some French guy.

It developed from there into something of a black-market industry:

I think the most we took was 37 boards. We got on the ferry and drove down, with paperwork that said we were the British surf team. The van would be loaded up to the gunnels with wax, wetsuits, boards, everything. And we would drive down to Biarritz. Some of the time we would have pre-orders from Jo Moraiz. He would buy some of the stuff and other stuff we'd sell directly on the beaches.

It was like a scene out of *'Allo 'Allo!* one night. Jo appeared, almost in disguise. We had to unload the boards in darkness and he gave me a bag full of French francs.

But the customs guys, they would see us with loads of boards and then when we drove back, they would ask, 'What has happened to the boards?' We would say, 'Oh, they all got snapped when we were surfing.' It was ridiculous some of the stuff we were getting up to. It was crazy. Then it turned into blanks. We were driving Bennett foam blanks [Tiki had the UK licence to make them] down there on trailers and that was when the French surf industry started.

It was the start of the real surfing boom. People don't realise how instrumental Tiki was in European surfing. Nobody else was making foam, when we were supplying Steve Harewood from Freedom, and he was doing the same – taking boards down.

One guy got caught by customs. They impounded his van and took all his surfboards. We were driving around Biarritz shitting ourselves because we had £40,000 of stuff, which in those days was a fortune. We didn't want to get discovered but we also needed to sell it.

Lizzy and I wandered into Biarritz. We passed Côte des Basques, looking down on the small waves breaking on the boulder-backed beach. This was where the Steakhouse, the epicentre of French and European surfing, used to be.

Kevin Cooke, who worked there in the 1970s, told me when I interviewed him:

> The Steakhouse was the place to go . . . at the top of the hill in Côte des Basques . . . that was the surfing hangout, where all the travelling surfers would go, read about in *Surfer Magazine*. We tended to dominate . . . our little van full of people made ourselves known there.
>
> A year later I went at the beginning of the summer and picked up a job at the Steakhouse. I worked in the evening washing pots. I had a room in the centre of Biarritz so I could surf Grande Plage. Had a really great time, surfing during the day, then washing up in the evening at the Steakhouse, getting my food and meeting up with loads of guys in the surfing world.

Masher (Martin Ward), when I interviewed him, had also mentioned the Steakhouse:

> The Steakhouse was where all the surf fraternity used to meet. The Devon boys would congregate there, and you would have the Cornish contingency and the Welsh boys were there and then you'd have travelling Americans, Australians. It really was a vibrant place to be. There was no us and them – no French animosity, no localism.

The universal thread of Biarritz in the 1970s was good times. Masher continued:

> Oh, it was amazing. Surfing without wetsuits in warm water. The whole French thing, you know. Being in France and living in a tent and eating French food and going to the Steakhouse at night.

Surf-wise it was eye-opening too, especially for Brits brought up on Devon or Cornwall's beach breaks.

BACK TO THE BEGINNING

Masher confirmed this:

The beach breaks between Chambre d'Amour to La Barre were incredible. As good as it gets. We would surf it on our own. I remember the first time I surfed Guéthary. We hadn't surfed reef breaks or point breaks prior to that. Amazing waves that broke in the same place, that weren't going to kill you but were still serious.

Walking around Biarritz brought us into contact with the commercial side of surfing for the first time since leaving home. We had cycled through surf towns with surf schools, surf shops and surf-themed bars and restaurants, but hadn't been anywhere like Biarritz. Surf boutiques and clothing stores sat side by side with chi-chi bars and hangouts in a unique Paris-meets-the-sea way. They made me confront what surfing was today: a multi-million-Euro business supporting individuals, shops, manufacturers and giant corporations. The 'Global Surfing Report 2024', a 387-page business report on the state of the industry, estimates, top line, that surfing in 2023 was worth €4.2 billion, with an estimate that, by 2030 it will be worth €5.5 billion.

Compare that with a few guys filling up a VW combi with blanks to sell to a French surf shop owner in a back street of Biarritz.

I found it mind-boggling how much had changed, and in less than 60 years. Yet Biarritz somehow managed to ooze cool and soul that made surfing still feel like a cottage industry. Even the big players like Rip Curl, who have two stores in Biarritz, keep a low profile, but have outlet stores on the industrial estates outside Seignosse and out-of-town headquarters in Hossegor. Decathlon,* latecomer to the surf party with its new Olaian brand, has its surf HQ in Hendaye.

I love surf shops and I love looking at boards and new developments, from the faddish to the functional, but I had no desire

---

* Decathlon, the giant French sports retailer, now have their own surfing brand, Olaian, selling boards, wetsuits, bikinis and all kinds of surf lifestyle gear.

to go shopping. However, we did pick out, out of necessity, stylish (and expensive) French pac-a-macs. To say it had been a bit rash to have sent our waterproofs home was a massive understatement: it seemed, from the brooding clouds over the peaks to the south, that we would need them.

We wandered the narrow streets of the old town watching the people. There were bars and restaurants everywhere, full of young, tanned surfy-looking people appearing to have a great time: cool-as-fuck, golden kids living a golden life.

Emily Currie, 2023 European women's longboard champion, and Bude local, travels to Biarritz regularly.

She told me:

> I immersed myself. I loved that kind of lifestyle. It's so much more relaxed than the UK. You wake up. You go surfing. You grab a coffee. Pastries, chocolate milk. You go surfing again and you spend your day on the beach or in the town. And you go back at night-time, and you repeat again. It was eye-opening for me when I was a fresh 16-year-old. There were parties with the surf crew. I was like, wow, so exciting! Wake up and go surf again.

Lizzy and I, not wishing to shy away from local delicacies, shared a plate of snails* over lunch, then bumped into Tony and Patricia Grant, friends from our phones, who had been following our journey on social media. They were sitting outside a bar having a mid-afternoon beer.

Just up the road, in a narrow back street near the harbour, we found a bar, Bar de Marine, and sent a picture of it home to Pete Vickery. In 1963 he had made it his 'local' while he was there because his local in Bude, the bar nearest to Crooklets Beach, was also called the Marine. I had promised Vicko I would find it but never thought for a moment that we would be able to, 60 years after he had been there, instigating an interesting meeting of cultures.

---

* When in Rome. I actually like snails, although they are a bit odd and, of course, a cliché to eat in Biarritz.

BACK TO THE BEGINNING

Vicko had told me:

On the last night, before we were coming home, we were in the Bar de Marine and we spoofed* for mopeds. You know, those ones where you drop the engine on the wheel. We won two. Bert won one and I won one. Then we had to get them back to England. When we came through customs, we asked if we had to have them taxed or insured. And the guy said, 'Where do you come from?' 'Bude, Cornwall.' 'No, you don't worry down there, mate.' The first night I went out on it, I got caught by the police and had to go to court.

It wasn't all one-way traffic. The French bought surfboards and we cleaned them out of mopeds.

Seemed like a fair exchange.

---

* 'Spoofing' is playing a gambling game, involving guessing the number of coins held in the hand. The loser usually has to buy a round of drinks or, as here, hand over their mopeds.

15

Where did surfing go wrong?

> *'This guy came up and asked, "Are you English? Do you play ping-pong? Let's play. A dollar a game?" My friend Roland arrived and said, "Hello! Boys, this is Miki Dora." He was trying to hustle us!'*
>
> ALEX WILLIAMS, 2024

Stage 14: Day 31 | From: Bidart | To: Hendaye | Distance: 30km

We checked the surf at Pavillon Royal at first light but an onshore wind was messing up the small waves, making them look very unappetising.

With nothing else to do except hit the road, we tidied up the apartment, packed up the bikes and set off for Hendaye, our last stop in France. The coastline south of Biarritz was beautiful: lush and green with small sand and rock bays, and small hills to climb. I didn't mind the climbs, which took us from bay to bay and into the steep back streets of Bidart. Lizzy was right: we were much fitter now we'd had 1300km of flat riding to tune ourselves up.

Things felt different here in the Basque Country. The landscape had changed. We had passed through the sandy flats and forest and now we were approaching Spain, the country in Europe with an average elevation second only to Switzerland. Many of the houses we passed, painted white with red- or green-painted doors and shutters, looked more like they belonged in the alps than to the dunes.

We crossed a railway line and wound our way into Guéthary, home to three famous surf breaks: Parlementia, Avalanche and Les Alcyons.

There are other spots to the south, such as Senix and Lafitenia, all of which have been surfed since the 1970s. The waves break over reefs, another sign that we were moving on from the beaches of Landes.

In the late 1970s and 1980s, if you were lucky (or unlucky) you might have bumped into Miki Dora, one of surfing's greatest characters, in Guéthary.

Dora was in the eye of the surfing storm when it hit America in the late 1950s. It could even be said that he was the storm. His influence on surfing cannot be underestimated. He was born in 1934, in Budapest, to a Hungarian Hussar and an American beauty. They moved with him to California in 1935, where his father opened a restaurant on Hollywood Boulevard. Dora's mother ran off with a lifeguard shortly after, so his early life was divided between Malibu and San Onofre, two of surfing's most famous haunts.

Miki became the best surfer at Malibu in the early 1950s – a master of the hotdogging* style – and, in doing so, became a legend. Watching films of Dora today it's easy to see why he got the nickname of 'Da Cat'. He was lithe and stylish, always seemingly on the brink, dancing on the edge of possibility, like a cat always landing on its feet. When everyone else was going straight, Dora was zigzagging through the surf and his life: a rebel with a cause who hated the mainstream finding the sport he helped make popular.

Surfing was deeply underground in the late 1940s and early 1950s. At Malibu, a crew of hardcore characters lived a different kind of lifestyle that was free and easy and not so different from the 'beach boys' of Waikiki; they surfed, dived and fished. Dora was among them. Brought up in military schools, he had come to resent authority and be distrustful of conformity. Surfing had given him freedom from

---

* 'Hotdogging' is a flamboyant style of surfing that originated in California in the 1950s and 1960s. It involved doing flashy stunts and sharp turns on the waves – sideslipping, 360 spins and head dips – that were only possible with newer, more manoeuvrable, wide-tailed longboards – 'pigs' – that Dale Velzy had started to shape in the 1950s. Some reports say that the first boards taken to Biarritz by Zanuck and first ridden by the French were Velzy-shaped pigs.

the crap of a standard postwar existence. A normal life wasn't for Dora. Sound familiar?

During this period a teenage Kathy Kohner spent time hanging out at Malibu learning to surf. Her father, Frederick, a Hollywood screenwriter, wrote a novel based on the experiences she had had at Malibu – in and out of the water – and had gushed to him or written in her diary. *Gidget, The Little Girl with Big Ideas* was published by Putnam in 1957 and sold 500,000 copies.

In 1959 the film of the book came out in the USA, starring Sandra Dee as Gidget. It was slated by the highbrow critics but was a box office hit, bringing surfing to the inland masses for the first time. Miki Dora doubled for actor James Darren, who played Moondoggie, Gidget's romantic interest. He also acted as a surfing consultant and stuntman.

Like Greg Noll going to Australia in 1956, *Gidget* was a moment that has passed into surfing lore. The sport was changed forever as the movie brought surfing to America's consciousness. The sport had its heroes and antiheroes in the form of surfers like Dora, music from Dick Dale (and, later, The Beach Boys), magazines (*The Surfer* started in 1962) and a brand-new industry keen to cash in on its success. *Gidget* spawned a bunch of sequels, a new surfsploitation genre and even a TV show in the mid-1960s.

Gidget, and the bandwagon that followed, brought crowds of new surfers to California's beaches, and especially Malibu. This was a problem for Dora, who until then had enjoyed uncrowded waves with a close crew of friends and enemies. He had had the best of it.

Watching films from the era is enlightening: in one, Dora kicks his board at other surfers' heads, pushing them off 'his wave' and throwing rocks at them like a petulant child. He was, in defence of his local break, which he felt was his, a colonialist: a local who didn't want anyone having what he had. He spray-painted swastikas on his boards and made Nazi salutes.

The question is there if you want to ask it: did surfing's commercialisation, of which he was a part, turn Dora into an arsehole, or was he one already? He would, famously, during the Malibu days and forever after, do anything to fund his surfing lifestyle, from hustling for small change to smuggling diamonds.

The surf world worships Dora as a hero because he was a stylish surfer. That he rode waves with panache, and was charming and intelligent, allowed surfing to ignore his racism, hatred and violence. Are you OK with that? Call me a heretic for not worshipping false idols, but I'm not.

Dora's attitude in Malibu is often said to be the start of localism in surfing. He was the original 'surf Nazi' who protected what he saw as his from outsiders. Really, he was just another arrogant wanker in the line-up, albeit one who ripped. Every surf spot has one.

Localism is a cancer that has spread throughout the surfing world, thanks in part to people like Dora. Those who have grown up near the beach, or who have spent a lot of time at a beach, see it as their patch. They resent outsiders and are prepared to fight to protect their 'rights' to the waves. It might be understandable in places like Hawaii, where local-born Hawaiians have taken back control of their waves, and get respect for it, as a direct result of colonialism, but it isn't right for every beach. Even with the righteous 'romance' of sovereignty, localism can still be ugly. Enforcing localism requires a breakdown in surfing etiquette, leading to violence and, at the least, a bad atmosphere. Nobody wants to be around when people are fighting.

Having to leave the USA, for various reasons, Miki Dora set off to seek perfect, uncrowded waves on an extended world tour, finding Guéthary along the way. His exploration made him a surfing trailblazer, funded by everyone except himself, through fraud and theft.

France, in the 1970s, must have felt like the California Dora knew of old: the water was warm, the food was great and the waves were good. Plus, there were fewer surfers. There was also a steady stream of English-speaking surfers to scam in a game of ping-pong. It was no coincidence that Alex Williams's encounter with Dora would be the way it was. It was what everyone came to expect. Yeah, but have you seen him surf?

After Dora's death to cancer in 2002 a plaque was fixed to his favourite bench on the terrace overlooking the waves at Parlementia, where he was often pictured sitting. It was stolen soon after, then was replaced, only to be stolen again. I guess what's good for the goose is good for the gander, right?

Ironically, such is Dora's infamy that I found myself in Guéthary, seeking out 'Dora's bench'. We rounded a bend and found ourselves looking at the sea and the old port of Guéthary. There, on a terrace with views of the reef, was a small park with wooden benches. I had downloaded a copy of a picture of Dora sitting on 'his' bench in the village and compared it with what I saw in front of me. The columns on the park's low balustrade looked identical: the bench was unmistakably the same. I wondered if this was the place. Did it matter if I was wrong? Not really. I went there to tell the story of Miki Dora and his place in surfing history.

Was Dora where surfing went wrong? Did localism kill surfing's soul?

A quick google revealed a Greg Noll-shaped Miki Dora 'Da Cat' model from 1966 – the best-selling signature surfboard in surfing history, as seen in Cité de l'Océan – was on sale for £21,000. Dora, despite hating everything about selling out, commercialisation and the mainstream, got a cut from each one sold. The only rules he lived by were his own.

Masher, a surfer who has lived a truly incredible surfer's life, got on to the subject of Dora when we met. He came across him often on his trips in the 1970s, often in France:

> I met Miki Dora a few times and he was a rogue. Every time I met him, he knew who I was. I wasn't a famous surfer but he would see me enough through Europe to know what we were up to. He would pretend that we had never met before. And I would think, hang on, you were having a beer with us a couple of weeks ago in the Steakhouse.
>
> He was into smuggling all sorts of things. Diamonds and all manner of stuff. He really was a nasty crook. You know people say Miki Dora 'The Cat' and all that? He was a horrible man.

There was no plaque on the bench. I sat on it anyway and Lizzy took a picture. I wish I could have seen what Dora saw when he sat here but it wasn't to be: the surf was flat. I had recently finished David Rensin's book, *All For a Few Perfect Waves*, about 'the audacious life and legend of rebel surfer Miki Dora' and so wanted to make him a part of the story (because he is). But, really, it didn't feel great hero-worshipping Dora. It would have been better to worship the waves instead.

The next beach south from Guéthary was Plage de Senix, a small cove with a few well-known waves. I had surfed here once before.

On that day there were a lot of people in the water but I paddled out anyway. As I waited for a wave, there was one guy sitting inside of me, meaning he had priority.

When a wave came that either of us could have caught, I asked, 'Are you going?'

He replied, 'Yes. But you go too!'

We took off together, riding the wave right next to each other, laughing. I had never met him before and he had given away his wave, an act of generosity I rarely see in surfing. Afterwards, in the car park, I thanked him.

'It was nothing,' he said.

We shook hands. He could have just said 'yes' and taken the wave and I would have waited for the next one. I reminded myself to do this more often: pass on the good vibrations and make someone happy. You just never know what might happen.

Lizzy and I continued towards Saint-Jean-de-Luz – a beautiful port town with narrow streets, great beaches and expensive boutiques that has long been the choice for well-to-do French and Spanish aristocrats – and cycled straight into a sea of excited people wearing black with red neckerchiefs. The streets were closed for the festival of Saint Jean and had been overrun with food stalls, stages and a huge funfair. We pushed the bikes through the throng down the main pedestrian street feeling very out of place.

The hill out of Saint-Jean-de-Luz was steep and long. It took us inland to avoid the fast coastal road of La Corniche Basque, a dangerous route (for cyclists) that runs along the cliffs for a couple of kilometres. Instead, we were treated to a climb up to the highest point in the area with views of the dark peaks of Spain in front of us and the Pyrenees to the east. The road, a single track for much of the way, passed through lush meadows and fields of maize separated from us by barbed-wire fences on rickety wooden posts. Farmhouses with red-tiled roofs and painted beams and shutters sat in huge plots.

We joined the Corniche Basque for the descent into Hendaye, the last town before the border, a holiday hotspot. It took us straight on to the long, straight seafront that looked over a yellow sand beach. The surf was looking good so we locked up the bikes and hit the water.

The waves were onshore but very surfable, although crowded. One of the better surfers, a handsome man of about 30 with a thick neck in a brightly coloured wetsuit, stood out. He could surf well but was hassling other surfers, whistling at people to get off his waves and dropping in on kids half his age. I got the impression he was the local hottie, who likes to make himself known. You might say he was dominating if you wanted to use that kind of language: the Miki Dora of this line-up.

I had a few waves and was really enjoying the session, sitting a little further out than most and taking some of the bigger sets that a lot of the other surfers didn't want. I was grateful to be there, surfing for the last time in France.

A set appeared on the horizon. 'Dora' was a little further out than me and, I thought, a little too far out to be able to catch it. I was in a perfect position, so turned to paddle. I noticed he started paddling too. I went for the wave anyway, as I knew he wouldn't be able to catch it. I was just about to drop in when I heard him whistle at me, a signal that would normally mean he had caught the wave and was going to go. I pulled back to let him go, but he hadn't caught it: he had whistled to stop me going even though he couldn't. A shitty move. I sat on my board and splashed the water with my hand in frustration. He had ruined the wave for me and yet he still remonstrated, saying it was my fault for paddling. He was in the wrong and he knew it but he kept up the righteous pretence. It was unpleasant: surfers around us started paddling away as if expecting trouble.

'No,' I said. 'You missed the wave.'

I didn't want a fight but I also didn't want to be bullied. He paddled away. How different from the day at Senix.

I didn't feel much like surfing afterwards, so caught one into the beach and watched him for a few minutes. He dropped in on a kid who had lucked out with a beautiful wave – possibly the best of his session – but had totally ruined it for him too. I hoped the kid wouldn't do this to the next generation when he was grown up. These things can get passed down, if we let them.

We stayed in a campsite at the back of the beach. It was damp and musty and felt a little desperate and unloved. The toilet block was way past its sell-by date, with broken tiles, bare wires and grubby shower trays. When I went to wash my hands I pushed a soap dispenser and a slug plopped out into my palm.

WHERE DID SURFING GO WRONG?

It wasn't a great end to our stay in France. Happily, it wasn't typical. I had loved being there: we had feasted on French food, scoffed bowls of *moules*, downed *pichets* of rosé and inhaled an awful lot of fabulous (if expensive) pastries. The cycling had been wonderful too. The surf hadn't been amazing, but good enough. If I was on a surf trip with the sole purpose being to catch as many classic waves as possible it would have been disappointing, but I was on a different kind of adventure and was grateful for every wave.

Since leaving we had covered 1300km. My knee was feeling OK, although it hurt a little on the climbs we had done recently. I felt the occasional sharp pain where my MCL had torn and a deeper throb where the new ligament had been screwed into my fibula. When I walked too far it ached. But it wasn't a deal breaker – I wasn't about to quit.

There had been shitty weather but then, I thought, we had been outside for a month, there was bound to be some rain. I loved that the life we had been leading was so very different from home. I hadn't missed sitting at a desk and was feeling all the better for it.

A few disasters had threatened to end the trip but we'd been lucky. If it hadn't been for Eric we could have been stuck in Soulac, waiting for spare parts like Sebastian had been in Brittany.

Next up were the mountains of northern Spain. The good times, I hoped, were not over yet.

Section 2
SPAIN

ATLANTIC OCEAN

STAGE 22
DAYS 47–48
126km

Tapia de Casariego

Playa de Bahin...

El Ferrol

A CORUÑA

Villalba

STAGE 23
DAYS 49–51
170km

STAGE
DAYS 44
107k

STAGE 24
DAYS 52–53
44km

Arzúa

Santiago de Compostela

S   F

STAGE 25
DAYS 54–56
185km

VIGO

A Guarda

PORTUGAL

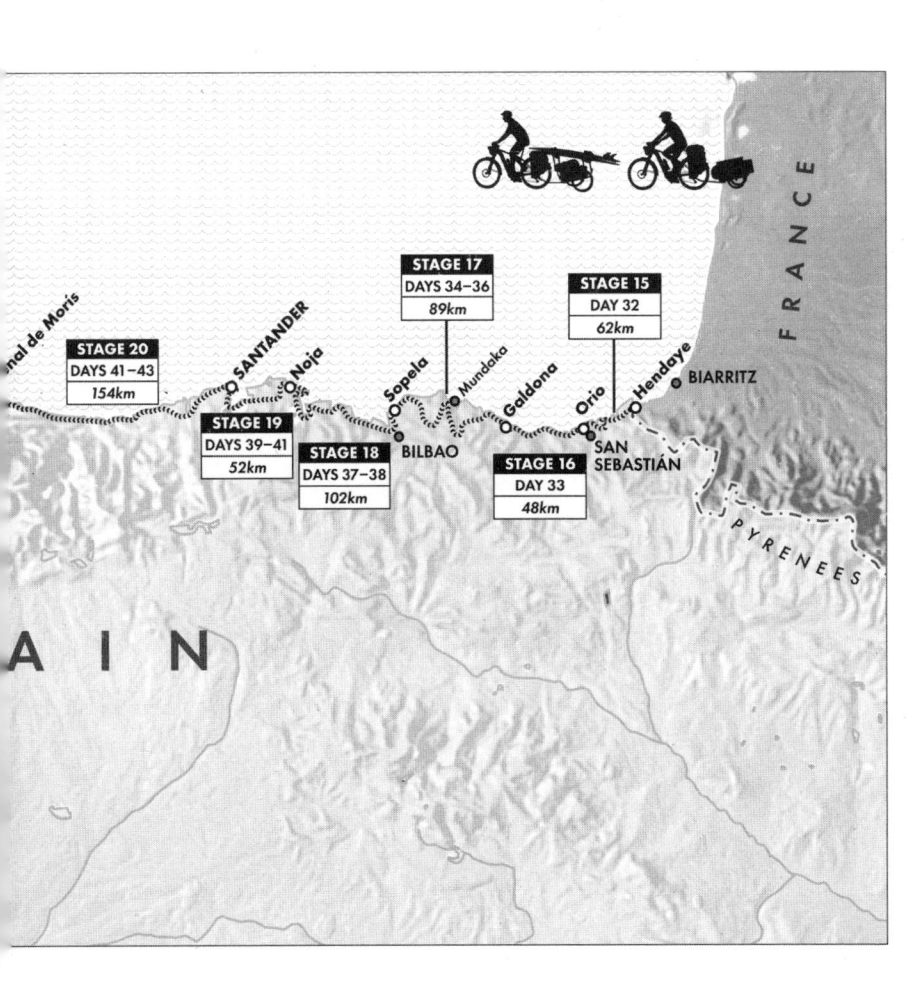

16

The worst day ever

'Stood in a tunnel beneath Franco's summer house at La Concha, looking for accommodation. My hands were so cold, I could barely use my phone, and my shoes were full of water.'
DIARY ENTRY: SUNDAY 23 JUNE 2024

Stage 15: Day 32 | From: Hendaye To: Orio | Distance: 62km

It drizzled all night and into the next morning, which wasn't very helpful because it meant we had to pack the tent away wet. It didn't look as if the weather was going to change, so there was no point in staying put, and we had seen worse over the last four weeks. We didn't bother with breakfast and hit the road: business as usual.

Except that this was the day we would cross the border into Spain.

We cycled out of the campsite and on to the Hendaye seafront, to a small coffee shop, where we sat beneath their awning and wrote postcards home while also watching the weather. The rain didn't seem all that bad – what's a bit of drizzle to the international surfing cyclist? – so we decided to continue into Spain, which lay just over the Bidasoa River. The crossing, far from being a big emotional achievement with tears and selfies, was tempered by the rain becoming more exuberant. With shoulders hunched and eyes squinting, we rode into the downpour across the bridge into Spain. And that was that. No customs, no fanfare. Just rain.

Irun was the place where we would leave the EuroVelo 1 cycle route (of which the Vélodyssée is a part) and begin to follow the Camino del Norte, an 800km-long pilgrims' route to Santiago de Compostela across the top of Spain. It hugs the coast, stopping off at a lot of beaches we wanted to visit, which meant we could save ourselves a bit of legwork with navigation. We would let it lead us – more or less – to the port town of Ribadeo, from where we hoped to head off around the coast of Galicia.

Eugene had given us the saintly gift of knowledge by insisting we download the Buen Camino de Santiago app, so we had information about hostels, routes and waypoints to hand. This inspired us to 'do the pilgrim thing', for which we needed accreditation, in the form of a Pilgrim's Passport, which had to be picked up in Irun and would then get stamped at holy sites along the way. If we made it to Santiago and had acquired enough stamps, we could collect our Compostelas – the certificates that would prove we had completed the Way of Saint James – and therefore deserved some time off from our inevitable purgatory.

There was only one place to get these passports that was open on a Sunday, somewhere called The Passionists, so we set off to find it.

The rain fell a little harder still, making it difficult to read my phone because of the drips from my helmet, and after an age of riding around mostly deserted streets, we found it. The only problem was, of course, that The Passionists was a church and it was Sunday. I pushed open the huge wooden door and looked inside. High mass was kicking off so I immediately withdrew, hoping I hadn't been seen. I didn't have the Spanish to ask for the accreditation or even to apologise for the intrusion.

We consoled ourselves that we weren't there to 'do the Camino' anyway, and cycled on towards the road to San Sebastián. We rode through sodden back streets and past the airport along a dual carriageway where cars roared by in a haze of spray, our hopes for absolution heading down the overflowing drains of Irun.

On the Komoot map of the journey our course shows a wiggle on the outskirts of the town. This was the moment we stopped at a campsite to shelter under their awning and faff about while deciding what to do. The wiggle was me pacing up and down, trying to get warm. My French pac-a-mac was keeping the water out, but wasn't wicking or breathing and my sweat was soaking me from the inside, making me cold and furthering my misery.

The options were simple: stop here and find a chalet or pitch or carry on. It was only 11 a.m. so, rather than fester all day in a damp caravan, or even a damp tent, we chose to carry on, despite the rain, which had eased a little at that moment. I flicked my kick-stand, pulled my helmet down over my forehead, mounted the bike and prepared myself for the biggest challenge yet.

Mount Jaizkibel was the only thing standing between us and San Sebastián. At 455 metres above sea level, the pass between Irun and San Sebastián was the first real obstacle we would have to tackle. While 455 metres might not sound like a lot to seasoned climbers, it was a lot to me. I was terrified and didn't know if I would be able to make it to the top. Was I capable? My hands were shaking in my sodden gloves and my heart raced in my chest as we pulled out of the campsite and straight on to the climb, an 8km slog of around 10 per cent gradient.

There was no messing about with foothills to warm us up and no shelter from the incessant rain and wind. We climbed straight out of the campsite and kept climbing. I put my bike into Blue Mode (Tour) and dropped down through the gears until I was in 'Granny Gear 2' (GG2), a slow and steady climbing gear. I didn't want to resort to using more power because of the batteries, but also because I wanted to see if I could do it. Was I able to call myself a proper cyclist yet? Only 455 vertical metres of climbing to find out. I regulated my breathing as much as I could. Slow and steady, in and out. No need to panic.

The road snaked around the mountain, switching back regularly. It was hard work and, at first, I was genuinely worried I wouldn't be able to do it. But, after having cycled 1300km already, I had a word with myself and set my determination to 'stop whining and get on with it'. I would pass the test, if only because there was no way around the mountain, and with no choice, other than turn around and go back or to push up the hill, I had to keep pedalling. I could feel the screw in my tibia as the pressure increased: it throbbed, a dull ache reminding me I had been under the knife. I felt the muscles in my backside and inside my thighs tensing and burning, my calves screaming: what the flipping heck are you doing to us?

I was attempting to think positive thoughts but I was tired, wet and miserable. I tried to focus on the countryside instead of myself, but the views were obliterated by a thick mist. Instead, I read spray-painted words of encouragement on the tarmac, presumably when a bike race had come up here. *Vamos!*

'Just keep pedalling. Ignore the voice in your head that wants you to stop. Take no notice of the part of you that wants you to fail. Let success prevail. You can do this.' My inner monologue was starting to sound like motivational trite.

I wondered if I was discovering the strong, silent, subconscious cycling spirit that those Lycra-clad, self-flagellating hard men and women of the mountain speak of. Hell, yeah!

In a small voice: 'Yeah, but it hurts. Hit Turbo!'

A shouty retort from the beta male inside: 'Do NOT hit Turbo.'

It took around an hour to reach the pass at the top. There should have been amazing views but instead the misty whiteout created a blank nothing beyond the side of the road. Water ran down the tarmac in rivulets and down my neck in cascades. I was completely soaked and my feet squelched in my shoes. Even so, I felt proud of myself. I had done it, and without the use of Turbo.

Lizzy was behind me so I waited for her to appear through the mist. I saw her headlight first: it shone brightly in the gloom as she plugged away at the last 100 metres. We hugged, compared our miseries, congratulated each other on the achievement and set off down the other side.

Lizzy, of course, wasn't in any doubt; she has crossed the Andes twice on an 'analogue' bike. I was the weak link and we both knew it.

The descent wasn't any less hairy, because of the wet road, although it seemed to be over rather quickly. It made me think that perhaps the ascent hadn't been such an achievement after all. A couple of sharp hairpins on deeply forested slopes near the bottom brought us suddenly on to a big road outside the town of Lezo, a San Sebastián suburb.

We followed cycle lanes into San Sebastián, which sounds easier than it was. The battery on the Garmin died and every time I looked at my phone to confirm the route the rain running off my helmet dripped on it, making it impossible to use. Whenever I needed to check our direction – which was quite often – I had to find a tree

THE WORST DAY EVER

to shelter under, take off my helmet and dry my hands and phone with a towel in my pannier. It was frustrating, time-consuming and, basically, shit. The Camino was signed with a depiction of a yellow scallop shell* against a blue background pointing the way, most of the time, but we lost it on the outskirts of the city and had to find our own way. We crossed over confusing motorway junctions, cycled past post-industrial wastelands, alongside railways and eventually came out on to the deserted beach at Zurriola, San Sebastián's surf beach.

Zurriola is described in 'The Surf Report' from June 1985 as: 'Fair but reasonably consistent break in the old part of the city. Surf is rarely good but it's a popular tourist destination worth visiting.'

The surf was 1–2ft and onshore with a few out. Not worth getting even wetter for.

With every turn of the pedals – as we cycled along the glistening seafront – I fantasised about being dry, strolling into San Sebastián's old town and eating a plate of exquisite *pintxos* (Basque tapas, that the city is famous for) in the sun. I had been looking forward to it and hadn't counted on it being wet. We rode into the old city, then along the cycle path that runs at the back of La Concha, San Sebastián's other, usually fabulous sandy beach, unable to find any shelter.

Franco's summer palace sits on a promontory that divides La Concha in two. A road passes underneath it in a tunnel, with a separate pedestrian tunnel. This small, damp-smelling and graffiti-covered underpass was the only place we could find that was dry enough for us to stop to hunt for accommodation online. Worse still, all the hotels we looked at were full. We found a hostel that was advertising a room available, only to find that it had gone once we had cycled up a steep hill at the back of the beach to check in. There was nothing else. Fuck. Fuck. Fuck.

The only option left to us was the campsite at Igueldo, a suburb of San Sebastián. Unfortunately, it was at the top of another mountain,

---

* The yellow scallop shell is a symbol of the Way of Saint James and is used in signage, along with a yellow arrow on a blue background. It represents the routes the Camino takes, all of which converge on Santiago de Compostela. Pilgrims often carry scallop shells because they were makeshift bowls and acted as the standard measure for alms given to pilgrims along the route.

the mighty Mount Igueldo, a peak of 181 metres with a climb totalling 345 metres. It wasn't the highest we had done that day but it was still another climb.

I got reckless and listened to the devil in my head, switching the bike to Red Mode (Turbo) and putting my head down to cruise up the steepest sections, confident we would find a place to pitch our tent, at the very least, when we got to the campsite. I didn't care by this time. I just wanted to be dry and warm and to get into my sleeping bag. I shouted back down the hill at Lizzy, who was settling in for another long, slow, steep ascent:

'Stick it in fucking Turbo! Come on! Let's go!' If Mount Jaizkibel was the first test, and I had passed, I definitely failed this one.

At the campsite reception I instantly knew it wasn't going to go well. The atmosphere was frenzied, with four receptionists fending off campers because they were full. There was, the woman said to me, a guest house down the road.

The man at the guest house spoke good English, which was a blessed relief, even if he couldn't accommodate us. A brief conversation – most of which I spent looking past him at the log fire burning inside – revealed that today was Saint John's Day, a national holiday, which was why everywhere was full. Didn't we know? No, obviously. He said there was a campsite 12km away in Orio, a town on the other side of the mountain, another 2km to climb and then it would be 10km down.

My bike, by this time, was low on battery and was showing a range of just 8km. What an idiot I was. I had spaffed all the power and now there was a chance we wouldn't make it to the campsite without my bike dying (riding an e-bike without power is horrible). Still, no point in flapping. I climbed the 2km in Green Mode (Eco) to conserve battery (it was tough and my legs screamed in agony but I fully deserved it) and then turned the bike off for the long, curvy descent. We should have been able to see the sea and the mountains but it was misty and gloomy: a filthy day that no cyclist should have to endure. A donkey in a field, mournful in its dripping coat, looked at us pityingly as we passed.

We found the campsite and pulled up to reception, trying hard not to look too desperate. The receptionist, sitting in her lovely dry office behind a sliding glass window, was apologetic.

THE WORST DAY EVER

'I have just one cabin,' she said, adding, 'Sorry, but only for one night.'

'Oh! *Fantastico! Sí, por favor.* We'll take it. *Muchas gracias!*' I said, barely letting her finish.

We fished out our passports, made a mess of the paperwork with our sopping cycling gloves, paid €100 and squelched across the campsite to a tiny one-bedroomed caravan with a shower and — best of all — heating. To me, right then, it was a palace.

With the radiators cranked up and all our things placed around the cabin to dry, including the tent, groundsheet, panniers and shoes, we showered, dressed in what little we had that was dry and trotted over to the campsite bar, a dour, canteen-like place with a tiled floor, metal and plastic chairs and Formica tables.

We ordered too many portions of *pimientos de Padrón* (fried green peppers), *rabas fritas* (fried squid) and *patatas bravas* (chips with a spicy pink sauce) and waded through them, undaunted by the grease. My oily fingers gripped a bottle of cold Spanish beer. It wasn't quite the streets of old San Sebastián but it would do. After the day we had endured, a plate of fatty fried potatoes could have passed as a plate of delicate and delicious *pintxos* in the city with more Michelin stars per capita than any city on earth. Almost.

The thing was that we *had* survived. We *had* climbed the mountain, and another one (albeit using Turbo). It hadn't been plain sailing. In fact, it had been absolutely shit. The hills of Spain, as predicted, had been terrible. My knee ached, my thighs burned and the screw in my leg throbbed.

But I had done it. And it was OK now. That was all that mattered. I slept like a milk-drunk toddler.

The gastronomic delights of San Sebastián would have to wait for another time. We couldn't go back, so instead, would press on.

We had business to attend to in Zarautz.

17

One for Burt

'We turned up with the boards on top of the car and they couldn't believe it. One of the blokes there was Graham Walker. He bodysurfed it. He caught a hell of a wave. They were wrapped in that as well.'

PETE 'VICKO' VICKERY, 2024

Stage 16: Day 33 | From: Orio | To: Galdona | Distance: 48km

I liked Orio. It felt a bit forgotten, sitting in a flat-bottomed, steep-sided river valley and left to its own devices by the motorway that bypassed the town on a long viaduct high above the port and apartment blocks. Those who found it discovered a little paradise, with a pleasure port, beautiful sandy beach, renovated art deco hotel, the campsite and a beach bar. We walked along the sea wall at first light and watched a couple of surfers catch a few waves, but nothing to get me excited. I was happy to save myself for the next town, a surfing hotspot with a reputation for excellent surf.

The morning brought sunshine and blue skies. We ate breakfast on the terrace of the cabin, watching the mist rising from trees on the steep sides of the valley. Everything felt brand new and with the whiff of possibility. Or was that steam coming off my shoes, still drying in the sunshine?

Yesterday was awful, but we were over that already. Today was going to be a better day. My legs were aching from the climbs we had done – Komoot was telling me we had climbed almost 1000 vertical

ONE FOR BURT

metres – about the same as scaling Yr Wyddfa, the highest mountain in England and Wales. I wasn't surprised my knee was grumbling.

It grumbled some more when we set off, crossed the river and almost immediately started climbing again. The road took us along the side of another steep valley, rising all the time, past farmhouses and meadows. At the narrow head of the valley, when the road was at its steepest, we passed fields of vines and, at the zenith, a winery.

We passed our first pilgrims trudging up the hill. Unable to see their faces, we could only judge them by their demeanour. Some looked weary, their shoulders hunched, while others skipped along, light in their boots. Some had the best kit, with no rucksacks,* while others carried big packs or wore clothes that had clearly been outside for a while. It was our first encounter with Camino pilgrims and we were happy to see them.

I tried out a greeting I had learnt, probably from Eugene, and was pleased to hear it back. On the steeper sections of the road it was grunted or spluttered more than sung, as the pilgrims, weighed down by the terrain, put in the holy miles.

'*Buen camino!*'

'*Buen camino!*' came the reply.

It means, literally, 'good road' but, as I had found out, was also a greeting to wish the pilgrim well on their spiritual or physical journey. It was lovely to hear the locals say it as we rode past: it made us welcome and felt like a spell, as if the words would protect us with their magic: 'Whatever your burden, go well.'

A little past the winery, on the descent, we rounded a bend and came to a viewing point. Below us lay Zarautz and its huge beach. It was a breathtaking sight: a blue sky, the sea looking glassy calm except for sets of waves moving through it, whitewater breaking on to the beach and the backdrop, beyond the town, of lush green hills. We could make out the shapes of the sandbars on the beach and the way the waves broke over them. It was perfect.

---

* Some pilgrims hire companies to transport luggage from one hostel to another, so saving them carrying it. I'm not sure how this affects their time in purgatory.

I wondered if this road was the same one that Pete Vickery and Burt Lovejoy had taken in the mid-1960s. It could well have been. They had travelled from the west, and the motorway had yet to be built. I hoped that we were seeing what they had seen all those years ago. Vicko had told me the story when I interviewed him, his eyes twinkling with mischievousness behind his Lennon-style glasses:

> We decided to see if there was any surf in Spain. You hear these stories, but it is true. We came around the corner and there was the best surf we'd ever seen. We went in and caught a couple of waves. Nothing spectacular but it must have been spectacular to the people in the town, because they went nuts and took us all back to the pub. Brilliant.

Vicko is always laughing, loves a pint, and is the heart and soul of Bude's surfing family. It shows in his sprightliness and constant presence at the beach: the surfing life has kept him young.

> We went to a place called Zarautz. And we were one of the first ones to surf there. We got taken up into the pub and given wine and everything.

And then, as if to qualify it, he added:

> A big long roll with cheese in it!

Whether or not Vicko was the first person to surf at Zarautz is moot. There is no way of proving it. But his stories of being cheered by the locals are not something you would make up. I believe him when he says it happened. What is difficult to work out is which year it was. It wasn't his first trip, which was in 1963. It was later, which means it could have been 1964 or 1965.

This predates the formation of the Euromar Club at Zarautz in 1967 and the first competition in the town in 1969. It may have been just after the first person to surf (just 30 kilometres away) in San Sebastián, at La Concha, which was in 1964. That was Spaniard Iñaki Arteche. His board, which he made himself, was based on the cover of *Life* magazine from October 1963, which contained what

we would call today a 'clickbait story' about actress Yvette Mimieux*
learning to surf for an episode of *Dr. Kildare*. Iñaki had never seen a
surfboard in the flesh so it is remarkable that he managed to make a
few of them in 1964.

It was a similar story with Félix Cueto, a man known as 'El
Inventor', who was inspired to make a surfboard by the cover of the
album *Surfin' U.S.A.* by The Beach Boys (that soundtrack again) that
his sister, an air hostess for a Spanish airline, had brought back from
the USA. Cueto had never seen a board in real life and yet, as a result
of his experiments, he was the first man to surf in Asturias, at Salinas
near the industrial port of Avilés. That was in 1963.

It is important to note here that in 1965 Spain was still 10 years
away from the end of General Franco's regime.† The state repressed
opposition, removed rights from those who opposed it during the
civil war and worked to an economic system of self-sufficiency and
limited trade that held the country back and kept it poor. There
was no open border between France and Spain like today. Life was
difficult. The Guardia Civil were brutal and the secret police (Social
Investigation Brigade) actively sought dissenters. The people were
told what to do, what to think and how to live, without the benefit
of cultural influences from outside Spain.

Surfing – the freedom of riding waves and the lifestyle that went
with it – must have been something so exotic and unattainable, a
manifestation of life outside. How did the local people react to the
first surfers and surfing?

Vicko and Burt were lucky enough to experience the best of it
first-hand. Burt, who had been ill with Alzheimer's, died in Australia
a month before we left for France, so I never got to ask him.

While a few Spanish soon-to-be surfers were experimenting with
board making, Vicko and Burt were the advance party bringing
surfing to the shores of Spain, even if there was no legacy from that

---

* Ms Mimieux is standing on the beach in the orange glow of sunset, wearing a bikini, staring straight at
the camera. She's standing next to a red surfboard. It represents, perhaps, all that was impossible to attain
in Spain in 1963.
† Franco died in 1975. After his death both major parties agreed to follow The Pact of Forgetting,
which demanded a purposeful, country-wide amnesia to move on from the atrocities of the civil war. It
remained in place until 2000.

first contact. It wouldn't be long before the isolated tribes of Spanish surfers began to coalesce, for more surfers to explore and for surfing to have an impact on those who found it.

Zarautz has been a settlement since 1237. Between the 14th and 17th centuries it was an important centre of the Basque whaling industry (the Basques were the first people to hunt whales commercially). Zarautz's first factory, a mill weaving linen cloth, opened in 1857. Isabella II, Queen of Spain from 1833–68, stayed at the nearby Palacio de Narros during the summer, so helping to kick-start the town's association with upmarket tourism. The railway station opened in 1895, bringing more high-profile visitors from all over the world, including Marlene Dietrich and Jackie Kennedy. The beach, at 2.8km, is the longest in the Basque Country.

In the 1950s people surfed on bellyboards that were known as *txamperos*. According to an interview with Javier Arteche (brother of Iñaki) on the website *My Paipo Boards* from 2011, the word comes from the Basque word for using the power of a wave: *txampa*. Like the *planckys* that were ridden in France, the use of *txamperos* declined with the rise of stand-up surfing.

Today, Zarautz is the epicentre of Spanish surfing. What started as the Euromar Club morphed into the National Surfing Section (part of the Water Ski Federation) and then, after a few fallow decades due to the changes 'brought about by the democratic evolution of the country' (their words not mine), became the Spanish Surfing Federation (FES) in 1997.

We weaved between apartment blocks on tiny single-lane streets behind the beach, ignoring the confusing one-way signs, until we came out at the eastern end of the promenade, on a stone-built terrace with wrought-iron railings. A lifeguard snoozed in a tower to the left of us. Below us, just above the beach, a cafe was serving a midweek clientele of beachgoers in various states of beach-undress.

The surf looked excellent, with peaks showing on the well-defined sandbars. It was busy, but not so busy that I would cycle away in the hope of finding better waves elsewhere, like I might have done in a van.

ONE FOR BURT

We locked the bikes and took our stuff down to the water's edge. I suited up and, before I paddled out, took a moment to think of Vicko and Burt and the adventure they had had in 1964 (or was it 1965?). They were not so different from the Spanish pioneers: Vicko had made his first board from plans in a book. Iñaki Arteche had made his based on the cover of a magazine. Félix had copied an album cover.

The first waves they rode are just memories, long obliterated by wind, swell and tide. That's surfing's ephemeral impermanence. Once the tide came in and their footprints disappeared, no one would have known they were ever there. Therefore, it is up to us, and the generations after, to remember and honour them.

'Cheers, Burt,' I said to myself as I waded into the shallows. 'Thanks for guiding me here. I will be forever grateful. *Buen camino.*'

I never knew Burt but it didn't matter. He was, and always will be, a part of the surfing tribe, just like me. I hoped his onward journey had brought him sunsets and waves.

In the water, I had a fun surf. The waves were good, the sun shone and the water was warm. Lizzy had a great time too: she got talking to an older guy with dreads under a sun hat who let her take the good waves and encouraged her to go for some she might not have otherwise. It was nice to see; sadly there aren't enough women surfing and even fewer women over 60. Age can make you invisible to the surfing crowd, no matter your ability.

After drying off we sat on a bench overlooking the beach and ate our lunch while watching the waves. If you must know, a big long roll with ham, cheese and tomatoes in.

The esplanade led us westward and on to one of Spain's most exciting stretches of coastal road, the N-634 between Zarautz and Zumaia, a section of 10km. I have driven it many times and love it, because it offers a rare opportunity to drive so close to the sea, but on a bike it was different. The road had a lot of bends and few straight sections, with no cycle lane, which made it difficult for traffic to overtake. The footpath was separated from the road by a continuous concrete barrier, which made it impossible for us to pull off to let traffic go by. With nowhere to go, we had to keep the pedals turning. It was exhilarating, with glorious views punctuated by scary moments as cars overtook us. Some of them were a little close, but nothing compared with what was to come.

There were a couple of people surfing the small beach at Getaria and one guy out rock-hopping barely big enough waves in the horseshoe bay at Roca Puta, the area's famous big wave spot. I surfed here on a bigger day on a previous trip with a friend. We had paddled out through a culvert under the road and surfed a left coming off the opposite side of the bay from Roca Puta. It was spooky, especially when a local surfer, wearing a wetsuit with a skeleton motif on it, paddled out and sat silently next to us.

From Zumaia we took the N-634 to the small town of Deba up an awful hill with no cycle path or even a hard shoulder, with fast traffic and no let-up. It was intense, tough cycling that was, at times, unnerving. After the previous day I knew I could climb it, so was more confident, but I still had to find it in myself to put my head down and grind away without panicking or getting out of breath.

After much wriggling, the road hit the coast high on a hillside outside Deba and followed it for the descent into the town. We freewheeled as the sea, far below us, came ever closer. With time to take stock and enjoy the scenery I was blown away by the coast: steep forested slopes led down to the sea far below us. I found it hard to believe that I was here, cycling, and loving it.

We didn't stop in Deba other than to stock up on provisions in a back-street supermarket before crossing a railway line to take a pedestrian bridge over the river. Once on the other side we picked up the GI-638, another fabulous coastal road with, thankfully, less traffic, but still some hills, which took us into Mutriku, a beautiful port town with a marina and colourful apartment blocks crowding into a narrow valley.

A punishing, steep and winding hill (it was an 'absolute bastard', if measured on the profanity scale)* took us to a campsite at Galdona and pushed our daily tally of metres climbed to another near Yr Wyddfa, if not a Scafell Pike. The site was old but excellent, and a little ramshackle compared with some of the corporate sites

---

* This is not a real scale but should be. All hills should be graded from 'a twat of a climb' to 'an utter tosser'. 'Bastard', though not a serious expletive, is up there with 'total fucker of a mountain', possibly because it's very satisfying to say.

we had stayed at in France. There were a lot of permanent pitches, some dodgy wiring and caravans that had been parked and then built around to make enclaves with chairs and tables, satellite dishes, picket fences and fridges under awnings.

The family who ran the site welcomed us warmly. The daughter, a dark-haired goth of about 22, spoke English and translated for her mother, who was very much in charge. She asked where we had come from. When we said we had pedalled from England she, genuinely impressed, exclaimed, *'Capullito! Tienes el culo de una alfombra!'*

'I will explain,' said the daughter. 'My mother says "Chapeau. But you must have an arse like a carpet!"'

I had to disagree, even though I knew where she was coming from. My arse was a bit sore after long days in the saddle but only in the sense that my sitting bones were bruised. Daily application of chamois cream to my nether parts had kept me moistened and had helped avoid any sores. My arse, far from being a carpet, was more like a slightly bruised peach.

We bought a couple of beers and sat outside the campsite bar in the sunshine at a table made from a beer barrel, writing our diaries. It was an excellent end to an excellent, if tough, day. We had done a lot of climbing. I reminded Lizzy of Eugene and his words of advice for us.

'Can you believe what Eugene said? "Northern Spain is easy. It's pretty much flat." Ha!'

'Bollocks,' Lizzy replied. 'It really isn't.'

18

Mysterious Mundaka

'I remember many things about surfing at Mundaka: fear, pain, elation, anxiety. Sharp points of focus that define the trip: catching a wave, paddling out. Jumping off the harbour. Important moments that have become more important over time.'
Diary entry: Tuesday 25 June 2024

Stage 17: Days 34–6 | From: Galdona | To: Sopela (via Mundaka) | Distance: 89km

We parked our peachy arses back on our saddles and set off from the campsite at Galdona on a steep downhill through a sun-dappled pine forest towards the coast road heading for Lekeitio, a place I was looking forward to. The road dipped and weaved around the coastline, following the contours as tight valleys with dripping ferns and waterfalls opened out to whisk us along exposed ridges with spectacular views of the Bay of Biscay 50 metres below us. The rolling was good, despite the hills, as the surface was smooth and easy.

This part of the coast, according to 'The Surf Report' of 1985, is 'rarely surfed because of steep cliffs fronting the sea and dangerous ripoffs. There are no places to park an unattended car'. It reminded me of the warnings I had heard from the old boys in North Wales. In the 1970s the Spanish Basque Country had a bad reputation. Vehicles parked up in out-of-the-way places – with kit inside and boards on top – were easy pickings for thieves coming out from under Franco's dark shadow.

MYSTERIOUS MUNDAKA

There were a few people surfing on the golden beach below the road that brought us into the valley that holds the town of Lekeitio, its river mouth and harbour. The waterfront, with bars and restaurants, sat on the other side of the river while an island, the Saint Nicholas nature reserve, which is separated from the mainland at high tide, sat offshore. The waves were small and closing out so instead of unpacking the wetsuits and boards, we stripped off and rode our bellyboards for an hour on the tiny but fun waves. The water was warm and the sun was hot. Afterwards, as we sat in a beachside bar, I enjoyed the familiar feeling of my skin prickling with the salt and sun.

The toughest climb of the day came between Lekeitio and Guernica, a cross-country trek to avoid going down the east side of the Oka River estuary, a shortcut that took us up to around 300 metres. I was thankful Lizzy had the Garmin. She informed me during the upward slog – which had sections of 14 per cent – that it warned her of upcoming climbs and their gradients with a colour change. Green was easy; dark red going into purple was very difficult. A couple of the sections we had ground our way through were dark red. I was glad I didn't know because I would have gone to pieces.

Mundaka isn't a stop-off on the Camino del Norte, which completely bypasses the area, going cross-country from Deba to Guernica and then on towards Bilbao. This meant if we wanted to pay our respects at this important surfing destination, we'd have to take a detour. It was, for me, not a question worth asking. Of course we would go to Mundaka.

The road from Guernica into Mundaka, a 10km straight, undulating grind, was busy with heavy traffic. Where the cycle lanes disappeared or were too narrow to use we took to the road. Lorries and trucks thundered past, giving us no choice but to hang on and keep pedalling. With a hot sun overhead and little wind my head felt like it was going to boil in my skull by the time we got to the campsite. I also noticed a weird smell coming from my cycling helmet. It was like pickled head, with vinegary overtones and a sweet, musky top note. It wasn't surprising: I had sweated in it for nearly 1600km, with most of the sweatiest days in the previous week.

Mundaka sits on the western side of the Urdaibai Biosphere Reserve, an area that encompasses the Oko Estuary from Guernica to Bakio and also includes a huge area of hinterland: 220 sq km in total. The town is focused on the harbour and most of the houses, many of which are medieval, face towards the sea. The church of Santa Maria, an unmistakable landmark that often features in shots of the waves at Mundaka, dominates the harbour. The town has a couple of beaches and is a centre for rowing and watersports as well as surfing. It is a beguiling, charming place: a Basque Country gem with oodles of history and soul.

The surf at Mundaka – a fast, barrelling wave that has been likened to an unstoppable freight train – is among the best in the world, not just in Europe. The waves break away from the harbour and into the bay over a shallow sandbar created by the River Oko.

Between 1999 and 2009 the world's best – along with their entourages, hangers-on and crowds – came to Mundaka for the Billabong Pro, an event that was part of the World Tour. It helped to put the town and the waves on the global surfing map although by then it was far from a backwater. Kelly Slater, 11 times world champion, was crowned world champion for the ninth time at Mundaka in 2008 after he needed to achieve an equal ninth to take the title. For a tiny town of around 2000 permanent inhabitants, that's big.

Before 1999 Mundaka was already well known and surfed regularly by locals in the Basque region as well as by travelling surfers from all over the globe. It had gained legendary status as being a perfect, hollow, if mythical, left.

It is hard to say who surfed Mundaka first. It may not even matter. But for those who were there in the early days and who stumbled upon it, the wave must have been an incredible find: not just because it's isolated but also because it doesn't work very often. Looking at the river mouth and estuary on a flat day you'd be hard-pressed to imagine a monster of a wave could break there.

According to Craig Sage, a wisecracking Aussie who first arrived in 1980, now owns Mundaka Surf Shop and who ran the Billabong Pro event, the place wasn't easy to find.

He told me:

You had to drive along the coast because there was no freeway. Some people have left Biarritz looking for Mundaka and never found it. Crossed the other side of the river. Well, it ain't here so we'll keep going, 'cos it's dead flat and you wouldn't think that there would be a wave here.

I liked Craig. His no-bullshit approach — life and family come first — was difficult to navigate, but I was glad to have 20 minutes of his time on the wall outside his near-perfect surf shop. I'd like to think that the fact we had cycled here from England was what proved to him that I was serious about the project and therefore worth chatting to.

He told me, while drying himself off after a swim, that it wasn't always easy for surfers in the town, especially before the death of Franco in 1975:

> It wasn't until I got here in 1980 that it was easier to be a foreigner here. You needed visas. You could only be here for a month. So, it was complicated to stay in Spain in those days.

Culturally there was conflict too. When surfers started coming by the vanload it must have been a big shock for the Franco-era fishing community of Mundaka and it took a major event for things to even out. On 16 December 1977 two foreign surfers saved the lives of two fishermen whose boat had been swamped on the sandbar. The surfers were invited to meet the mayor, a gesture that marked the beginning of a better understanding between the people of the town and the surfers, but, as Craig said, it wasn't so cut and dried:

> It was hard in those days as there were a lot more fishermen, boats and captains and they resented the fact that we were coming here and having fun on the waves while they had to go and work.
>
> And then also, trying to steal their girls. There were quite a few fights and a lot of resentment towards us. Understandable. I'd be pissed off too if I came home after fishing on a boat for three or four months and you find some long-haired hippies are trying to chat up the girls. I doubt there was a traveller who came through here who didn't either meet or fall in love with a girl.

Spain also had that reputation for being difficult. Friends from North Wales were always complaining about having their stuff ripped off. In the 1970s, when Spain was still under Franco, the people were poor. Surfers, with boards and equipment, though often relatively poor themselves, had a lot more than the locals.

Alex Williams told me a story about being in Mundaka in 1977:

> There wasn't much surf, so we went to Bakio [a town a little way along the coast]. We were parked by the beach and Roland looks at the car next to us and says, 'That's my old board bag I had stolen when I was here two years ago. I wonder if my board's in it.' He wandered over, opened the bag and there's his blue [Westhouse Tom Hoye] board! So, two guys came back and he said, 'This is my board. It was stolen.'
>
> After about 15 minutes, there were about 30 people around us and we were trying to explain and everyone's getting a bit ... tetchy. I saw two Guardia coming along on their motorbikes and stopped them. They said, 'You guys with the board, follow us.' They took us to Bermeo police station. Big fat police chief who's not interested at all. Plaster coming off the wall. A twisted light flex coming down from the ceiling with the ends just twisted around two terminals of a light bulb. We were thinking, do we really want to be here?
>
> Roland said, 'This is my board. It was on the car. It was stolen two years ago.' The police chief said, 'Well, can you prove it?' And Roland said, 'Yes, I can. If we take it out of the bag, there's a fix at the back there. Dig it out. I filled it with a red washing-up sponge.' The guy gets his knife out, digs into it and there's the red washing-up sponge. So then, things changed. They're then saying, 'You're not going to beat up these guys, are you? You're not going to kill them?' Then we left with the board and board bag.

As I was sitting on the wall waiting for Craig to finish drying off, I had a text from Carwyn Williams.

'I'm back from Bilbao. Anytime you want to pop in, let me know.'

'Cheers, Carwyn. Might not be able to as we are in Mundaka.'

'Mundaka! Go and see Craig at the surf shop. Ask him about the time I slept by the church.'

'I will. I'm with him now!'

MYSTERIOUS MUNDAKA

Craig never told me the story. He had things to get on with.

Lizzy and I had lunch on the terrace overlooking the harbour that was the 'command centre' for the Billabong Pro when it rolled into town. Sitting there, watching the comings and goings of the boats, the tourists, the locals and with the river running in the estuary beyond, I felt myself becoming ever more entranced by Mundaka, whereby, on previous visits, the waves had scared and (figuratively and literally) scarred me.

Before leaving for Europe, I had been to see Doctor Dave Sweet, a lifelong surfer from Bude who travelled in Europe in the late 1960s. Over a coffee at Rosie's Cafe at Crooklets Beach (a far cry from Mundaka, I must admit) he described to me how he discovered surfing, influenced, of course by an Aussie lifeguard, and how he thinks he may have stumbled upon Mundaka on a trip to Biarritz in 1969:

> When we were small, my mum always used to take my sister and I to Summerleaze.* My mum loved the water and would spend all the summer down there with us. One year, there was an Aussie lifeguard called Pete Le Hay surfing a good wave off Cross Rock. It was phenomenal. I remember sitting on the beach, watching him catch these beautiful right-handers. It was a lovely day and it looked fantastic and I said, 'That's it!' My dad was very much into cricket and soccer and all that and I said, 'No. I'm surfing.'

And about that trip?

> We found this nice left-hander. And I think it was Mundaka but I can't swear to it. It was this lovely left-hander coming in and there was a harbour and all the rest of it.
>
> So this old guy came up and we couldn't understand very much. Andy was asking, 'Are we the first people to ever surf here?'

---

* Summerleaze Beach in Bude.

The old guy said, 'No, no. You're not the first.' We had a Union Jack sticker on the car and he pointed at it. Rodney Sumpter with his Union Jack surfboard had been there the year before!

Rod Sumpter was a supremely cocksure and brilliant surfer and self-publicist who was born in Watford but grew up in Australia. His parents left the UK as 10 Pound Poms in 1952 but he returned to the old country in the late 1960s, having won various junior contests around the world. He was, some have said, the de facto junior world champion in 1966. Rod starred in the classic surf film *The Endless Summer*, putting him at the vanguard of surf exploration in the good old days when longboards were king. His signature surfboard, the Britannia model, made by original UK board builders Bilbo, was famously emblazoned with a Union Jack.

Was it that board that the old guy had seen? Possibly. Maybe.

Matt Warshaw, founder of the organisation The Encyclopedia of Surfing, describes the hard-to-get-hold-of (I have tried) Sumpter as '. . . literally and figuratively, a moving target. Researching him for the encyclopedia was difficult. We couldn't track him down [he is very much still alive], and there wasn't much source material. Eventually, my take on Sumpter was that he surfed like Nat and scammed like Dora.'

The reality, according to Corky Carroll, one of the world's first professional surfers and surfing pundit, wasn't on the scale of Dora, but still had a whiff of likely lad about it. Here, from The Encyclopaedia of Surfing, he explains:

> In 1966 they held the World Surfing Championships in San Diego. Rodney didn't qualify for the Australian Team so, realizing that being born in England might have some sort of value, he contacted somebody in the British government and got them to recognize him as a British surfer. He then rushed over to England and threw together a surfing contest with himself and the three or four other dudes that surfed in England at the time. This became the "National Championship." Naturally, Rodney won and was therefore the British Champion. This not only got him into the World Championships but got his way paid and all expenses covered as the "champion" of his country. Nine of the ten Aussies,

MYSTERIOUS MUNDAKA

meanwhile, had to pay their own way to America. And, being a very competitive dude, Rodney wound up in the finals, getting 5th. He placed higher than all the Aussies except Nat Young, who won the event. It was a great coup.

It could well have been Sumpter who found Mundaka. Or maybe he had heard from someone in Biarritz that there was a magical wave somewhere in northern Spain and had gone to look for himself. We will never know. But it's a good story and I like Doc Sweet's version: they were looking for surf, happen upon one of the world's best river mouth breaks and discover they had been beaten to it by Britain's best surfer and slipperiest waterman.

I surfed Mundaka in 1998 while on a month-long surf trip with a friend. We took the ferry to Roscoff, drove down the west coast of France and, after a huge swell had challenged us beyond our abilities at Lafitenia in France, moved on to Mundaka. We slept in the van on a boat ramp by the river after surfing the beach at Bakio before the swell arrived. When we woke at dawn we were confronted by the biggest, cleanest, most perfect – and terrifying – surf I had ever seen.

I snapped pictures in the blood-red half-light of a couple of surfers taking huge waves, mesmerised but also very afraid of what was to come. I was in my 30s, fit and strong and had been surfing a lot back home, but I wasn't prepared for anything like this. We jumped off the harbour wall and paddled into the river, allowing the flow to take us out to sea and around the back of the peak, which was breaking at about 8–10 feet (2.4 to 3 metres), maybe more, off the sandbar. I paddled so far beyond the breaking waves – and the take-off point – that it took me a while to paddle back to anywhere I might have stood a chance of snagging a wave. The locals dominated the line-up, catching the best waves, getting tubed and making it very hard for outsiders to catch anything.

My friend took off on a huge wave under the peak and cartwheeled down the face inside the tube. I saw the whole thing as I was sitting on the shoulder looking directly into the swirling vortex. As he went over the falls he put two huge dents in the back of his board with his shins.

As you may well imagine, it didn't do a lot for my confidence. When I did manage to catch a wave though, it was wonderful: a fast, if unspectacular, ride for what seemed like miles at a speed I hadn't gone on a surfboard before.

Sitting out the back between sets an Australian surfer paddled up to us and said, 'Well at least you can now go and tell your mates you surfed Mundaka at 10 to 12 feet.' I didn't know what to say or even what to make of it. I detected a little sarcasm, even if it did confirm the size. Thinking back, I think it must have been Craig.

After being in the water for about three hours I was exhausted. The wind changed direction and messed up the surf, making what had been monster waves breaking cleanly into monster waves breaking all over the place. The usual way to get out at Mundaka is to take a wave into the river and then drift up to the harbour mouth with the current. I was afraid that if I missed the harbour, I would be pulled out by the current again and have to try and catch a wave in. Instead, I paddled for the boat ramp, which was about 100 metres further up the river than the harbour mouth. The current pulled me beyond the ramp, so, instead of drifting and then panic-paddling into the harbour, I tried to climb the rocks between the two. As I was hauling myself out of the water and on to the rocks a set of waves came through. The first one knocked me off my feet and the second dragged me back into the water. The third one rammed me like a charging bull into the rocks. I climbed out of the water with a bloodied hand, cuts on my feet and bruised shins and back, my board a shredded mess.

The waves Lizzy and I surfed at Mundaka were very different. We were keen to get in before any crowds appeared, even though the surf was tiny, so we paddled out from the boat ramp when the tide was still quite high and dropping. The current made it difficult to line up on the inconsistent waves but, when they came, they were bowly – not a shade on what it can be though – and I was surprised how much fun it was. The peaks jumped up quickly, with a short, steep drop and a tapering wall. It required a quick bottom turn and then a top turn on the wall before it fizzled out.

We surfed with a lad who was on a foamie without a leash. His friend, driving a speedboat, towed him back up the river each time he drifted too far out to sea. When he lost his board, both Lizzy and I paddled it back to him to save him a swim. Lizzy got a lift back to the boat ramp, being pulled behind the boat, and I – true to form – beached myself on the rocks because the current was too strong to allow me to paddle back to the boat ramp. This time, I clambered out intact.

We stayed at the campsite in Mundaka, which is on a hillside overlooking the river a little out of town. Its onsite restaurant, which had sublime views across the estuary, ran an odd ticketing system that made us feel completely useless and very hungry, hangry and frustrated. It was our first encounter with the Spanish way of life – eating late in the evening – and it came as a shock. We couldn't fathom out how the ordering system worked, despite asking the bar staff, and found ourselves eating at 10.30 p.m., having gone to the restaurant with the intention of eating at 8. Everyone else seemed to know the system and worked it perfectly: people who had come in an hour after us got their food ages before us.

We watched as Spanish kids, having to wait an absolute age to eat, entertained themselves during the long hours before food. We had felt sorry for the women in France, some of whom appeared to be starving themselves. Here in Spain it was the kids who were starving. They played up – I knew how they felt – and the intensity of the noise in the restaurant rose steadily.

Leaving Mundaka was hard. But that was because of the mountain that stood between us and Sopela (formerly known as Sopelana), our next stop, rather than anything else. That said, I could easily have stayed longer, despite the surfing crowds Mundaka now attracts. At 400 metres the mountain wasn't a biggie in real cycling terms, but it was up there with the one we had climbed on our first day in Spain. I hardly slept the night before and had an anxious morning before we set off. Packing up took ages: I dragged my feet and pissed about in a fit of procrastination and self-pitying angst.

When I started to see spray-painted messages on the tarmac during the roll up to the foothills, I knew something special was coming, and not in a good way. That the road we were on was favoured by cycling events filled me with dread as we wound our way through meadows and pine forests and steadily upwards in a constant stream of sweeping bends and contour-following curves. When the gradient became steeper I changed down through the gears until I was in GG1. I heard Lizzy laugh behind me: she had noticed, for the first time on the trip, the Garmin had changed from a tough red-grade climb to an absolute bastard of a what-the-fuck-were-we-thinking? purple. That was about the same time as my left thumb weakened and deftly flicked the power button to Purple Mode (e-MTB) for a section that was about as steep as we'd climbed anywhere. A bastard of a twat of a climb. Thankfully it didn't last long and it soon went back to being merely an absolute bellend of a mountain.

I sweated and puffed and tried to stay positive throughout the whole miserable experience. The final kicker was a false summit with a short section of downhill – the relief! – before cranking up to a steep blind bend to finish. I was pooped, my helmet stank and, when I got to the top, a light drizzle reminded me the mountain was most definitely in charge. I realised that I hadn't taken in any views on the way up because I was focusing on pedalling, and now I was at the top there weren't any.

Back on the flats on the other side Lizzy and I got passed by a young couple in full cycling kit on expensive-looking road bikes. They looked sexy and fit in their Lycra as they whizzed by and gave us a cheery '*Buen camino!*' I felt about as far from sexy as it is possible to feel in my filthy shorts, sweaty top and with yesterday's cycling shorts and bikinis drying off on the makeshift surfboard drying rack.

I wondered where they were going. I imagined they would cycle home to a modern, minimalist apartment, shower off in a walk-in wet room and then proceed to have noisy, mightily-thighed sex on white Egyptian cotton sheets in their king-size bed. Afterwards, I projected on them a dinner, by candlelight, at a reasonable time, with no ticketing system.

Lizzy and I, however, would continue on to Sopela, where we would find a wet pitch on a sloping campsite, throw off our grubby things, cook our dinner and fall into bed, too knackered to do anything except say good night.

I suggested that we go to Decathlon and buy some sexy cycling kit. I was getting a bit tired of my merino top and shorts.

'What then?' she asked.

'Go to a hotel.'

'Then what?

'We take it off.'
'Then what?'
'Fall asleep, I expect.'

The beautiful cyclists' shapely backsides disappeared into infinity, leaving us cruising the roads outside Mungia towards the coast and then crossing the river in Plentzia on an elegant, arched footbridge. A cycle path ran alongside the river and then headed inland and up a hill towards Barrika, a small settlement on the cliff above a series of beaches.

One of them was Meñakoz, a dangerous big wave spot that was first surfed in the early 1980s. Before that is the beach at Barrika, a beautiful spot at the bottom of a steep cliff with fingers of rock stretching out into the bay.

Lizzy and I surfed here on a hot summer's day in 2021. We walked down to the furthest end of the beach, to a peak that was breaking beautifully over sand and rock with just three people surfing it. We paddled out and sat in the channel just off the take-off zone, to show the locals that we weren't there to muscle in on their waves.

The waves broke beautifully – not huge, but regularly. The water was so clear that I could see the bottom and the rocks below. Watching the waves break from the side gave us a grandstand view of the surfers. They were ripping. Each time they took the set waves I paddled into the peak to take the next one, so giving them the choice waves and trying to make it obvious I wasn't going to be a dick. We did this for a while until they invited us to surf the peak with them. We sat chatting with them in the sunshine between sets. It paid off to have taken the time to show our respect. If it happened at home I would have felt aggrieved if someone paddled out and tried to surf all the best waves. I wasn't about to do it here.

We stopped for a coffee at a cafe above the beach before we cycled on to Sopela, one of the busiest beaches on this coast and the location of the last campsite before Bilbao. From here we would be able to catch the metro into the city and make up for missing out on *pintxos* in San Sebastián.

I knew exactly where to head.

19

The slippery streets

'I need to try and not become overly cautious. It would be sad to lose the freedom of riding a bike. I must keep believing in myself. Too much caution causes stress and just makes things worse.'

LIZZY'S DIARY ENTRY: FRIDAY 28 JUNE 2024

Stage 18: Days 37–38 | From: Sopela | To: Noja (via Bilbao) | Distance: 102km

The metro into Bilbao from Sopela only took about 30 minutes. Once we had put up the tent, pumped up the mattresses and set up for the night, we unhooked the trailers and cycled to the metro station. Our reward for getting this far – 1609km since we had left home – was to head for Bilbao's old town, the Casco Viejo, with the sole purpose of scoffing as much tapas as we could. We had missed out in San Sebastián and we weren't about to do so in Bilbao. No, sir!

Aside from travelling by ferry, this was only the second time we had been in any form of motorised transport since leaving home (we had caught a bus in Biarritz). I felt as if we were back in the land of normal people, doing normal things. I found I hadn't missed it at all. We hadn't watched television for five weeks and had never been bored. I felt more like myself than at home.

'I must remember to take this back into my old life,' I thought.

We walked out of the station and straight into a hot and busy night in the old city. The narrow pedestrian streets, full of bars, cafes and shops, were thronging with people. We made our way to the

THE SLIPPERY STREETS

neoclassical-colonnaded-delight-cum-family-meeting-place-cum-football-pitch-for-kids Plaza Nueva, where we had the choice of any number of *pintxos* bars with a mouthwatering selection of treats waiting on the bar tops. We chose one, ordered a random selection and, when it came to us on a series of small plates, unashamedly stuffed our faces full of croquettes, anchovies, chorizo, squid, egg, bread and cheese in various combinations.

My legs were so stiff from the previous few days of cycling that I could barely swing them over the bike in the morning. We had been in Spain for a week, with just one day off from cycling, and had ridden 240km. Each day had brought us at least 800 metres of climbing, sometimes more.

That day, I knew, wouldn't be any easier, although the challenges were not just about hills. We had to navigate our way through Bilbao, somehow, and had originally planned to stay at Playa Joyel beach campsite, which Google told us was only 90km away. We didn't think it was possible and set our sights for Castro Urdiales, a port town 40km away. Distance-wise it would be an easier day.

How wrong I was.

We followed the route Komoot* had set for us out of the campsite and west out of Sopela, up a hill towards the coast and the mouth of the River Nervión that bisects Bilbao. It took us up a half-finished road that ended at a parcel of woodland where a tiny track disappeared into the trees. We pushed the bikes and trailers through the branches, squelching in the mud and catching our legs on brambles and stinging nettles. I mounted up and began to pedal but before I could get too far my trailer overturned on a tree root and I came to a grinding halt, jumping off into the undergrowth before I fell.

The woodland track eventually brought us to a mossy tarmac road at the top of a hill. I freewheeled down towards a junction, happy we were out of the woods, so to speak. Behind me, though, I heard Lizzy skidding with a swooshing, rubber-on-wet-tarmac

---

* Komoot is brilliant, but occasionally it would send us off on routes that were completely unsuitable for our bikes and trailers. We'd find ourselves looking at climbs, old river beds or at paths that could kill us and have to recalibrate. Tsk, Komoot, you did it again!

kind of sound, immediately followed by a crash, the clattering of water bottles rolling down the road and Lizzy shouting out in shock and pain. I stopped, fearing the worst, and turned round. She was sprawled out on the road, the bike on top of her, the handlebars turned back on themselves. I dropped my bike and ran to her. She crawled out from underneath the bike and sat in the middle of the road, head in her hands, crying.

She had a bloodied knee and calf and one elbow had a nasty scrape. It didn't look bad enough to need medical attention but bad enough to make my nettle-fizzing legs stop bothering me. She hobbled to the side of the road and sat on the pavement examining her injuries. Thank goodness, at least she hadn't been hit by a car.

While Lizzy composed herself and examined her injuries, I pulled the bike upright and looked over it: one of her bar ends was shredded and the front wheel was a little buckled but it was still rideable. The disc brakes weren't affected by the buckling, which was a relief.

She had pulled on the front brake and the front wheel had skidded, sending her tumbling. I taped up the bar ends and consoled her in my usual clumsy way. I hated to see her in pain and distress. It wasn't her fault. The road was slippery. This kind of thing could have happened to anybody.

With the only thing to do to get back in the saddle – what other option did we have? – we set off cautiously, reaching the river and following it upstream through Bilbao's suburban towns. We navigated pedestrian crossings, speed humps and traffic lights, eventually coming to the hulk of the steel transporter bridge* in Las Arenas. We only had to wait for a few minutes before we were able to push the bikes on to the gondola that was slung on wires beneath the frame of the bridge. We joined a bunch of other cyclists and half a dozen impatient drivers jostling to get their cars in prime position for disembarking. Our bikes were too long to be squeezed on to the front of the gondola so we were wedged in by cars either side of us. It took moments to cross the river but saved us a few hours of cycling. At the other side we bullied our way off, blocking the way of motorists revving up behind. We slipped into the Bilbao traffic, following the route Komoot had set for

---

* The Vizcaya Bridge is a UNESCO World Heritage Site and the world's oldest transporter bridge.

THE SLIPPERY STREETS

us, through Portugalete and out towards the AP-8 autoroute, where a long pedestrian bridge took us over a huge junction. The bridge led us on to a delightful greenway that was like a mini bicycle motorway, carrying us into countryside: the perfect antidote to having had to assert ourselves in frightening traffic.

The greenway followed an old railway line out of Bilbao, taking us through a corridor of luscious green away from the factories, warehouses and apartment blocks of the valley floor. After climbing for 7km we hit the apex and began a steady downhill to the tiny beach town of Playa de la Arena, where the cycle path stopped abruptly at the beach car park in front of a wide sandy beach. We followed the Garmin on to a clackety wooden boardwalk across the beach, a footbridge over a river and on to an old road around the coast. We passed a few pilgrims and wished them a *'Buen Camino!'* before diverting on to the N-634 for some awful but scenic climbs. The AP-8 autoroute seemed to be ever-present, crashing through the countryside in tunnels and over viaducts while we weaved around the contours of the hills. The swooshing noise of the traffic on the motorway was constant.

On a steep downhill just before Castro Urdiales the steering on my bike became heavy and unresponsive and threatened to throw me off. I pulled over as soon as I could – on to a pavement in front of an apartment block where people were hanging out of their windows watching the traffic – and discovered I had a puncture. Bugger. Oh well. Just get on with it. There was no point in being upset or paralysed by failure. Lizzy had already brushed herself off once today.

We just had to keep moving.

We flipped the bike over, took off the wheel, replaced the inner tube, flipped the bike back over, reattached the trailer and cycled away, sadly to no applause or even recognition from the glum-looking, empty-faced onlookers.

Keen to see how bad the damage was to Lizzy's front wheel, we found a scruffy, old-fashioned bike shop in Castro Urdiales, where we met another saintly mechanic and – through the miracle of Google Translate – managed to communicate the fall, the buckled wheel and the need to get it fixed, *por favor*. As usual, the mechanic, a slow-walking, kind-faced man in his 60s, got to work, charged us virtually nothing and wished us well.

The only campsite within cycling distance that night offered us a space in a muddy field with an extended family taking up most of it with four or five caravans and various cars. They went out for the evening and returned in the small hours, their cars pulling up right next to our tent. We heard a woman fall over drunkenly, lose her shoes and stumble about right outside. I lay awake for hours afterwards, unable to sleep, listening to the sound of the rain on the flysheet.

We had a lie-in the next morning because it was still raining. I felt very sad, dreading another day of constant climbing, and tired from being kept awake. Spain so far had been tough and it was showing: for the first time I felt like I had had enough. Unzipping the tent to go to the loo in the drizzle was a pain. I fantasised about stopping somewhere nice for a few days, perhaps with a pool and sauna and some lovely food.

The route we took in the morning didn't help. We headed away from the campsite through a series of scrappy villages above the motorway, passing pilgrims so we knew we were on the right path. It was hard going at times but the mountainous terrain meant there was no other way if we were to avoid busy roads or the motorway. Barking dogs and the hiss of traffic below us made up the soundtrack.

We were following the Camino again, which meant there were some sections that were tricky for the bikes but would have been easy on foot. We passed under the AP-8 motorway and then followed the route up a steep, rocky slope, at the top of which we could see a road. We knew the drill: downshift, whack up the power and gun it. It became so steep and unstable that I couldn't get any grip or pedal anymore and had to jump off my bike, to avoid falling off it, about three-quarters of the way up. Lizzy dismounted before it got critical. We helped push each other's bikes to the crest and over it on to tarmac. There we found ourselves on another slippery descent.

I went first, slowly. Lizzy followed me, very cautiously, but fell off on the steepest part when her front wheel slipped out, again, the same way it had the day before. Her water bottles clattered off down the road. It wasn't as bad as the previous day's crash but it had unseen consequences. Lizzy is tough, and has done a lot of difficult things in her life, but this was the last straw. She got back on the bike again but began to fear downhills, which resulted in her going at crawling speed down steep slopes from then on. On some of the steeper roads,

THE SLIPPERY STREETS

particularly on gravel surfaces or when it was wet, she got off and pushed. The fear of falling is very real when you still have the scabs to remind you. I rode past her on the steepest slopes, making myself useful checking our route while waiting at the bottom.

Even though the surf was looking good at Laredo when we cruised along its wide seafront we weren't really in the mood to surf. Its beach, a 4km-long sweep of sand backed by dunes and an esplanade like a cheap version of San Sebastián, pushes out into the mouth of the Ría de Treto, behind which is a wetland and nature reserve. We had hoped to get a small ferry across the river to save ourselves 20km of cycling (and to look at the left-hand point break that works on big swells) but, when we got to the end of the sandy spit, we realised that there was no way we would be able to push our bikes through the sand and lift them up on to the boat.

A few dead ends (to locate a non-existent shortcut) later and we found our way on to the flats skirting the estuary on a road with unforgiving traffic. Lorries carrying anchovies (they were pictured on the sides) from the canning plants in Santoña tickled our panniers as they roared past, sending the day's stress levels to previously unreached heights.

I was very happy when we arrived in Playa Joyel. We pushed the bikes through the security gate and into a sea of playing children, giddy with holiday excitement. We found a good, flat pitch, put up the tent to dry it out, pumped up the beds, showered, put on a wash and sought solace in a beer or two in the campsite bar.

We discussed the previous couple of days over a pizza: they had been hard, but never dull or bad enough to make us want to stop and go home (apart from that morning's mini-wobble). Far from it. I wasn't unhappy and neither was Lizzy, just a bit shell-shocked. She had bruises too: an extra bonus.

The Camino had taken us down some rough tracks and difficult paths, but it was keeping us away from the main roads where the traffic was unrelenting and perilous. It was an OK trade. The trip was still delivering and was constantly evolving: our fortunes changing as quickly as the weather.

I swigged from my beer, feeling tired but happy. We had survived another day.

20

La Primera Ola

'I saw an advert for Barland surfboards in the magazine Le Bateau. *My sister went to Bayonne so I said to her, "Go there for me and tell me what you see." The next evening my sister rang. "Jesús. There are some boards. Beautiful." I said, "Buy it! I will try to get it to Santander."'*

JESÚS FIOCCHI, SANTANDER, JULY 2024

Stage 19: Days 39-41 | From: Noja | To: Santander | Distance: 52km

The beach at Playa Joyel (Noja) was stunningly beautiful. A crescent of golden sand with a rock island at its eastern end and several smaller islets and a river mouth towards the west. A few small waves were breaking off the islets on the western end. A couple of surfers were catching the biggest sets on big boards.

It was a hot day so, in no real hurry to get moving, we spent an hour bellyboarding in the shallows. The waves were powerful enough to give us a few fun rides in the crystal-clear water and to make us feel like it wasn't all about slogging our guts out on the bikes. We were here to surf and have fun.

Our rigs had been attracting attention again: a Spanish guy started talking to us at the campsite. He said he wished he could persuade his daughter to go cycling with him. When she arrived, he introduced her to us. Then, when we were packing up, he brought us a gift of a couple of croissants from the campsite shop and called us his *amigos*.

Later, when we were stopped at the side of the road checking the Garmin for directions, a car pulled up and the driver asked us if we were lost, then, clearly wanting to know what we were up to, asked us about where we had been and where we were going. We chatted to them in our semi-passable Spanish, explaining our mission. I loved these encounters. Seeing people's eyes widen as we told them our plans was always a thrill. I don't know if they thought we were mad, brave or just plain stupid. Either way it didn't matter. I could cope with being all three.

When we reached Playa de Somo after a thankfully easy day's riding along the coast a Portuguese dude* started a conversation about the boards outside a surf shop. He made us feel welcome. On the way to the campsite, buying groceries in a tiny shop in Loredo, the owner said our boards were beautiful.

More fun encounters and a chance to learn a little more Spanish.

Playa de Somo is a huge beach on the Bay of Santander with surf schools, surf camps and a surf shop. At its southern end there is a sand spit that juts out into the bay and offers quiet bathing: a complete contrast to Santander across the channel. A small ferry carries beachgoers here from the city in the summer. The beach at Somo is shaped like a jawbone, faces roughly to the north, and along its length there are peaks, with the biggest waves at the eastern end in Loredo. Somo is open to more swell than El Sardinero, the beach in Santander where surfing started in Cantabria.

Loredo, however, was the site of a significant moment in Spanish surfing history. In the early 1970s a group of local surfers created a commune, the 'House of the Hippies' as it became known, at a remote farmhouse called Casa Lola. They started making surfboards under the brand Tablas de Surf Santa Marina [*tabla* is Spanish for 'board'] and so established the first surfboard factory in Spain, setting the tone for a way of living that was alien to many during the dying days of Francoism.

The brand went on to become Geronimo Surfboards in the late 1970s. It later metamorphosised into Pukas Surfboards and, in doing so, became a part of the fabric of surfing. Pukas opened shops in San Sebastián and Zarautz and, in 1978, organised a competition at

---

*I call him a dude because that's exactly what he was: bare-chested, skinny, long, salty hair and baggy shorts. A proper surfy dude.

Zurriola in San Sebastián, which ran for many years. In 1988 they, along with wetsuit giant Rip Curl, put on Spain's first professional contest at Zarautz.

We pitched up at the campsite at the eastern end of the beach that overlooks Playa de Los Tranquilos (Loredo) and Santa Marina Island.

The pitches, as is common on Spanish sites, were on top of each other, with little space between one tent and the next. Much of the site was taken up with permanent pitches: knackered caravans left for years, being added to over time to make them ever more ramshackle and sad. Awnings covered in green algae were weighted down with used water bottles filled with rancid-looking liquid or cement. Fake grass or plastic tarpaulins covered any of the pitch not already covered with awnings or decking. Nature was being kept at bay, missing the point of camping.

We surfed at Loredo in the evening among a soup of surf schools and then surfed at Somo the following morning: at first light there were already a couple of surfers in the water surfing a glassy 3ft peak. The waves were powerful for their size and it was fun. I managed to catch a few speedy runners but most of the waves I caught were just 'suck, tuck and duck' closeouts.

As I sat in the water waiting for the sets, I looked over towards Santa Marina Island and remembered the Super 8 film of it I had been shown by John Cutts, a surfer from Bude who now lives in Australia. On big swells there is a fast right-hander that breaks over rocks on the island's western side. Santa Marina is the site of a big wave contest, the Santa Marina Challenge, and is regularly surfed by local surfers. The island gave its name to the first iteration of Pukas.

The grainy and dusty film shows the Fiocchi brothers, Jesús and Rafa, two of Spain's first homegrown surfers, surfing it in the spring of 1972. It is an important, rare document and shows how spots like Santa Marina Island brought surfers together. John, and his travelling companion, Roger Tout, a board shaper, met the Fiocchi brothers in Santander. The brothers showed them Santa Marina.

LA PRIMERA OLA

The film marks an important intersection, just as the 'House of the Hippies' did a couple of years later.

Jesús was also featured in a documentary, *La Primera Ola*, a film about the beginnings of surfing in Spain in the 1960s and 1970s. Keen to meet him, I tracked him down and arranged to interview him on his boat, *Surf*, in Puerto Chico, the marina in the centre of Santander, when we were passing through the city.

Surf is a beautiful wooden tuna fishing boat. Jesús, a slim, sprightly man of 82 years (although he looks younger), welcomed us aboard and invited us into the cabin, where there was a galley, a bedroom and seating area. Fishing rods were suspended from the ceiling and old pictures of family, friends, fish caught and surfboards ridden lined wooden panels between the large windows. Jesús told us he spent most of his days on the boat.

Jesús's story is incredible. He grew up swimming, spear fishing and sailing. In the early 1960s he spent his summers in Biarritz with his family, which is where he first saw surfing, although he had bodysurfed at El Sardinero, the beach close to his home in Santander. In 1964, while looking through a French boating magazine (Jesús and his family worked in shipping), he saw an advert for Barland surfboards in Bayonne, which was, at the time, just a couple of years old. Jesús's sister and father were going to Biarritz, a six-hour journey in 1964, so he asked them to visit the Barland factory and buy him a board.

Because Jesús was keen to avoid paying customs duty on the board, Michel Barland agreed to smuggle it across the border and leave it to be picked up by the coach of the Santander football team, who were playing in Irun, close to the border. The board made its way back to Santander, and to Jesús, who took it out at El Sardinero on 23 March 1965.

People were intrigued, as Jesús told me:

In the top of the blank, the *tabla*, there was 'Barland, Bayonne' and I painted over it. Nobody will know from where I got it. People asking me, 'Where did you get it?' At the time, my grandfather was working in a shipping company in Santander. And I say, 'I got it from Australia. I told the captain, he was coming back to Santander and I told him to buy it and bring it.' So, for one year, it was a lie.

You could argue that Jesús held back the development of surfing in Spain, but so what? His two brothers started surfing too, and together with a few friends (Jesús was the only one with a car), they began to explore, finding Santa Marina in the late 1960s and surfing it on their own for the first few years.

The first national competitions were held in Spain in 1971.*

There were six competitions in Spain: two in Asturias, two in Santander and two in the Basque Country. I won one competition, came second in others and third in another. So I became the '71 Spanish champion. My brothers were second and third.

Jesús went to France to compete in the first European Championships in 1972 – the first Spanish surfer to do so.

John Cutts, talking about his trip, in 1972, on the way back from discovering waves in the Canaries, told me:

Santa Marina is now well known, but back then, the only people that knew about it were Jesús and Rafa Fiocchi. We met them in Santander, and they took us there. Spring 1972, I think it was.

You take off 10–15 feet off the island, away from a big slab of rock. So, an angled take-off and it barrels off from there. The first year, it was way too big for me. It was double overhead. Then the second year, I was more experienced in riding a lot bigger waves. It was well overhead, like sometimes one and a half times overhead and barrelling off. It was incredible. And nobody there. Just Alfie and myself. The Fiocchis were working. We were there about three or four weeks, and I don't think we saw anybody else.

Lizzy and I chatted with Jesús for a couple of hours as the seagulls squawked outside and the breeze rattled the rigging of nearby boats. When he told us that he had met Gordon Clark (of Clark

---

* The first competitions were held in Zarautz from 1968, but the first national series of competitions was in 1971.

LA PRIMERA OLA

Foam)* while he was travelling around Spain on a motorcycle in 1974, I felt a further connection with surfing's wider history. Gordon Clark wasn't in Europe to surf but the Fiocchis took him to Somo. The relationship resulted in one of Jesús's friends, Carlos, going to work for Clark in Laguna Beach in California and starting his own surfboard brand in Spain, and the Fiocchis themselves visiting California in around 1976, staying with Hobie Alter,† the father of modern surfboard manufacturing.

Jesús was charming and humble, but clearly loved playing his part in surfing's history and enjoyed talking about it. Because he was there in the very beginning of surfing in Spain he made connections all over the surfing world. He enjoyed the golden period before everyone else got there – he had made it his own – and could appreciate it for what it was and for the fact it will never be the same again:

> I had the luck of being alone. I mean, with two or three more people in the water. For 10 years. Maybe more. Because the new surfers were young people. They didn't have cars. Now, everyone has a car. This is over!

We took pictures of ourselves with Jesús and left him to his afternoon pottering about on his beloved boat, while we headed to a hipster bakery on Santander's quayside for a cake and coffee. Our food arrived just as the enormous Brittany Ferries ship, *Pont Aven* – the only opportunity we had to go home early – slipped out into the estuary.

I felt no pangs of homesickness as I watched our last lift home depart. We still had a month and a half to cycle, were still only 1700km into our journey (that I had estimated to be 3000km)

---

* Clark Foam revolutionised surfing by creating foam blanks used for making surfboards. They enabled the shortboard revolution of the late 1960s and allowed surfboard shapers to build lighter, shorter boards.
† Hobie Alter was a manufacturer of balsa surfboards in the 1950s. Clark worked for him in the beginning to create a viable foam product that could be made at scale.

and felt like we belonged more here than there. We were roughly halfway through our time and distance. To give up now would have been devastating. I was tired but I still had more to give and was determined to see it through.

I sipped my tea and watched as the ship disappeared. Getting here, to Santander, from the campsite at Somo, had been an adventure in itself: we took a tiny ferry across the estuary. When it came to disembarking, we had to detach the trailers and drag them off by hand before passing the bikes to each other across the bow as the captain manoeuvred the boat alongside the quay. As usual, when under pressure it was a bit fraught, but we had done it: another obstacle overcome.

There were plenty more to come.

21

Trouble in paradise

'Some days it can be so overwhelming. The map is huge, the distances we cover, relatively small. We have cycled every day – bar three – for the last 43 days and covered a lot of map – inch by inch – but the task remains.'
INSTAGRAM POST: WEDNESDAY 3 JULY 2024

Stage 20: Days 41–43 | From: Santander | To: Arenal de Morís | Distance: 154km

Riding out of Santander took us to the lighthouse at Cabo Mayor and then through villages and settlements on the northern side of the city, following a ridgeline between the sea and the valleys inland. The roads were quiet and the going was good, bar the odd hill, until we got near to Torrelavega, when we had to ride on the main road to cross the Río Saja. Impatient traffic made the going tough for a few kilometres. I had to stand my ground, ride positively and be damned if there was a queue behind me. If I moved over too far into the gutter, cars would overtake too closely for my liking and that was much more frightening than having intolerant drivers honking at us.

After another day of almost constant climbing, even though the hills were small, leading to another day's total over 800 metres, we arrived at the fabulous clifftop campsite at the royally approved resort of Comillas. In the late 19th century the Spanish royal family holidayed here (but probably not on the campsite, even though it's very nice). These days, so I hear, members of the nobility continue to take their royal holibobs in this part of Cantabria. Antoni Gaudí's spectacular, if slightly bonkers (true to form), tiled art deco masterpiece, El Capricho, a summer residence built for a wealthy nobleman, is a popular tourist attraction in the village.

Once Lizzy had chosen a flat enough pitch (she was in charge of finding suitable pitches due to her perfectionism – I was often too tired to care but glad to be horizontal), we erected our official summer residence and went for a swim and bodysurf on the small beach below the campsite. It had been hot in the saddle all day so I did a bit of pathetic *ooch*ing and *ouch*ing on the way in while she plunged in without hesitation.

While wandering around the campsite to look at the views from the better pitches at the cliff edge, I got talking to a middle-aged lady from Cornwall, who was staying in a black camper van. I noted that she had the best spot and that we had stayed on it the year previously: big mistake.

Within five minutes, she had told me all about herself with gusto, leaving no detail out. I found out the value of her house ('Wow! That's a lot!') and that she swims every day, back in Cornwall ('Oh, well done *you!*'). I also found out the restaurants in her home town are expensive and that she swims every day. Did I say she mentioned that?

She also told me what they were having for supper, which did sound rather scrumptious, if a little smugly put: grilled seabass and Greek salad with a glass of fizz ('Sounds lovely.'). We were having a kind of veggie ratatouille with aubergines, courgettes, onions, tomatoes and potatoes that was easy and delicious but wasn't bass with fizz.

Unfortunately, the ratatouille took ages to cook, due to a problem with fuel, which, during the hungry moments of waiting, made me want to throw the whole lot, plus the Trangia stove, over the cliff. We had found it hard to find methylated spirits in France to replace the limited supplies we had brought and had, so far, failed in Spain. Having visited a few hardware stores, the nearest we could find was cleaning alcohol, which was 96 per cent pure alcohol. It worked, but burned cooler than meths, so making any meal – or even boiling water – take ages. For a hungry camper who had climbed almost the equivalent of Slieve Donard (850 metres) again – for the eighth time in nine days – it was torture.

I would have happily gone out to eat but we were still having trouble with Spanish restaurants, in that they didn't start cooking until 9 p.m. and we were too hungry for dinner at 8, never mind 9 or 10. That is, I suppose, what culture shock is.

I sat and watched a pot barely boil, half wishing I was in my van cooking on its lovely induction hob. But then I remembered why I was here, that I was having a great time and should not be envious of anyone else, at any point, especially pompous women in VW campers.

When Lizzy was clearing up she met the woman at the washing-up station, got the house value thing, the restaurant thing and the swimming in the sea each day thing ('Well *done*. I do too.') plus some new information: how they loved going off-grid in their van because they had recently installed solar panels.

Lizzy came back, a little vexed.

'That woman!' she said. 'All she did was talk about herself.'

'And her house?' I offered.

'A million. And how she likes to camp off-grid.'

The woman walked past, a picture of smugness and superiority. 'I was just telling your wife how jealous you were of our dinner.'

'Oh right. Well, it *sounded* nice but I wouldn't say ours was . . .'

She wandered off.

Lizzy, noticing the van, asked, 'Is that her van? Does a van like that have a bathroom?'

'No,' I replied.

'So how do they go off-grid if it hasn't got a toilet?'

'Porta Potti?' I offered.

'So a bucket then? What a joke. Her house might be worth a million but she still has to shit in a bucket.'

Lizzy, I should say here, has washed in rivers, wild camped her way across Europe and South America and been at the rougher end of the camping experience. Performative campers who say they are going off-grid because it sounds like the thing to do, do not wash with her, in a river or otherwise.

I was a little jealous of seabass and salad, but wouldn't have admitted it because I didn't want to acknowledge the entitlement. Here we were, on our silly bikes, living like paupers while she pretended she'd be happy with shitting in a bucket (and yet was staying on a very plush campsite and using their facilities). Well done *you*!

We wandered into the old village of Comillas to take advantage of the one cultural difference between home and Spain that would work in our favour: the hardware shop was open until nine. We bought a couple of bottles of 99 per cent proof rubbing alcohol, which we thought we'd try. We sat down in the square for a drink (not the rubbing alcohol), watching local families play keepie-uppie and taking their evening *paseo* as the light faded and the day fizzled out to a lovely, slightly less tense end.

Packing up early to avoid our new friend, we pedalled away from Comillas on a very bumpy cycle path through the Oyambre Natural Park and then over a steep hill to Playa de Merón, a fabulous surfing beach a little to the east of the river estuary and town at San Vicente de la Barquera. I love surfing here, and have done so for years. It's not the world's best wave but it's always a great place to hang out and spend time. The last time I surfed here the waves had been fantastic and I had made a friend in a Spanish surfer who had rescued my board after my leash broke. On another occasion I had surfed a small but perfect peak on my own that was breaking so regularly I was able to surf a right, then a left, then a right. That's a rare thing indeed.

The surf was 3–4 feet (0.9–1.2 metres) and clean and not quite as perfect but fun all the same. The line-up was international, with Dutch, German, English and Spanish men and women surfing. I liked that. It felt good to be back here but even better to have got here under my own steam.

Playa de Merón has been surfed since at least the mid-1960s. According to Daniel Esparza's essay 'Towards a Theory of Surfing Expansion: The Beginnings of Surfing in Spain as a Case Study', Peter Viertel, who was responsible for bringing surfing to France, used to spend his holidays in San Vicente de La Barquera and surfed when he was here in the early 1960s, so inspiring locals to surf too.

We bullied our way across the bridge at San Vicente, making wishes,[*] and headed into town, breathless. The Garmin, and the Camino, sent us up the steepest road we had encountered yet, a narrow lane that seemed to go straight upwards. The route, an absolute bastard of a climb, though short and sharp, led away from a busy roundabout and on to a back road high above the town. Just as I was gearing up a car slowed down

---

[*] It's said that if you can hold your breath all the way across the bridge then your wishes will come true. We couldn't, although you might say they (the wishes) did.

in the middle of the road to let someone pass. I knew that if I stopped I would fall off or roll back down the hill on to the roundabout, so I had no choice but to carry on. I shouted at the driver to continue but he stopped right in front of me. I swerved around him and into the path of the other driver, who had to stop to avoid hitting me.

I waved an arm about in a 'rumbunctious European style' at the driver while simultaneously trying to thank the car that had stopped for me. It must have been a confusing sight for all, especially since my raving was mostly in English: exactly what bike-hating motorists expect from cyclists.

From the top of the road we could see, to the south-west, the mountainous hulks of the Picos de Europa, a small but mighty range of limestone giants with peaks of up to 2600 metres. I had been nervous about crossing this part of Spain because of the hills, but, as luck would have it, the coastal foothills of the Picos were not as steep as I thought. Since leaving the Basque Country the climbs were less severe and although there were lots of them, we enjoyed a relatively easy day, finishing up at an amazing campsite called Camping Entreplayas in Llanes that overlooked a beautiful, red cliff-backed cove, Playa Puerto Chico, where we bodysurfed a fun shore break that left us skidding on to the hard sand on our stomachs. The town, a medieval fishing village with thick city walls, narrow streets and a picturesque harbour surrounded by restaurants, cafes and bars, was a complete revelation. Beyond the city walls, a steep limestone escarpment of over 1000 metres rose up from the coastal plain, a constant reminder of Spain's ever-present mountains.

Having cooked successfully using the newly acquired rubbing alcohol, we wandered into the town for a mooch and a drink. We agreed, while going over the last few days, that we were dealing in different scales when it came to hills. Climbs that I saw as near-impossible feats of human endeavour and fortitude were, to Lizzy, just foothills, as if I wasn't feeling inadequate enough. In her diary Lizzy wrote: *'Martin's massive hills are mostly quite moderate. Oh, how far he has come though — no tears or even moans.'*

Let's put that on the record.

The conversation didn't end well though, as it turned to where we were going next. Looking at what we still had to achieve, it now seemed, to me, that we might have to make some compromises if we were to stand a chance of making Sagres in 90 days. We were only

400km into Spain and we had yet to navigate the remote region of Galicia and its crenellated coastline in Spain's north-western corner.

I wrote on an Instagram post that day: *'How naive to think it would be *just* 3000km to Sagres when we are already approaching 2000km and are *only* around 400km from the border with France. Porto, and Portugal, is 600km by the most direct route.'*

Going around the coast of Galicia, nice as it would be, I felt would take too long, be too difficult and risk us not making Sagres in time. I felt we should at least consider taking a more direct route, going cross-country through the region, following the route of the Camino, to Santiago de Compostela instead of hugging its coastline. If we completed the Camino del Norte we would cut off a bit of the corner and still have finished an amazing achievement. To Lizzy, this felt like I was trying to take Galicia from her. She fought hard against it, on principle, if nothing else. She was being told 'no' and, for someone who has had to put up with a lot of 'no' in her life, particularly from men who have tried to get the better of her, it was mildly triggering. I felt misjudged and frustrated for wanting a compromise to keep the journey on track. Once again we were both carrying too much baggage, only this time it weighed more than just a spare battery ever could.

It was a sulky, unpleasant exchange that could only be cured by getting back on the bikes and riding, which we did the next morning. By the time we arrived at a town called Poo we had both had a chance to reflect, and while we still hadn't agreed a route forward, we were back to being bezzies. Cycling had cleared the air and made us realise that there were bigger things to think about, like getting a shot of me in front of the Poo sign. It is never not funny. Every love needs a Poo sometimes.

We had passed from the region of Cantabria into the region of Asturias on leaving San Vicente. Asturias is often called 'Green Spain' for its verdant countryside, and perhaps a touch of rain. The cycling was fantastic and took us along the coastal plain to amazing beaches at Borizo and Barro and then through lush meadows, around an estuary with a church overlooking the water, past elaborately decorated *hórreos** on stone stilts, and on beautiful rough roads through forest

---

* *Hórreos* are raised granaries, usually built from wood, atop capped stone pillars.

slopes with steep descents. Lizzy dismounted for the worst of them, choosing to push rather than risk skidding on the gravel.

We lunched on bread and cheese on the beach at Ribadesella, watching the surfers but declining an opportunity to get wet due to the rising tide that was making the waves a little fat. It was unfortunate that we had turned up a bit late but that was all a part of what we were doing. We couldn't stop and wait for a few hours for the tide to drop, because we had a time limit to think of.

The beach, a sweep of sand at the river mouth of the Río Sella, with clear blue water and a jolly esplanade, backed by grand houses, was lovely. Being able to park the bikes right on the path above the beach was our reward for cycling here. Despite driving through Ribadesella before I had never stopped, simply because, as with Zarautz, there is little to no parking available for vans like mine.

The end of the day brought us a few surprises. The Desfiladero de Entrepeñes, a steep-sided gorge, took us up a right twat of a climb (read that as 'a bit steep' on the Lizzy scale) on the N-632, during which I was puffing and blowing (but not crying or moaning – go me!). We crossed the motorway and climbed another arse wipe of a hill into Caravia, a small settlement with a huge church at its heart. We stopped at the church to have a drink and something to eat and to shelter from the rain that had started to fall again in big, fat, sock-and-mood-soaking globules.

I knew there was a campsite halfway down the hill, with a beach at the bottom where there was good surf. Lizzy and I had stopped there before. I wanted to end the day, desperately, because I was exhausted, hungry and cold. Lizzy wanted to carry on, in favour of exploring new places. I stood my ground and after a brief strop (from me), we freewheeled down the hill towards Camping Arenal de Morís and a chance meeting that would mean so much. The surf, as we cruised down the hill, was looking pretty good too.

We pulled into the campsite and stopped at reception to check in. As I was walking through the door, a booming voice bellowed:

'Mister Dorey!'

I turned around to see a giant of a man, with a smiling face and freckles, bearing down on me.

'We've been following you!' he said.

22

Saint Ben and the boys

'Meeting up with Ben and the boys was a total blessing. We got fed and looked after, and found out what an incredible family they are and all they have achieved. A real treat.'

LIZZY'S DIARY ENTRY: SUNDAY 7 JULY 2024

Stage 21: Days 44–46 | From: Arenal de Morís | To: Playa de Bahínas (via Gijón) | Distance: 107km/1982km

It took me a while to work out where I had met Ben after the initial, very disarming man-hug. His name eluded me at first too, but then I remembered: he had looked around our van a few years ago. Thankfully, graciously, he introduced himself to Lizzy as Ben from Widemouth. He was with his son, Zeb, and his friend, Sam, on a boys' surf trip to celebrate finishing their GCSEs.

Ben said he had been following my posts on Instagram and knew we were close by but was still amazed to see us. I was a little surprised myself, and surprised to feel this as a minor intrusion. We hadn't expected to bump into anyone we knew, especially at such a tiny, out-of-the-way place like Arenal de Morís.

But, as with all small miracles, you don't always recognise them when you first see them.

We set up the tent and then headed to the beach for a surf. Ben and the boys joined me. The waves were onshore and messy but still a lot of fun. It was good to surf with people from home and it reminded me that surfing is an activity undertaken by a tribe sharing a common joy. Surfing is, and should be, about community as much as it can be about solitude.

We hooted as a local surfer, taking off down the beach from us, dropped into an absolute beauty: a big wave that curled behind him in an angry tunnel of spume. He rode it well. We were happy to be able to see it: that was how it was done.

We left the campsite early the next morning so we could get some kilometres under our belts. Plus, it was raining so there was no point in hanging around. Having looked at the route to Gijón – where we had booked a hotel for two nights to get some rest and shelter from torrential rain that was forecast – I knew there were some big hills to tackle. What lay between us and four stars of comfort was pain. While leaving early saved us about three hours of fannying around with breakfast – we were on the road by 8 a.m. – it cost us dearly later.

Food can be an issue for the long-distance international cycling-surfer, and especially for those who have issues with food. It was becoming a flashpoint between us and tensions were rising daily. Perhaps this was a reflection of the difficult conditions we had been encountering in Spain: the hills, the weather, the cooking fuel. Until then it hadn't really affected us: as long as we had supplies and could cook (or navigate the menus in restaurants) things were OK.

Our usual routine meant we ate breakfast, started late, cycled in the middle of the day, stopped for a sandwich at lunch and then cooked in the evening. This meant we had to stop daily to undertake what I see as the devil's task: shopping for supplies. I watched the bikes while Lizzy shopped, then, naturally, complained when she came back with bursting bags. All the food went in my panniers, I should add, so I was the one hauling it.

Lizzy, like anyone, needs food to be able to function, of course. Food is fuel but also dopamine that helps her to be clear-headed. Without it she can become moody and anxious, can't concentrate and feels down – symptoms that point to neurodiversity. Food, in a chaotic and sometimes confusing world, offers comfort, balance and, above all, control. Shopping is a part of that control. Without the safety of supplies, or the knowledge that food will be available later, Lizzy can panic.

Food, also, can't be any old fuel. The quality of the intake needs to be controlled – it needs to be nutritionally balanced too. And when you are cycling, it needs to be enough. We were burning through calories at an alarming rate. At this stage, I was losing weight fast.*

I have different issues around food. I can go all day without eating because, like the primitive I am, I think that hunger motivates me. Plus, I can't be arsed to eat when there are more exciting things to do. As long as I know there will be something to eat, at some point, no matter what it is, I will be happy. On this trip, despite growing issues, I was trying to be a happy pragmatist.

However, I also have restaurant anxiety. This is mostly about the fear of being forgotten, not understanding the menu and waiting for ages for food to arrive, but also includes being unable to cope with overcrowded restaurants that have too many tables for the space.

Imagine, if you will, someone who wants to order as quickly as possible, in a country where the kitchen doesn't open until 9 p.m., sitting with someone who can't choose because they are hungry and overwhelmed, the menu is in another language and there is too much on it, and who needs to make sure the food they do order is nutritionally balanced.

I wouldn't go out for dinner with us either.

That day it was breakfast that drove the wedge between us. Its absence ramped up the tensions, failed to put a cap on intolerance, forgot what it means to be nice, couldn't deal with the lack of control (while losing it at the same time), and pushed the collective anxiety over the edge of a two-day-long precipice that could only be cured by the timely reappearance of Saint Ben.

At Colunga, a small village an hour into our ride, I suggested we stop at a cafe for breakfast. Lizzy didn't like the look of it and said she wanted to stop for a bowl of yogurt first (from our supplies) and then stop for breakfast further on. 'Why can't we just stop for breakfast?' I wondered. Stopping twice was just pissing about and wasting time. We had hills to climb.

I cycled off. My way of taking back control. I am an arsehole sometimes. Lizzy can be equally difficult, but, unfortunately, she can't do much about it – because of the effect that being hungry can have

---

* Don't worry about me at this point. I was carrying quite a lot of excess baggage, mainly as a result of sitting on my backside for many months the year before.

on her emotions – whereas I could try harder. I should learn to accept her teetering on the edge as a sign to back off and gently take control, but only really gently. Of course it's easy for me to write this now, but at the time I was fuming.

We sat on a bench overlooking the square in Colunga while Lizzy ate her yogurt and then went next door to a cafe for a ham and egg sandwich and a coffee for Lizzy and a shit cup of tea for me. Soon after she was back to her normal self, as if nothing had happened, dopamine restored.

I was still brooding. I just wanted an easy life, but an easy life didn't always come easy. You had to work at it.

Back on the bikes, and feeling a little happier, we took the AS-258 out of Colunga and hit the AS-330, a wiggly road that led us into the hills. It was tough going but just a warm-up compared with what was to come. We crawled up the shady, single-track road as it wound up a mountain in a series of sharp bends around steep-sided valleys with gushing rivers hidden in the trees. There was precious little traffic and it was a great ride. All the time, though, I had the next climb at the back of my mind.

We could have pulled off and cooled down at Playa de Rodiles, a stunner of a beach with high cliffs at either end, a river-mouth break and a forest of eucalyptus behind the dunes. However, it was 6km out of our way and 6km back. I was ambivalent about going there anyway, having spent a few days there in 1998 after I had been whacked and mashed up at Mundaka. Back then, I had spent the first session watching my friend surf perfect, spitting 6–8ft tubes over the sandbar at the end of the river mouth. Each wave had peeled off into the bay with a precision that I hadn't seen anywhere before, apart from at Mundaka. It has been said that if Mundaka didn't exist then Rodiles would be the best river-mouth wave in Europe.

I had paddled out the next day, when it was smaller, with a surgical glove taped to my hand to protect my injuries. Even though it had only been about 4ft – head high – I had taken out a 6ft 10in pintail (designed for bigger surf) because my 6ft 2in fish-tailed board couldn't handle the speed of the drop and the race down the line. With a few vans of travelling surfers and a bunch of locals it had been crowded and the atmosphere tense. That was the trouble with

Rodiles. It had a bad reputation for localism: if you surf the beach it's fine but try and surf the river mouth and it won't be.

I wasn't up for that today. The locals can keep it (which, sadly, is exactly what they want).

The next big climb started outside the town of Villaviciosa, where the valley floor began to fall away and we passed between whitewashed houses and *hórreos*, climbing steadily into the eucalyptus plantations on the upper slopes. Gaps in the trees showed us where and what we were: tiny figures in an enormous landscape, with low mountains to the south of us on the other side of a huge valley, the motorway going through tunnels and across viaducts below us. Looking down, I could see the way we had come snaking up the hillside. I geared down to GG1 and powered up to Purple Mode (e-MTB) for the steepest sections, some of which were up to 14 per cent.

The descent, a winding, steep freewheel down to about 50 metres above sea level, was a short-lived joy. Almost immediately we climbed again to 250 metres through forest and meadow. The countryside was beautiful but – fucking hell – it was tough. I was tired and could barely appreciate where we were and what we were doing, even though at the end of it there was a four-star hotel.

We got lost on the descent and couldn't find the right path into the city. The Komoot route was leading us to a rough track disappearing into the forest. We stood at the entrance to the path looking at the screen, confused: it didn't seem right. A mountain biker came past and explained it was an OK route but might be a bit difficult for the trailers on some stretches. It was the best way to the city. He cycled off down the path.

OK then.

The track nose-dived into the eucalyptus forest and quickly took us on a few turns for the worse. It was a forestry road with deep ruts, rocks and mini water-cut ravines that turned over my trailer and got Lizzy pushing her bike. Without trailers it would have been a blast. A few miles of chiropractic riding and a fair bit of pushing later we came out on the N-632, a little surprised to be so close to the city. We picked up a cycle lane that followed a river, taking us under bridges and skirting the heavy traffic, until it brought us to the city centre and Gijón's beach, Playa de San Lorenzo. From there it was a short dash across six lanes of traffic to our first taste of anything approaching luxury in six weeks, the Hotel Silken Ciudad, where, I was reassured, they had sheets and a bed you didn't have to blow up each night.

We locked the bikes in the garage, went up to our room, made a mess of the giant whirlpool bath and slept for the rest of the afternoon.

With nothing much to do the next day except wander around Gijón looking for food in the rain, we ate tacos at a shared table in a crowded restaurant, later than hoped, and with my back to the room. It wasn't my idea of a relaxed night in the city. Lizzy wanted something other than tapas, which was fair enough but in the end caused her to be overwhelmed and unable to decide and unable to let me decide for her. It felt like an impossible situation, resolved with a less than perfect compromise that turned eating into nothing more than, it seemed to me, an exercise in fuelling up.

We hadn't charged up the Garmin before we left Gijón, which meant that we ground to a very sudden stop when we were attempting to leave the city. It didn't help the simmering tension, but at least we had scoffed a huge hotel breakfast so food wasn't today's issue. We muddled through after some exchanges that would best be forgotten. The hotel stay was supposed to be a chance to recharge – figuratively and literally – and yet it failed on both counts.

Still, being back on the bikes was a tonic and the weather had perked up. We followed a road through the suburbs and into the surrounding hills that was like the tail of an angry cat. It took us up and down a few steep but short hills, past a rusting, disused steelworks, under a roaring motorway and alongside a railway before coughing us up like a four-wheeled furball into a yawning Bagpuss of a valley with patchwork fields, whitewashed farmhouses, orchards and big skies. How did that happen? One minute we were cycling past the rusting hulk of a steelworks, the next we were cruising through benign, fairy-tale countryside.

The scenery changed again on the approach to Avilés. We entered a seriously industrial landscape of railway yards, steaming pipes, stacks of steel girders and filth, dirt and rust. We were pulled over by the Guardia to allow a peloton of about 100 riders to fly past us at about four times the speed of our little convoy. It was like being overtaken by a high-speed Lycra circus in a *Mad Max* film.

An old railway transformed into a greenway took us into the heart of Avilés along the river and past the huge bases of wind turbines waiting to be lifted on to ships docked in the river. Rusting steel sculptures stood tall on the waterside, providing an interesting contrast to the Oscar Niemeyer-designed International Cultural Centre we also passed, with its bright colours, curvy shapes and wave-like exhibition space.

We rode past pilgrims, walkers, joggers and families, following the Camino through the deserted docks and out to the river mouth and Playa de San Juan, the easternmost end of Playa Salinas. We stopped in the car park to check the surf and noticed Ben's van.

It was, as it turned out, the small miracle we'd been needing.

Ben was in the middle of making lunch. When he offered some to us we didn't turn it down. It was Sunday and no shops were open so we had nothing to eat anyway. A cup of proper English tea and a sausage sandwich later and we were checking the surf with Ben and the boys. I was keen as mustard as it was looking good, but Ben said to wait. They had surfed here before and knew when it would be at its best.

It was agony waiting for the tide to come up but it was worth it. Overhead sets came rolling in, one after the other, breaking in regular peaks. A channel at the north end of the beach made the paddle out easy. We surfed for a couple of hours, trading waves and hooting each other. I managed to catch a few set waves that felt great, with a big drop and a wide-open shoulder. Everything felt good.

Salinas was the first place in Asturias to be surfed, by Felix Cueto, the inventor I mentioned earlier who made his first board in 1963, based on the cover of The Beach Boys' album *Surfin' U.S.A.*. People were already catching waves at Salinas with inflatable mattresses, but until Felix turned up with his home-made board – it was made of plywood covering a frame like an aeroplane wing – no one had managed to stand up to surf. He was later joined by a local man who had bought a Barland Rott in Biarritz.

Felix's second batch of boards were made from epoxy resin and polystyrene, a precursor to 'modern' epoxy boards, because he couldn't get expanded foam to use with fibreglass and polyester resin. In 1968 he surfed Rodiles for the first time. Later, he also bought a British-made Bilbo in Biarritz.

Ben offered to cook for us that evening – he sensed our need – and gave us directions to a campsite they had found, around 15km to the south, at Playa Bahínas. While they went to buy supplies we cycled off

SAINT BEN AND THE BOYS

to find the site, a wonderful, family-run campsite in a tight valley at the back of a beach. Quiet and peaceful, with none of the seasonal pitches we had come to expect, the campsite felt more like it belonged in the Lake District than in Spain. We explained to the owners that we were with the English people and they gave us a grassy pitch adjacent.

While Ben cooked and the boys played football, we drank beers from the bar and sat in the sunshine, feeling very blessed to be able to resolve our day this way. Ben, it became clear, was sent to us when we really needed him.

Ben was an ordained priest. But he wasn't like any other priest I have ever met. He was over 6 feet tall, well-built and freckled, with a bald head, a big white and ginger beard and a very soft, measured way about him. He sailed, surfed, skied and worked as a mountain bike guide, mechanic and youth worker. He explained to us that he was now co-ordinating the Church's response to climate change. I listened, eager to allow him to inspire me. He spoke about himself and his family in a way that only being away from home allows. In letting us into his life he gave us the space to slow down and reassess ours. We didn't need to say anything about what our journey had been like the last few days. I felt he knew.

A wave of calmness engulfed me and spoke gently in my ear: everything will be OK, if you let it.

We cooked breakfast for everyone the next morning with supplies bought from the campsite shop. Before we left, Ben gathered Lizzy and me in his huge arms and said a Celtic blessing. My usual reaction would be to snigger at anything like this, but I didn't: I was grateful that we had found him and was sure it wasn't by accident:

Deep peace of the running wave to you
Deep peace of the flowing air to you
Deep peace of the quiet earth to you
Deep peace of the shining stars to you
Deep peace of the source of all peace to you.
May the deep peace of Jesus
Christ the author and founder of peace be with you always, Amen.*

---

* Celtic blessing adapted by Ben.

23

A decent cup of tea

'57km today, which means we smashed the 2000km mark! That's a lot of time in the saddle. I never thought I would do that, never mind towing two surfboards.'

INSTAGRAM POST: MONDAY 8 JULY 2024

Stage 22: Days 47–48 | From: Playa de Bahínas | To: Tapia de Casariego | Distance: 126km

Another day, another 800 metres-plus of climbing. And to think that our friend Eugene had said that northern Spain was flat. I was getting used to it, little by little, and wasn't so daunted any more, but it was tiring. A day of doing 57km felt like more, even though I know proper cyclists do much more than that daily, and climb more. Still, I was getting fitter and my back was aching less and less each day. Sebastian had been right: cycling makes thing better.

Even though my knee grumbled on the biggest climbs, I felt more like me than ever. And that me wasn't afraid to climb hills or to go surfing on crowded beaches, loved being outside all the time and knew that shitty times wouldn't last forever. I was learning how to be a better travelling companion too. We were getting better at being ourselves.

Despite this, the spectre of Galicia was still hanging over us. We hadn't decided what to do. Would we cut across country and miss the coast out altogether? Would we cut some of it out to make it quicker? Would we attempt to cycle its 1600km of coastline?

We agreed to wait until we got to Tapia de Casariego, where we would meet up with Tony Butt, a British big wave surfer, oceanographer and environmentalist. Tony, we decided, with his local knowledge and wisdom, would be able to help us decide.

On leaving Playa de Bahínas we picked up the N-632, the old road, as it wound its way west through hilltop villages and open country and then took us on a rambling course along the coastal strip between the Asturian mountains and the sea. We stopped for lunch at the incredible La Concha de Artedo, a stunning white-sand beach backed by pine forest. We spotted it through the trees while cruising around its eastern headland. The road led us into the back of a narrow valley, under a huge concrete viaduct, over which the motorway ran, and down a cobbled lane to the pebble ridge at the back of the beach. We pushed the bikes on to the ridge, stripped off and leapt into the sea. The water was warm and clear. There were only a handful of people on the beach, some of them starkers. I was tempted but, when I fell asleep on the beach, I kept my shorts on. I didn't need sunburn on top of tired legs.

The roads followed the contours of the coast, in a pattern that took us into tight, wooded valleys, around hairpins where rivers gurgled under the road, and then up and out of the valleys to farmland dotted with houses. We crossed the motorway a few times, sometimes going under viaducts, at other times crossing over on bridges. On one steep section I saw griffon vultures circling overhead as I sweated my way up. I never gave them the chance to feed on my weary corpse. I had more to do than lie down in the road and die.

We overnighted in a campsite in Cadavéu, a small village on the coast. It had a pool and a bar, which was all we needed. We turned in early – about 10 p.m. – but were kept awake by children running about until the small hours, big, noisy family meals being eaten just before midnight and dogs barking continuously.

The morning brought sunshine, and a downhill into Luarca, another beautiful port town, for coffee and a croissant (*cruasán* in Spanish) before hitting what felt like flatter countryside. In Navia we stopped at a bike shop to buy a puncture repair kit. The owner admired our Brooks saddles, telling us that he used to work for them: a nice encounter. Despite the countryside rolling more than rollicking, by the time we had spun into Tapia de Casariego in the afternoon we had climbed another 960 metres.

It started raining heavily – in fat, chin-dripping, neck-chilling, sock-soaking drops – so we sheltered under the awning of a cafe above the beach and messaged Tony. While the rain fell in sheets on the road and our bikes, we waited, me sipping the worst cup of tea I have ever tasted. While I know it wasn't the bar's fault for not knowing how to make a cup of tea in an English style, I had tried, and failed, to ask for hot water with cold milk. Whatever I asked for, the milk came frothed and hot. I was on the point of giving up and ordering a coffee when Tony arrived.

His first saintly act was to teach me how to order a cup of tea. (He texted me a few days after we met so I would have a record of it: '*Té negro (que sea English breakfast y no Earl Grey si es posible, por favor) con un poquito de leche fría en una jarrita aparte, eso es, leche fría, gracias.*')*

With a half-decent cuppa in front of me, I began to thaw out.

Tony is a well-respected surfer who has been ploughing his own furrow for a long time. He is well known for a column that ran for over 20 years in *The Surfer's Path* magazine, and is an explorer and pioneer, who has discovered waves in and around Tapia and Galicia. It all started with a few trips while he was a student at Plymouth Polytechnic.

Despite being 64, Tony was full of energy, the result of a life not lived on the sofa:

> I decided to just get the ferry down to Spain every couple of weeks or once a month, for a few days, and just relax. That was about ... just over 30 years ago. One day, I decided not to go back.
>
> The first trip was in 1979. I went with three other mates, and we were 17 or 18 years old and we didn't have a clue. We went on the ferry as foot passengers from Plymouth. We had boards and

---

* This translates as: 'Black tea (English breakfast or if you don't have that, Earl Grey if possible, please) with a small jug of cold milk, if not, just cold milk. Thank you.'

rucksacks and we walked around the town, trying to explain that we were surfers. We found out that if we got this little boat from where the ferry is, you end up in a place called Somo. So, we got this little boat across and camped in the dunes in Somo for two weeks and just surfed there.

Tony didn't really look like a typical big wave surfer, whatever it is that they were supposed to look like. He was slight, intense and bald. I liked him because he likes to do things differently. His niche was big wave surfing, a passion that has resulted in him pioneering spots in Spain that are now well known. He continues to search for waves, always moving on when the jet skis and circus moves in.

Later, on another trip, we got a map out. I had this idea that a straight piece of coastline might coincide with nice, flat reefs. We got there and I remember driving along on this road, over this bridge, and out of the corner of my eye, I spotted this wave. So, we paddled out there. Today, it's one of the best waves in Spain. Now, everyone knows about it, but then, nobody was surfing there. We were waiting for the locals to turn up but there were no locals at all. It's near where I live now.

Eventually other people discovered it. But on those little trips we never surfed with anybody else for about seven years.

What does this prove? That it's still possible to find new places to surf in Europe? Possibly, but only if you have the knowledge and dedication of someone like Tony.

I thought it was all over, discovering spots, then surfing them for 10 years. Somebody would come along with jet skis and invite a load of cameras. Then it would all be over. And it was like a cycle. That would happen again. And I thought there's nowhere else to discover. There's nowhere else to find that experience any more.

And then a couple of years ago, me and a friend discovered this place in Costa da Morte. It felt like it was 30 years ago. It took two winters to get out there.

It took us about an hour to paddle out through a beach break and then along the coast. The wave is in front of a cliff. The first time, we got one wave each and we were out there for four or five hours. When we got in we hugged each other. It was an amazing experience, even though we only got one wave each. We were in total flow the whole time. Nothing else existed. Just the mission of getting into this wave and surfing it.

I wondered if surfers like me would ever be likely to make that kind of discovery. In my 30s and 40s I surfed a stretch of coast that was almost always quiet. If you worked hard you could surf alone or with just a few friends. It meant getting up early, walking or scrambling, and, at one time, involved going out in boats. Like Tony, we tried to outwit everyone else and surf without other people to spoil it. On the mornings when I arrived at the beach to find no one else surfing, everything felt new. There were no footprints on the sand and no sign of anyone else. On those mornings, with empty waves rolling on to the reef, the world was beginning again.

Tony was living proof that it is still possible to find new places to surf, if you have the time and patience. Alternatively, if you were like me, you could just get up before anyone else.

Surfers – unless they leave slicks of sunscreen or plastic fibres in the water – live in an ephemeral world. After each wave has been surfed, their wake – and any proof of their existence – disappears almost as quickly as it was made. The water, displaced by fins and rails, returns to itself. On land, however, it may be a different story. Travelling surfers can end up leaving indelible marks on the communities in which they travel, whether it's opening the door to more surfers and tourism, or even creating new families and people.

Waves are nothing more than water, supercharged with pulses of energy from storms thousands of miles away. As surfers all we are trying to do is be present at the precise moment the energy runs through the water so we may slide down it. Every wave, therefore, is a new discovery. It wasn't there before and it won't be there afterwards. There might be others but they won't ever be the same. Capturing that moment is what surfing is about. The context may change – you may surf with friends, in new places or with hostility in the air – but the moment is unique.

The rain eased and the conversation came to an end so Lizzy and I left Tony, got back on our wet saddles and headed to the campsite at Penarronda. We hadn't really discussed the Galicia problem but Tony had fired us up. Galicia is one of European surfing's last frontiers and it would be a shame if we decided to skip it. But 1600km was a lot to add to our journey.

There was a familiar figure at Penarronda when we pulled in. Ben, Zeb and Sam were walking back to their van, surfboards under their arms, when we were checking in. It was a great surprise, but also not a great surprise. I wondered what it would be that we needed this time, aside from an evening under their awning sheltering from the rain. That they had a purpose in our lives now was indisputable. I just had to work out what it was.

Talk, over evening beers, turned to bike maintenance. Within a few moments, on Lizzy's request (I would never have asked because I am a man), our bikes were upside down, being given the once-over by Ben, who had, as we had found out from talking to him, been a bike mechanic and mountain bike guide in his younger days. He diagnosed worn brake pads on Lizzy's front wheel, showed us how to change them and, while he was at it, changed mine too.

In the morning, at first light, Lizzy and I went for a bellyboard at the beach. We walked down the boardwalk and through the dunes and found ourselves alone on the sand. It had rained overnight and the marks left by yesterday's sunbathers, surfers and dog walkers had gone. There was no wind and the small surf was clean and crisp, breaking left and right on a sandbar at one side of the beach. For all we knew, we could have been the first surfers.

Ben blessed us again before we left. He laid his huge arms on each of our shoulders, towering above us. It made me feel safe, as if he had given us a talisman for the coming miles. We didn't know if we would see him again but made rough plans to try and catch up in Santiago de Compostela, if we went that way.

When we cycled off to meet up with Tony again we felt brand new. I was confident the bikes would last the distance and that made me happy. They had been the biggest extravagance for the trip and it seemed to me they had been worth it. Aside from a little damage from Lizzy's falls, and spokes broken because of too much weight, they were holding up amazingly. We had covered over 2000km since leaving home and all we had had to do was change a couple of brake pads. I called it a win.

Tony introduced me to Nathan, an Australian surf school owner who was married to a local woman, the daughter of Adela, bar owner and founder of a long-running surf competition in Tapia de Casariego, the Goanna Pro. In turn, Nathan introduced me to Rob Gulley, one of two brothers who were the first to surf in Tapia in 1968. Their story made me realise that what happens on land is equally important as what happens in the water. The traces of that first visit – by complete chance – resonate today.

We met Rob Gulley outside Adela's bar in the centre of Tapia on a warm night. The town was preparing itself for a regatta and the harbourside was buzzing with people and excitement. Rob sat at a table on the street where he could see and be seen, his blue pilot shirt, big shoulders and peaked cap making him look like a retired airman. He was full of energy and spoke quickly, flitting from subject to subject, interrupted only by people coming past to say hello. The house Rob had shared with his Spanish wife sat behind us on the quayside. His grandson was rowing in the harbour.

Everyone knew everyone, and because of that, it felt like home.

Rob and his brother Peter arrived in Tapia in the summer of 1968 on a trip from Australia to the old continent. Their father, a seaman, had encouraged them to go to Europe and to explore. When they arrived in Tapia they had already travelled through France, Portugal and Galicia.

Rob explained, in his curt, no-nonsense, scattergun way:

> We came here and found this wave. There was nothing else there. Just a grass hill. Pulled up and got the boards off. Within about 10 minutes, there's a couple of kids on the hill watching. It was a great little wave. Just one after another. A right and a left. There were no other boards, so we had no problem. Surfed all the afternoon.

They packed up and left but, when they got a little further down the coast, Peter persuaded Rob to turn around and go back. It was to be a big decision that had a huge effect on the town, and the brothers.

We went back, and the surf was still good, so we stayed there. Next thing, there were about 20 people on the hill watching us. We tried to communicate but I couldn't speak Spanish. I pointed to the board and they nodded, so I took a couple of kids on to the beach and gave them a push of the board. Then they obviously went home and told someone about us. Next thing the people in charge of the office of tourism in town came down. Through an interpreter, they asked us to stay until they could get some cameras up from Madrid to film us surfing. They wanted to promote it as something in the town for people to come and do. We said, 'OK, why not?' They invited us to a big lunch and said the cameras would arrive in a week. They turned up three months later.

By that time we knew everyone in town. We'd been invited to every house in town for dinner. When we did have to leave, I left my board with the tourism office. Half the kids in this town learnt on that one board. It was a Bennett.* It's been restored now. We came back in '69, with two more boards. The same people were here. It was great. Stayed another two or three months.

My brother and I ended up in Vietnam. When that finished, I worked for a few years and came over here in '76. Met a girl, my ex-wife now. I've got a grandson and granddaughter here now. I'll be rowing with them tomorrow in the regatta.

Peter took his own life in 1991. According to his last requests his ashes were scattered at the beach in Tapia. There is a memorial to Peter, and a friend of theirs, Tony Alonso, another surfer who came to Tapia with Peter and Rob in 1969. The Pro Competition, which takes place at Easter each year, is held in Peter's memory.

Rob told us all about the Aussies who came and stayed. He introduced us to his daughter-in-law, who was walking past. We then

---

* Bennett Surfboards was a company set up by Barry Bennett in the 1950s. Tiki in North Devon had the UK licence. The logo was said to have been designed by John Severson, founder of *The Surfer* magazine. Today, Bennett makes longboards and rescue boards.

met David Nielson, whose father Colin came to Tapia with Rob in 1969, met a local girl and stayed. It was a story of a community, not of two brothers discovering a wave.

I liked Rob a lot. He was down to earth, though a little random, as if his stories of his life in Tapia and the people who had travelled through couldn't wait to get out. His influence on the town is undeniable. As a result of him and Peter 'discovering' Tapia new lives have been made. Rob has become an elder statesman. The town, in return, honours the brothers for bringing surfing to Tapia.

But, as Rob said:

> I didn't do anything special. We just happened to be the first ones to surf here, that's all. I couldn't win a surf contest if I tried.

He didn't really need to say any more. The story reminded me of Nick in Labenne, Carwyn in Le Penon and Craig in Mundaka. Surfing had brought these people to Europe and Europe had, in some way or other, cast a spell on them.

Their lives were intertwined, joined by the same invisible thread.

24

Galicia the enigma

'Today's thoughts: you worry it's going to be difficult but often all turns out well and things turn up when you need them. You just never know when you set out what there is ahead of you.'

Lizzy's diary entry: Friday 12 July 2024

Stage 23: Days 49–51 | From: Playa Penarronda | To: Teiraboa Basecamp | Distance: 170km

Galicia, the region of Spain that sits at its north western corner, was deeply symbolic for Lizzy and me. It is remote and difficult to navigate, with a coastline of around 1600km that is extremely convoluted. When our relationship was still young, we had pushed the sofa aside and spread out a map of Galicia on the floor of my flat, planning an escape, far from prying eyes. A few months later we drove on to the ferry at Plymouth and set off. As usual with these things it never quite worked out the way either of us had hoped. Despite returning later and exploring the Costa da Morte (a section of Galicia's coast) and the coast from A Coruña to Foz, there was still something unfinished about Galicia: it remained an enigma, remote, vast and difficult, almost within our grasp, but not quite.

We took the decision to take the most direct route – cross-country to Santiago de Compostela from Foz and then on to Vigo on the coast and over the Río Minho into Portugal – rather than going the long way round the coast. This was painful, but necessary. It meant, for the time being, that our business in Galicia would remain incomplete.

Of course Galicia would always be there for us. After speaking to Tony Butt about his discoveries on the Costa da Morte I felt like the tortuous and difficult coastline held even more promise, even if it would be impossible to cycle in the time we had left. There were future possibilities, if only those possibilities meant fewer crowds and wilder spaces. Plus, we would get a chance to tell Galicia's story.

But that was all for another trip.

Taking a more direct route, however, would allow us to follow the Camino to its conclusion at Santiago de Compostela. Sadly, we wouldn't be able to pick up our Compostelas (holy redemption certificates for finishing the Camino) because we had failed to get ourselves Pilgrim's Passports in Irun. To qualify for redemption we would have had to get those passports stamped twice a day for at least the last 200km of our journey, at churches, auberges or hostels. This explained why the route we had been following – the Camino Norte – had taken annoying diversions at regular intervals to take us into villages with churches.

We passed a lot of pilgrims daily. Some of them, by this time, would have been walking for weeks. Some may have been walking for months. They looked hardened, determined, stoic, as if in the head-down-crack-on part of a great ordeal, which, of course, they were. The Camino del Norte is considered one of the toughest Caminos (there are at least nine routes pilgrims can take to get to Santiago de Compostela) and it seemed to attract more men than women, although not exclusively.

With our chances of atonement blown, it didn't matter whether or not we got our stamps. We didn't need a certificate to prove we had suffered. You just had to take one look at us to know that. I had lost about 5kg while in Spain, our kit was filthy and our tyres were beginning to go bald.

On leaving the campsite at Penarronda, Ben had blessed us again. It meant a lot to me. His presence was a timely intervention and saved us, possibly quite literally:

> May the peace of the Lord Christ go with you, wherever he may send you.
>
> May he guide you through the wilderness, protect you through the storm.

May he bring you home rejoicing at the wonders he has shown you.
May he bring you home rejoicing once again into our doors.*

The first day of cycling from Penarronda to A Gaivota, a campsite on the eastern side of the Ría Foz, was the easiest day in terms of climbing we'd had in Spain yet. There was none. Even so, crossing the river at Ribadesella, the border between Galicia and Asturias, on a narrow path at the side of a motorway bridge, was difficult. With our panniers brushing either side of the path we pushed the bikes to avoid catching a handlebar on the bridge's handrail. We could have easily been flung into the river about 30 metres below us.

Despite heavy rain pinning us down a couple of times, the cycling was fantastic. We followed the coast for a lot of the way on small roads above low cliffs with views of the sandy beaches below. A few people were surfing small waves at some beaches. We arrived at Playa de las Catedrales between maelstroms and sat with a cup of coffee looking down the coast towards the stacks, arches and caves that the beach is famous for. It's so popular that you need to book a place to be able to access it.

The rain persisted all night and into the morning, which meant we had to pack up the tent wet. Everything felt damp and musty and we started the day cold and not looking forward to what was to come. We were heading away from the coast, and into the mountains.

It didn't take long for the route – heading inland towards Santiago – to start climbing. At first we followed the N-634, the old road, up a wide valley, but then the route diverted on to small, quiet roads in the hills. At Lourenzá we passed the Monasterio de San Salvador and its baroque church, the facade of which was designed by Fernando de Casas Novoa, the architect of the cathedral at Santiago de Compostela.

We left the town on the N-634a, the old N-634, and it immediately took us on to two switchbacks and two big-ish climbs to Mondoñedo, a beautiful village in the hills at the head

---

* From a Northumbria Community morning prayer.

of the valley. We pushed the bikes through winding, narrow streets, trying to find the route out through the tourists and market-day people-traffic. A quiet lane took us between the houses and out into green fields on a narrow road that snaked up into the hills and to a junction where the road we needed was blocked off with a barrier: road closed. We ploughed on regardless, careless, allowing the Garmin to lead us further into the hills, around more hairpins and along the side of a valley, climbing most of the time. Between breaks in the trees – and between the beads of sweat – I could see fields and forest below us in a narrow valley. On the opposite side, running along the ridgeline, a series of wind turbines were turning slowly, just like my tired legs.

By the time we cycled past the next sign saying the road was closed we were too heavily invested to turn back. We debated it but decided we would risk carrying on. How bad could it be? On other occasions we had been able to get through roadworks and blockages. It was a constant grind to keep going, dragging my trailer slowly up one steep section, only to find another climb ahead. At the heads of little valleys, rivers rushed under the road and then dropped away into the valley. The road had no crash barriers. The further we went, the more remote it felt and the more we had to press on: it was way too late to turn round.

I was out in front going into the hairpin around a steep gully cut into the hillside by a river when we found out why the road was closed. It had collapsed into the ravine and the tarmac that was left – a narrow, buckled piece ripped apart by the landslide – leaned heavily towards the chasm between the trees, in the process of falling down the mountain. I stopped and pushed the bike slowly over the deep cracks in the road on the tarmac that was left – a strip a couple of metres wide – looking down into the void (while also not wanting to look down into the void).

We continued to climb, passing through a few scrappy hamlets where dogs barked and cars lay abandoned in messy yards, and rejoined the N-634 at the highest point of the journey so far, 540 metres above sea level.

I was exhausted and felt like I was riding through treacle. We stopped at a spring by the side of the road to eat lunch, a tin of sardines each in half a loaf of bread.

'Welcome to PMT,' Lizzy said, out of the blue. 'This is what it feels like.'

The N-634 was long and straight, with traffic rushing by and long, slow climbs and descents, all above 450 metres. The rain came and went. When it got heavier than just a bit of a shower we sought shelter under a huge tree at the bottom of a dip, on a long straight section. We sat on the Armco barrier behind the bikes, which were just inside the white lines, and waited while it bucketed down. Cars and lorries roared by, splashing us with spray.

Two articulated lorries approached, one from each direction. They were both flying, thundering towards us. As they got closer, I could see they would pass right where we were sitting.

'Are they going to slow down?'

'Doesn't look like it.'

'Jump! Now! Go!'

We leapt over the barrier and into the foliage on the other side. As the lorries passed, I felt like I had been hit with a sonic boom. The bikes wobbled on their stands and the spray washed over us like a wave.

'They weren't going to stop, were they?'

'Not a chance.'

I pulled out my phone and started looking for somewhere to stay. I had had enough. There were no campsites within 80km. But there was a hotel in the town of Vilalba and it looked as if they had rooms. It was a Parador, too, one of Spain's national, state-owned luxury hotel chains. The Parador at Vilalba was built in a castle tower and had a secure garage where we could lock our bikes.

We checked in and went up to our room. The room had dark wood panelling, chairs like thrones, and a shuttered window overlooking the tower. It also had a bed I didn't have to blow up. That was enough for me. I had a shower, hung up my stuff to dry and sat down on the bed. I lay back to test the pillows and fell asleep almost immediately.

Cycling cross-country to Santiago instead of cycling around the coast of Galicia, it turned out, was the right thing to do, because we had been following the Camino Norte for so long. We would never have made the rendezvous with our friends in Sagres if we had, but it was still disappointing to miss out what I felt was an important part of the story.

The plans for getting home – driving our kit back to Santander and getting the ferry – allowed us a few days to relax. Lizzy and I decided that we would spend those spare days in Galicia. We would visit the surf museum in Valdoviño, a small surfy town on Galicia's coast, that is devoted to Galician surf history, and meet up with Jesús Busto, a historian and writer, who lived nearby.

So, while we might be jumping about in time a little, now – while Galicia is on our minds - is the time to talk about its surfing history and our meeting with Jesús at his beautiful home in Doniños, a small beach town about 8km west of Ferrol on Galicia's north-west facing coast. Doniños has great surf and has been a focus for Galicia's surfing scene since the 1970s. We got there a couple of days after leaving Sagres, two days before our ferry home.

We squeezed the van between the narrow gateposts and parked in the lush, wild garden. Waiting for us were Jesús, a slim and athletic man of about 55, and his elf-like wife Helena, both surfers. Their home, a modest wooden chalet overlooking the beach, was every bit as perfect as you might imagine a Spanish surf shack could have been. We sat in the conservatory and talked about surf history and Galicia.

Jesús pulled out a book and flicked through the pages until he found a picture of Rob Culley leaning out of the window of a white Bedford van with British plates, from 1968, before they discovered Tapia de Casariego, heading down a hill towards Pantín, a beach that's a few kilometres to the north of Doniños.

The Pantín Classic, a professional surf competition, has been running at Pantín Beach since 1988, thanks to the Ocean Surf Club (Galicia's first surf club), headed up by its president, Vicente Irisarri. The competition has grown from a staple on the European circuit to a stop-off on the World Surf League (WSL) Qualifying Series. Over the years it has attracted some of the biggest names in surfing including Joel Parkinson (world champion in 2012) and Coco Ho (pro surfer and star of the surfing film *Blue Crush*.Vicente Irisarri retired from the Ocean Surf Club in 2005, passing the job of co-ordinator to Jesús in 2006 and 2007. Since 2008, after the club handed over the competition to Club Praia de Pantín, Jesús has devoted his spare time to surf history and has researched Galician surfing extensively. His knowledge is vast.

In its early years the roster of British surfers competing in Pantín reads like the story of 1990s British surfing. Names like Grishka Roberts, Russell Winter, Spencer Hargreaves, Gabe Davies and, inevitably, the smiling Welsh workhorse, Carwyn Williams, made regular appearances between 1990 and 1998.

Mike Raven was one of them. He placed second in the second Pantín Classic in 1989. I knew Mike because he grew up in Bude. Today, he lives in Portugal – another one who stayed. The first time I met him was in early 1989 while surfing in Tenerife. He was doing a photo shoot for Alder Sportswear with photographer Peter Cade. At the time he would have been 16 or 17 but was already European champion, having competed all over Europe.

Mike had explained to me on a Zoom call before we left for France:

> I think the reason the Brits were so prevalent at the time in Europe was that we had a decent contest scene at home. We were used to competing and travelling. Bob Westlake, who set up Alder Sportswear, sponsored the Surf Scene 1000 surf contests in the UK, which was a proper circuit and gave us competition experience. It spread to Europe and morphed into the EPSA [European Surfing Federation]. At the beginning we were more used to competing so we did well more often.

By the late 1980s and 1990s British surfers had found Galicia, and Pantín. But in the early days, as Jesús explained, surfers bypassed Galicia in favour of going to Portugal, Morocco and the Canaries. Between 1969 and 1975 just a handful of foreign surfers travelled to Galicia. It was just too big and difficult to manage, with bad roads, big distances, no information and surfing conditions that change all the time.

As a result, Galicia didn't have the influences that Australian and British surfers had brought in other areas in Europe. Jesús went on:

Sometimes it is difficult for us too. All the waves break over sandbanks, and the sandbanks change a lot. We have a wave here that is called 'the Ghost'. In the morning it could be good but, in the afternoon, nothing. How is this possible? It is the same tide, the same size wave, the same wind, the same direction. But it changes a lot.

Other factors, aside from the geography, that affected surfing in Galicia were social and economic. Galicia had always been poor compared with the rest of Spain. People who wanted to surf in the 1960s and 1970s couldn't simply drive to France and buy boards from Barland like others had done. They had to start from scratch, making their own foam and formers. Even then they often didn't have transport.

Early inspiration in Galicia came from Félix Cueto, the very same surfer who built boards in Salinas in 1963 based on the cover of *Surfin' U.S.A.* He moved to A Coruña in 1967 to study, so kick-starting surfing in that area. Jesús continued:

> They took maybe five years to discover Doniños. And you can see Doniños from A Coruña. But for them to go 50km to the north was an adventure. Also, not many people had cars! It was very difficult.
>
> In the '60s and the '70s, Galicia outside the cities was very, very poor. They didn't have much education. It was a poor place inside of Spain. Still is. So, I think that things happen here in other ways.

By that Jesús meant that DIY culture existed in Galicia. Francisco 'Rufo' Tizón was the trailblazer in this regard. After a lot of experimentation (and failure) Rufo dissected and copied an imported board. He then found out about Barland in Bayonne and went to buy foam blanks, but couldn't afford them. The only thing to do was to make his own, building concrete moulds to create the blanks. Rufo opened Galicia's first surfboard business in 1972 but not before an outside influence – a South African called Darryl (somewhere along the way his surname has been lost) – helped. Darryl had been sailing from the UK and had stopped in A Coruña for repairs. He met up with Rufo and the two became friends, with Darryl passing on his knowledge of surfboard making.

Rufo, and others, also had to swim against the stream because the sea was viewed very differently in Galicia to other parts of Spain or Europe, as Jesús explained:

> The sea has a very strong significance in our culture. We are a seafaring community. But normally the sea in Galicia means death, work, losing your family. So, the pioneer surfers had problems with this kind of thinking. People didn't understand that someone could go to the sea for pleasure. We don't have the same culture as the UK, where you go to the sea for your health. Most people thought the sea was dangerous.
>
> The pioneers gave permission to surfers of my generation. Their gift was to show that there are other ways to have a relationship with the sea. You can enjoy it.

Socially, surfing brought new ideas to Galicia too. One of Jesús's books is called *Otro Mar*, meaning 'another sea', implying that surfing has given Galicians new ways to look at the sea. He explained to me:

> Maybe the main change in Galicia is the way people thought about surfing. Surfing showed us that there are other ways to live. With Franco, for most people, there was only one way. They told you how you had to do things. How you had to think. But when you have surfing, music and a different culture, you say no. You can be yourself.
>
> Thirty years ago people said surfing is for those who don't want to work, they smoke marijuana ... And now, maybe, surfing is a normal thing.

As I sat listening to Jesús I felt that I had happened upon the soul of surfing, or at least a part of its soul: the part of it that respects the past and wants a better future. Here in Galicia, professional surfing contests sat side by side with surfers looking for nothing more than waves to ride. There was room for people like Tony Butt too, explorers on the edge of possibility, pushing big wave exploration without the circus that can go with it.

I could understand why Jesús wanted people to know about the history of surfing. It's important for us to understand where our sport has come from. In Galicia, surfing's roots were humble. They had done it their own way, despite poverty, social pressure and an ingrained fear of the sea.

> Every day is different. It is very different between winter and summer. In winter in Galicia, it's possible to be in the water and to be alone with your thinking. Maybe you feel more connection with the sea. I don't like to be with a lot of people around me speaking. Because I want to be in the sea. My mind goes to other places. And sometimes there is a lot of tension in the water and I don't like it.
>
> It's like the case of Miki Dora. He was a horrible person. I don't want people like Miki Dora as my friends, you know. But he was a very good surfer. So, other people say, 'Wow, Miki.' I don't like this about surfing: if you are a good surfer, you can do things that are not good. In other communities this wouldn't be the case. I don't understand this kind of thing in surfing. If you are a good surfer, you can do whatever you want. That's not good.

As I ate my way through the breakfast menu at the Parador, I thought of where our next surf might be. Galicia's coast is convoluted, with the Rías Baixas and the Rías Altas (lower and upper rivers) creating a series of peninsulas and deep river valleys. Many of the surfing beaches, like Doniños, are on the Atlantic-facing coasts, at the end of the peninsulas. Our route would take us across the region and across the Rías Baixas, where they were navigable by bike, a day's cycle from the nearest surf. So, more than likely, I thought, we wouldn't see any surf until we had passed Vigo, almost 200km to the south. That was disappointing, but necessary.

I sampled just about everything from the buffet in anticipation of another long day in Galicia. Breakfast was so big, in fact, that we managed 50km before stopping for lunch. Most of that was on the N-634, then, after an old stone bridge looked like it was going to lead us to another tricky offroad section, we forged a path that took us into Guitiriz and then into beautiful countryside. We passed meadows and chestnut groves, followed rivers into boggy flatlands with huge lumps of granite – a bit like weathered tors – in the fields. The road began to rise gently then took a sudden turn upwards with a couple of sharp hairpins, topping out at 650 metres above sea level, another record for the trip, at a wind farm. We stopped and took in the views of the mountains behind us. The descent, a gentle roll through forests and meadows, led us into some small hamlets past smallholdings on undulating roads with the occasional granite outcrops, with some steep drops and sharp climbs. There seemed to be flowers everywhere, including *Verbascum, Echium*, umbellifers, grasses, ferns, daisies, buttercups and bird's-foot trefoil (arse-split ring-pain). In the woods, eucalyptus, firs, chestnut and alder. We hoped, perhaps, that we had left the rain behind too.

By the time we reached Teiraboa Basecamp, a campsite 40km from Santiago, we had covered another 72km and climbed another 1000 metres. We also realised, while cooking our dinner, that, bar the odd stay in a hotel, we had been outside all day every day and it felt wonderful.

I was finding the hills easier too, as I had learnt how to settle in to a climb: keep up the revs, don't let lactic acid build up, just keep turning. For someone who claimed he didn't have the mental fortitude to climb, I was surprising myself. Galicia was giving me something that had eluded me for so long.

And tomorrow we would ride into Santiago de Compostela.

Until then we went through the same old routine that had been disrupted by the real bed at Vilalba: eat, erect the tent, blow up the mattresses, spread out the sleeping bags. Shower. Sleep.

25

Santiago de Compostela

'We don't feel entitled to anything, and appreciate all the tiny luxuries of life as a cycle tourer: good food, a warm sleeping bag, a comfy bed and shelter. A warm coat. A beer.'

DIARY ENTRY: MONDAY 15 JULY 2024

Stage 24: Days 52–53 | From: Teiraboa Basecamp | To: Santiago de Compostela | Distance: 44km

Another awful night's sleep, with dogs barking, children screaming late into the night and people wheeling suitcases past our tent at first light (what was all that about?). Being inside a tent was no insulation from the outside world. We might not have been able to see anything but we could hear absolutely everything. And wheelie suitcases, when trundled around at first light, on a quiet campsite, were absolutely deafening.

Breakfast, sitting on stone benches, wearing everything in a cold north wind, didn't help.

Soon after setting off for Santiago, the temperature began to rise. Overexcited pilgrims were everywhere when we got to Arzúa, a small town near the campsite where the Camino del Norte converged with the Camino Frances. It brought pilgrims together for the final, exuberant 30km of their walk and the atmosphere was excited and full of anticipation. Large groups of young people cheered us as we went past. Lone walkers trudged along. Some pilgrims waved flags, while others sang. Two teenage boys carried their friend's pack, as well as their own, slung across a wooden pole, while their friend limped alongside, smiling. A piper walked with one group, marking their progress with music.

There were lots of bikers too, mostly overtaking us, mostly looking terribly professional in sexy Lycra and flapping gilets. One, on a road bike and in full kit, wished me a '*Buen camino*' and handed me something. 'For good energy,' he said. It was a home-made energy bar.

It was all going so well.

The walkers headed off on a path that was impossible for us, which sent us on a route that took us to a huge road junction and into a maze of railway lines, flyovers and motorways, on a gravel track that was too deeply rutted and rocky to ride. It ended in a narrow tunnel going under a motorway in land that had been marginalised by development. We ate our lunch by the side of a disused railway, in the shade of a flyover, sitting in the dirt. Another new low.

Lizzy wasn't feeling well – a result of getting cold the day before and generally being run down – so I steered her as gently as I could towards the city's campsite, a busy, shady site on terraces cut into a steep hillside overlooking the city, to rest and recoup before cycling the final few kilometres to the end of the Camino at Santiago's cathedral square. There was no point in pushing at this stage. Our glorious entrance into Compostela, the field of the star, the place where Saint James's remains were re-found in the 8th century by a hermit shepherd, would have to wait.

We checked in and set up the tent in a damp and rather depressing corner reserved for tented campers. Lizzy complained about aching and feeling shit. She needed food, rest and some love.

We had made a rough plan to catch up with Ben and the boys but a brief text told us they wanted to move on to find more surf, so it was a pleasant surprise to see them as they were checking out. As usual their appearance was timely. Ben had bought me some new cycling gloves, as he'd noticed mine were falling apart. He also had another blessed gift for us: knowledge.

'What are you doing this afternoon?' he asked me.

'Not sure. But not going into the city,' I replied.

'Then go to the mall. It's five minutes away. All-you-can-eat sushi. And a great barber.'

With that he took his hat off to reveal his huge freckled head, de-fluffed.

I looked at Lizzy.

'Great plan.'

'Sushi sounds wonderful,' she replied, wiping her nose.

Getting a decent haircut in Spain is easy if you have a bald head. However, as I found out, getting a good – or even passable – haircut in Spain when you have a full head of hair and lack any kind of Spanish barbering vocabulary, is near impossible. I sat in the chair and realised I didn't know what I needed to ask for. I pointed at the sides and back of my head and said *'numero uno'*. I then stroked my chin and said, *'y la barba'*. I sat back and let the barber do his work, whatever that would turn out to be.

It might not seem special to get a haircut in a gigantic modern shopping mall but it felt like it to me. Sitting still, with nothing to think about, while the busy barbershop buzzed, clipped and snipped around me was a delight. I closed my eyes, leaned back and let the barber shave my neck, snip my eyebrows (they were getting a bit whizzy) and wet-shave my face. I listened to the music on the radio and the chatter of the barbers and could have been in a back street somewhere, enjoying one of life's finer pleasures.

I opened my eyes and looked at what the barber had done. Without the words to utter anything different, I simply said, *'Si, esta bien.'* I had a number one all around the back and sides and a bit of fluff on the top, with side bits that stuck out either side of my temples. It would look fine under a cycle helmet.

Afterwards we filled up on all-you-can-eat-sushi, which was a welcome change after weeks of cooking rice and vegetables (!), and then returned to the campsite where we fell asleep in the sun on the grass around the tiny pool. Lizzy was feeling worse with every passing hour, so with the aim of allowing her a little luxury to help her to feel better, I booked the Parador in Santiago for the following night.

The Praza do Obradoiro, the meeting point in Santiago for all pilgrims, was buzzing when we pushed the bikes into its north-eastern corner in the morning. It was huge, and full of excited,

SANTIAGO DE COMPOSTELA

exhausted people. On the eastern side, the Cathedral of Santiago provided a focal point for those streaming into the square. The two bell towers, baroque masterpieces of fussy, flouncy sculpture, ornate ironwork and delicate pillars, with a sculpture of Saint James dressed as a pilgrim atop, looked down on the plaza. Opposite, with a colonnade of hefty square pillars, sat the Palace of Rajoy, the HQ of local government in Galicia. On the southern boundary the College of San Jerónimo, now the seat of the rectorate of the University of Santiago, watched studiously over the square. On the northern side lay our bed for the night, somewhere behind the decorated facade and big glass doors of the Hostal de los Reyes Católicos, a hostel and hospital for pilgrims that was built by Queen Isabella I of Castile after her own pilgrimage in 1486. It was finished in the early 1500s and continued to be used as a hospital until 1953, when it became a hotel. Today, it is the largest hotel in the Spanish Parador network and has been described as the most beautiful in Europe.

My eyes had watered with the cost when I booked it but I figured it would be a fitting way to mark finishing two-thirds of our journey. Lizzy needed rest. And besides, fuck it, we had cycled over 800km in the last three weeks, towing stupid, overweight trailers and surfboards and being rained on most days. Of course it was worth it.

Before we checked in to what would be our most luxurious and lavish hotel stay ever, we stood in the square and took it all in.

Full of relief and joy, I wasn't tired, because I had only cycled a few kilometres to get here from the campsite, but I still felt the miles in my calves. Lizzy was full of cold and snot, and smiled through the sneezes. I was determined to enjoy the moment: a collective, exuberant success, whatever the journey, on reaching the end.

Pilgrims and tourists of all ages, colours and nationalities thronged into the square from every corner, as they do each day. Some of them were crying while others stared up at the cathedral, in awe of this most sacred of places. Pilgrims sat, their backs against the pillars of the Palace of Rajoy, packs laid out in front of them. Large groups sang together while waving huge flags. People chattered and hugged, smiled and cried. A man played the bagpipes in one corner while a tourist train weaved between the crowds, people aboard snapping away at the pilgrims, at us and at the square. Cyclists pushed their bikes through the crowds.

The atmosphere was electric. People were emotional and exhausted, having reached the end of their walking or cycling journeys, some of which had started in France, southern Spain or Portugal, or even from farther away, like us. Some would go on to Cape Finisterre, to the Atlantic, but for many this was the end of weeks and months of walking or pedalling, adding a certain 'what next?' to the atmosphere.

People of all nations were there, but there was no one like us. Our bikes, trailers and surfboards stood out and attracted attention and we had our picture taken by tourists and pilgrims, smiling, arms in the air, celebrating. A Japanese family had their picture taken with us and then took some with our phones for us. People asked us where we had come from and joked that we wouldn't need the surfboards in Santiago.

Some commented, 'They have surfboards. Why?'

I explained, 'We have surfed and cycled our way here from England.'

'Ohhh. Wow!'

A middle-aged English woman in cycling gear said, 'That looks fun. Not,' as she walked past us, looking down at our bikes.

I let it drip off me like a blob of unwanted rain. Nothing could stop me from enjoying my accomplishment and the happiness it brought. I had cycled up some bastard hills and a few absolute twats of mountains to get here. I had pedalled my heart out (and only resorted to Red Power on a couple of stupidly steep roads with teeth-shattering cobbles). She had no idea.

It had been fun, the greatest adventure. I hadn't even cried, and it wasn't over yet.

We wheeled the bikes towards Spain's most beautiful five-star hotel, as you do, and checked in. What frauds we were! Then again, since this was originally a hospital for the benefit of pilgrims – we had the excuse that Lizzy was ill – we had every right to haul our snotty, smelly, damp, muddy, sweaty, filthy selves through the huge arched glass doors of this incredible, historic building.

The concierge helped us with our panniers and waited for us while we parked the bikes and locked them up among the Porsches and Range Rovers in the underground garage. Our room, one of the cheaper ones admittedly, was at the back of the hotel, reached by crossing two cloistered quadrants and then walking down a

SANTIAGO DE COMPOSTELA

creaky wood-panelled corridor decorated with religious paintings in crimson and gold leaf.

We slept for a few hours then went out to explore Santiago's narrow back streets and tourist honeypots. We bought stickers for the trailers and commemorative scallop shell bracelets to mark the occasion of completing the Way of Saint James. As usual we bickered about what and where to eat but settled on an enormous paella and a few beers in a restaurant that was full of tourists just off the Praza do Obradoiro.

That night we sat in bed and watched Spain beat England in the final of the European Cup. It wasn't the only thing Spain was winning at. They had won at paella, architecture, hotels, atmosphere, mountains, rain and cycling adventures, although France had given them a good run for their money. We absolutely loved it. As the Spanish side lifted the cup in a boisterous, noisy, ticker-tape climax, Lizzy and I celebrated getting this far with a few of our own in the huge, creaky wooden bed.

26

The last days in Spain

'Feel shit. Knackered. Just about managed 50km today to bring us within a snuffle of Portugal at Redondela. Great riding conditions but I've picked up Lizzy's cold and it's whacked me.'

INSTAGRAM POST: TUESDAY 16 JULY 2024

Stage 25: Days 54–56 | From: Santiago de Compostela | To: A Guarda | Distance: 185km

Normal service – and by that I mean being grubby, tired cyclists – resumed in the morning. We toyed with the idea of staying another night at the hospital for weary international surf-bike tourists and sick (and rich) pilgrims but at €280 a night I baulked, instead scoffing a couple of courses of eggs and bacon and staying as late as we could before being thrown out. My only regret was not stuffing my pockets with bread rolls at breakfast.

The concierge opened the big glass doors for us when we left and walked out into the plaza and a valet followed us down to the garage to pack up the bikes, probably to make sure we didn't scratch any of the expensive cars they were looking after for other, wealthier pilgrims who had driven to Santiago.* Stepping out into the throng of new arrivals made me feel a fraud, like the TV presenter who pretends to sleep in the jungle for the camera but goes off to the

---

* There are no Compostelas for people who drive to Santiago.

nearest hotel when it's switched off. Had the hard miles we had put in been invalidated by five-star luxury?

I saw other guests leaving, with piles of suitcases they couldn't manage, and marvelled at how they travelled. Did their money simply buy them help? Is that what it means to have the cash for luxury travel? To not have to carry your own bag, drive your own car, open doors for yourself, blow up your own bed or cook your own food. It seemed ridiculous to me. All the fun was in the struggle. Without it I would be someone else.

Our way out of the city started on big roads then took us on to smaller roads and finally on to paths and gravel tracks following the Portuguese Camino (Camino Português) towards Porto and Lisbon. Where before we had followed the yellow arrows towards Santiago, now we followed blue arrows pointing away from Santiago. Many of them were hand-painted on the back of road signs or on walls as afterthoughts: the going home arrows.

Cycling away from Santiago meant we could, for the first time, see the faces of the pilgrims walking towards us. Some were lost in contemplation while others smiled and said hello. Some were in pain, others wrapped in clear plastic capes, easily spotted in hi-vis jackets or living the dream in Camino T-shirts. They seemed a jollier bunch, in general, than those on the Camino del Norte. Among them were old and young. There were more women too, and more young women especially. Maybe the Camino Português was less of a macho get-it-done-slog than the Norte and so attracted a crowd with nothing to prove.

The path took us through farms and small settlements. In places it became rough or even cobbled, passing springs, granite *hórreos* and covered wash houses or weaving between houses on narrow concrete paths. We passed chicken coops, barking dogs, vines growing on wire strung between granite beams, and fields of maize. In the verges I saw a riot of flowers: daisies, fennel, angelica and evening primrose. In wooded sections, as we rode on sun-dappled lanes, I saw groves of eucalyptus, pine, chestnut and alder. Most of the riding felt like it was downhill too, which made it seem easy. Galicia was being beautiful for us.

We camped at a site on the river at Carril and felt like we were back where we belonged.

Lizzy was feeling better after a night in the hotel but I was going down fast. I'm not saying that I suffered more than she did but it came in the night and it hit me like an incontinent, snuffly, cough-train. I felt awful. My nose was streaming and I was hot and cold, unable to settle in my sleeping bag and constantly needing to pee. My teeth hurt too.

Unfortunately, the campsite, unlike others we had been on, was deadly quiet after 10 p.m. The only noise piercing the silence was the sound of zips, and not in a good way, because going to the loo involved a lot of zips. Normally the ripping of a zip is a sound I quite like but not on this peaceful campsite or with this regularity. Each time I needed a pee – again – I had to unzip my sleeping bag, pull on some shorts and zip them up, unzip the inner tent, unzip the flysheet and then zip up the inner tent. I couldn't do it quietly, no matter how hard I tried. It was like pulling off a plaster.

Returning from the toilet – it was only a short walk over crunchy gravel – meant doing the same in reverse: a total of 10 zipping sounds shattering the delicate peace of the night like a sonic pickaxe. If we both went, it would be 20 zips because our tent had two entrances. I felt sorry for the other campers but what can you do when you are ill, middle-aged and need to pee and blow your nose all night? I would have been worried about me if I was a camper on that site, kept awake by the constant comings and goings of the ailing English cyclists.

The Camino Portugués, once we had reached it again in the morning, took us on some lovely back roads and on ancient byways with walls lined with mossy boulders. We forded a river nervously, watched by pilgrims taking the dry-footed way over a too-narrow clapper bridge. Occasionally the route would be marked with mini shrines, where pilgrims had left gifts and prayers to Saint James. The offerings consisted of scallop shells, ribbons, messages written on stones and even faded photographs of people, children and families. On one, a cross on a back road, we found a pair of worn-out boots.

Once again, though, as we entered the corridor taking traffic and trains south to Pontevedra and Vigo, the pastoral spell of backwater Galicia was broken by modernity, ploughing its way through the countryside, cutting the old roads off and sending us down paths beneath viaducts and beside railways. Dwarfed and marginalised

THE LAST DAYS IN SPAIN

by infrastructure, we pushed our way down steep, rocky pathways, across dry river beds and over rutted paths, long-forgotten byways bypassed by concrete. We were inland, crossing the neck of the peninsula that separates the Río Pontevedra from the Río Vigo. We crossed the Río Vigo on the Ponte Medieval de Pontesampaio, a narrow medieval stone bridge with a cobbled carriageway strung between two tiny villages with steep, winding streets. It was a picture postcard kind of affair and demanded a couple of selfies and a group shot.

By the time we arrived at Camping Cesantes in Redondela we had completed another 50km, climbed 800 metres and were just about ready for food and rest. Under normal circumstances we would have passed the campsite and driven on, based on how it looked, but I was so knackered, I had to stop. The entrance to the site, down a narrow lane lined with breezeblock walls topped with chicken wire, suggested it might be yet another high-density camping experience where we would have to pitch up between sad caravans. When we were met by a huge, sweaty, bald-headed man in a filthy vest pushing a wheelbarrow, he seemed to confirm it.

However, as we were learning, appearances in Spain could be deceptive. The man welcomed us with a toothy grin and showed us to the office, where we were greeted by two women with big smiles, who seemed to be surprised to see us but welcomed us warmly anyway. They checked us in, charged us almost nothing and then showed us to a part of the site devoted to tents. Unlike in other campsites, where tents seemed to be an afterthought, the area was in a small orchard with lush grass, views of the sea and lovely dappled shade. A path from the orchard led us down to the beach, a huge arc of sand with a long sandspit that stuck out into the estuary. Kite surfers whipped across the water between the beach and a couple of offshore islands. In the distance, across the bay, the twin towers of the Puente de Rande, once the second longest cable stay bridge in the world, stood tall, silhouetted by the setting sun.

I wouldn't have chosen to stay at this campsite, or even visited this beach, but I was glad we had. Hidden in plain sight away from the tourist trail, the area was frequented by locals and Spanish, with few tourists, making it feel more genuine. The site was basic but perfect and all we needed.

THE WAY OF THE WAVES

Thomas, a slim, bearded German man in his 70s, had also found the site. He pitched up next to us when we were cooking. As he was fastidiously putting up his tent, he told us how he had been to buy it at Decathlon because his old tent – that he had spent 350 nights in – had started to leak. He took a while to work out how to put up this new, unfamiliar shelter. When it was up, I remarked that it looked like a good tent.

'It's new,' Thomas said. 'I bought it today at Decathlon. The other one wasn't waterproof any more . . .'

Thomas then told us the whole story again. He told it to us again in the morning, too, which made me worry about him. Was he suffering from dementia?

Thomas told us that he cycled alone, for long periods, doing long distances, mostly on main roads, and had done for some time. I wondered if cycling enabled him to live in the moment and have a simple, uncomplicated life. When you cycle there is no past, and to some extent, no future, so there is nothing to remember if remembering is a problem. When you are on a bike there is nothing but being on the bike. You travel a line where memory means nothing.

We hung up our stuff to dry and then, when we had a chance to see it all laid out, bickered about how much stuff we had. I felt we could have travelled lighter. Lizzy disagreed. We packed up in silence, but, before we left, we hugged, as we always did. Whatever issues we might have navigating our life together and each other's special powers, getting back on the bikes always seemed to erase the memory of anger and hurt. It always faded with the steady turning of the pedals. That was the joy of being on two wheels. No past and no future. Just the road.

We took a few back roads through the village at Cesantes and then found ourselves on a busy road, trying to work out how to get to the Camino, which was on the other side. Cars were streaming past us and joining from a junction, making it difficult and dangerous to do a U-turn. I could see a side road on the opposite side, a little further up. The side road would, I hoped, lead us back to the path. I shouted to Lizzy to follow me, stuck out my arm and – fuck it – pulled out into the middle of the road. The traffic behind had no choice but to brake hard behind me, coming to a grinding halt. I stopped, waiting for a gap in the traffic, still holding up the cars behind. When I got the chance, I raced across the road with Lizzy trailing me. Cars hooted and honked as we went.

The side road took us up, very steeply, from sea level to 250 metres in a couple of kilometres. Unashamed, I dropped down the gears to GG1 and slipped into Turbo, one of the few times I had used both. A couple of hairpins took us to the top, where a woman was selling Camino-based trinkets from a makeshift stall at the side of the road. We stopped to browse and look at the view. We could see the campsite, the Ponte de Rande, the cars on the road below us and, in the hazy distance, the peninsula we had crossed yesterday. How far we had come! It seemed unlikely, impossible even, to think that I had cycled all that way, from beyond the horizon.

The path, now flat, disappeared around the wooded mountain. We followed it through the trees, admiring the views when they appeared between the branches, passing pilgrims, some of whom were open-mouthed that we should be on this steep hillside with bikes and surfboards.

The descent was equally hairy, with a few tricky switchbacks forcing us to push the bikes. We descended into the suburbs of Vigo and on to a greenway, a cycle path following the track bed of an old railway. The overhead power lines had been retained and they now carried lighting, and stations, renovated into public spaces, were painted with murals. The smooth path brought us into the centre of Vigo, alongside the river, past its pleasure port and through its huge dockyards. I wished cycling at home could be safe and easy like this. Town planners from the UK need to take their holidays in places like Vigo, Nantes and La Rochelle.

We cycled out of the city and around the coast through coastal resorts and beaches until we reached the tourist town of Baiona and the campsite that would be our home for the last night in Spain. We had completed another 50km but, despite the hill in the middle, had only climbed around 500 metres.

Camping Playa Baiona sits on a finger of sand at the head of the Río Minor. On its west side is the Playa Ladeira, a wide, sandy beach that is open to the Atlantic. On the east side the site overlooks the Marisma da Ramallosa, a wetland nature reserve that fills and empties with the tide. The river runs in deep muddy channels until the area is flooded by the incoming tide. As the tide ebbs, the water rushes out through a narrow channel at the tip of the sandspit.

We pitched up and walked to the end of the point, swimming out into the clear water of the river and letting the outgoing tide pull us out into the bay. The sun was hot and it was a perfect way to allow the late afternoon to slip by. We decided to eat in the campsite's restaurant that evening – it overlooked the beach – so we had a lot of time to kill before the kitchen would open.

Even though we fell asleep on the beach, had long showers and dawdled as much as we could, our hunger drove us to the restaurant before the kitchen opened. We nursed beers as the sun dropped over the ocean and the people on the beach slowly packed up and returned to their pitches.

For us, getting into bed at 11 p.m. was a late night.

At 12 p.m. the music started. It woke me with a start, because it sounded like Christina Aguilera had crawled into the tent with us and was knocking out some of her shittest Europop with a mariachi band. They were competing with a DJ to make the most annoying noises.

'Oh God, no. Please no.'

'What the fuck is that?' Lizzy said as she woke up too.

Once we had worked out that the music wasn't coming from the tent next door, or even from the campsite, I got dressed and went to have a look. On the seaward side of the site I could see that, across the water, on the other side of the bay, at least 3km away, the Fortaleza de Monterreal, a huge fortress, was lit up with pulsating lights. Beams from spotlights penetrated the night sky, searching, no doubt, for the last sleepers. The music boomed like a barrage.

With nothing to do, I took my sorry arse back to bed and tried and failed to get to sleep. The music finally stopped at 2.30 a.m.

I woke to the sound of firecrackers at 8.

'Why is Spain such a noisy country?' I asked no one in particular.

'It's fiesta season,' Lizzy offered.

'Yeah, but why does it have to be so fucking loud?'

'That's how they do it.'

'Do you think it will be like this in Portugal?'

'Don't know.'

'Are you ready for it?'

THE LAST DAYS IN SPAIN

'Yeah, I suppose so.' She didn't sound sure.

Spain had a final gift for us, as if she was sorry she had kept us up all night and wanted to make amends. Leading away from the campsite, around the wide bay, past the fortress, between the road and the sea, we found the most perfect cycle path, a fast-running, smooth-surfaced olive branch painted in brilliant gold. A yellow brick road guiding us towards the frontier with Portugal and on to the final leg of our journey.

The path ran just a few metres above the water, a gilded strip between the scrubby, granite boulder-strewn hills and the glittering sea. Cycling along, with no lumps or bumps to unseat me, no traffic to kill me and no dogs to bark at me, I forgave them all. The drivers, dogs, DJs and crack-of-dawn ordnance had kept me on my toes, on the edge of my saddle, awake into the small hours and up too early. But so what? Does it really matter if tea isn't important to Spanish culture? Not one bit. That was my problem, not theirs.

As the north wind picked up and pushed me gently along, I was ready to come around. Spain, I thought, did cycling well. There had been difficult, busy roads and frightening moments, but we had survived. The love I held for my bike had never waned. My love and respect for Lizzy grew each time we navigated some kind of tricky middle ground, unseated a strop or clipped a spinner into the boundary.* There was no *voiture-balai* bearing down on us.†

The tough bits hadn't been because of Spain or Spanish culture. It wasn't Spain's fault that I had an issue with hills or restaurants. It wasn't their fault that we found their exuberance, excitement and noise a bit much sometimes. We were the stumbling blocks: a couple of stuffy English cyclists, living in a bubble, held back by habits yet desperate to escape them.

Nevertheless, we had become, partly at least, acclimatised. We killed time until dinner. I had climbed some 15,000 metres in the last few weeks (without once throwing my bike down in a

---

* Fuck me. I don't watch or understand cricket and here I am, in a section about being in a foreign country, using a cricket metaphor. Classic. Speaks volumes. I didn't even go to public school.
† Have I saved myself with this reference to the broom wagon? Doubtful, but worth a try.

hissy fit). We had muddled through with shit Spanish. We had found *amigos*.

And soon we would have to learn how to do it all again.

In the meantime, though, until we reached the border at the Río Minho and had navigated the uncertainties of the crossing, we had the Golden Camino. It took us, smoothly and quietly, through forgotten villages, to empty beaches and headlands, never too far from the sea and always under the mountains. What could be better? The sun shone, the boulders sparkled like glitter and the sea twinkled azure, reflecting the deepest blue sky.

Adiós y gracias, España.

All is forgiven. It was us, not you.

Section 3
PORTUGAL

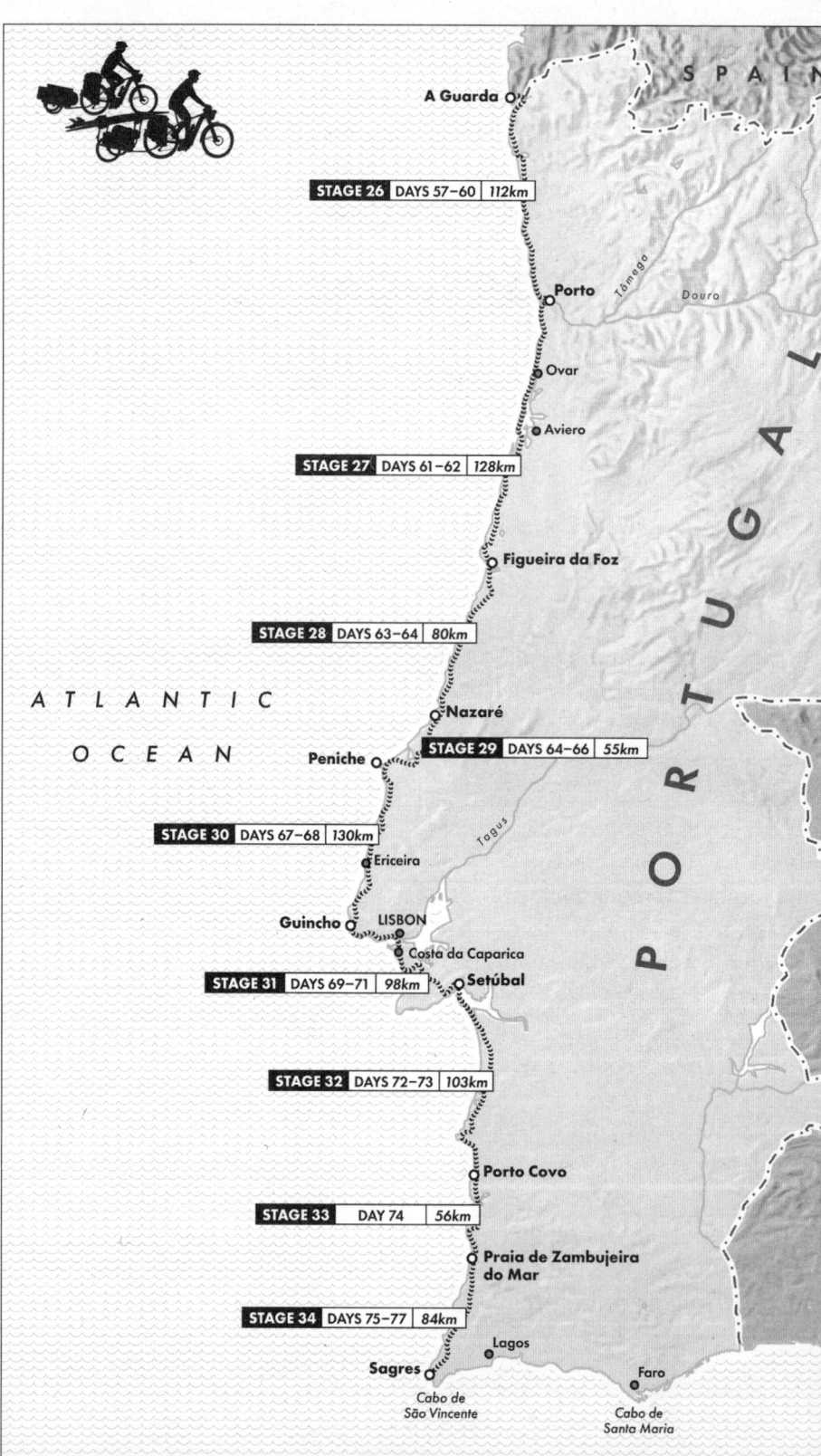

27
A sanctuary in Âncora

'Sagres – our end point – is now just 750km away. Between us and there are a lot of great places to pass through . . . Lisbon, Porto, Peniche, Ericeira, Nazaré . . . Magical adventures.'
INSTAGRAM POST: FRIDAY 19 JULY 2024

Stage 26: Days 57–60 | From: A Guarda | To: Porto | Distance: 112km

There was no question we would have to make the crossing from A Pasaxe, the port just to the south of A Guarda, across the Minho River to Caminha, the first town on the Portuguese side of the border with Spain. If the ferry operator refused to take us then we would have to backtrack 15km upstream to the nearest bridge at Vila Nova de Cerveira and then cycle another 15km downstream on the Portuguese side. That would be an afternoon's ride. I really didn't fancy it.

We booked a transfer with the 'official' operator. I was optimistic the ferryman would accommodate us, however hard it might be. Until then not one had refused us passage, even if getting the bikes on had been difficult. This crossing, however, was the most uncertain.

A Guarda was the last town we passed through in Spain before the crossing. It sat on the coast a few kilometres from the mouth of the Minho, the border between Spain and Portugal. We cycled in on the Golden Camino and immediately felt like we had reached the end of the world. There were a few people eating lunch at a beachside restaurant and a few people on the beaches, but when we cycled through the town's centre, it was deserted.

The ferry 'port', which consisted of a pontoon sticking out into the river and an extensive, disused quayside, was quiet, apart from a few speedboats buzzing across the river and a tout trying to get our business. The boats, carrying pilgrims with packs, moored up on the quayside, not on the pontoon.

I received a text from the ferry operator: *'Warning! Taxi-mar (Bar do Ferry) and other pirate boats are unsafe competitors because they do not have an authorized port in Spain, and they will also lie to you by saying we are not operational.'*

Pirates on the river! Wow. That sounded exciting. People making illicit border crossings! We really were in the borderlands, at the ends of the earth. As always there was an air of apprehension and expectation.

Our boat came, on time, and pulled up to the pontoon. It looked much like the other boats, was the same size, had the same size engine, and looked to be in the same condition. The difference was that we could embark on the pontoon, which meant wheeling the bikes down a ramp, although it didn't make it easy. The ramp was wide enough for the bikes themselves but it had a 90-degree turn, making it impossible to get the trailers down unless we disconnected them, removed the panniers and manhandled it all on to the pontoon.

The skipper, Captain Forense, was cool about it all, even though we weren't, despite admitting he had never carried surfboards and trailers before. Everything had to be lifted into the boat separately, with the bikes and trailers taking up most of the space. He still managed to squeeze in a couple of German cyclists and their bikes too. It took 10 minutes to load everything but felt like no time at all. Lizzy, nervous about the crossing, leaving Spain and trusting her bike and kit to Forense, fussed and fretted, trying to keep control in an unfamiliar situation. It was making her so stressed that we were halfway across the river before she had manged to tie up her lifejacket properly. At the other side it took longer to unload the bikes and luggage than it did to make the crossing.

With trailers hitched up again – and back to normal – we posed for photos with Forense and then set off, heading south. Outside the port, a little way down the coast, we stopped by a bench overlooking the river and sat down.

'What are we going to do now?' Lizzy asked.

I could tell by the tone of her voice that she was close to tears.

'Where are we going? What are we doing?'

'We are going to find Howard and Laura,' I said. I was excited that we had reached Portugal and couldn't wait to get going.

'I don't know them. How are we going to talk to people?' Lizzy asked. 'I can't speak Portuguese. We haven't got any food. What are we going to take to Howard and Laura's? Where are we going to sleep? Who will be there?' Then she added, sadly, 'I loved being in Spain.'

She pulled a tissue from her bar bag and wiped her eyes. Even though Lizzy and I had travelled through Portugal before, in a van, it felt new. Cycling made things different and Portugal, seen from the saddle of a bike, was a new country, with a hard-to-understand language and different customs and culture. Everything felt new and overwhelming: the crossing, the lack of food, the not knowing. I understood, but couldn't help other than to offer Howard and Laura. Once we got to their place, I was sure, things would be OK, but it was easy for me to say. I knew Howard well enough to be confident he would offer us a safe space but couldn't be sure of anything else, really.

I must admit I felt a little lost myself. We had just about got used to being in Spain and now Portugal felt different. In the short cycle from the ferry we had been passed very closely by a few cars and that had spooked me a bit too. Everything was uneasy, frantic even.

We cycled out of Caminha along the coast to Praia de Âncora on a mix of quiet roads and cobbled cycle routes, stopping to buy a bottle of Mateus Rosé (what else?!) and some Portuguese custard tarts for Howard and his family (an ironic gesture, obviously) as well as some other supplies.

Vila Praia de Âncora, a pretty town on a small river, with a harbour and a long seafront overlooking a lovely sandy beach, was busy. Groups of old men sat talking on the low wall separating the esplanade from the sands. Striped canvas changing huts sat in rows at the back of the beach. A few small waves were breaking on the sandbar on the other side of the river, which was emptying into the sea via a wide, shallow channel.

THE WAY OF THE WAVES

We locked the bikes on the seafront and paddled across the river to bodysurf in the waves beyond. Lizzy needed some water time before jumping headlong into the unfamiliar. The sea, as always, worked wonders, its ability to calm and restore never underestimated.

It took us a while to find Howard and Laura's house, which was hidden away down a cobbled lane and behind a stone wall with big double gates. We pushed the gate open and wheeled the bikes on to the drive. Ancient vines in their bright green, early summer exuberance, reaching out across a framework of tall granite pillars strung with wire, provided dappled shade. A rack of surfboards leaned against the stone house and a set of steps led up to the first floor. The kitchen door opened and Howard, Laura, their daughter Rosaline and youngest son Hugo, and the dog, Bear, spilled down the steps to greet us, a groundswell of peace and tranquillity.

I was sure that this place would give us something – I wasn't sure exactly what – but it became very clear that things were easy and relaxed and Howard and Laura were exactly the kind of people Lizzy would love.

We sat down at the wooden table in the kitchen and wine was opened. Laura went back to chopping vegetables. Howard talked.

Howard is a surfer, actor and brand owner.[*] You may have seen him in the Waitrose Christmas adverts. He's handsome, tall, with long red hair and a beard and is always being cast as 'the Dude' because that's what he looks like. He's thoughtful, intelligent and articulate with a dash of insecurity and fuck-it-just-do-it bravado that comes from being an actor: a singularly unique trait to the profession. Laura, pale-skinned and elf-like, with long silvery blonde hair, is a teacher, artist and mother of three. She's a considerate and powerful woman, giving Howard the space to talk and be himself while quietly checking in where necessary.

The two of them have been constant travellers and adventurers. Their latest adventure, the house in Portugal, had been their summer residence since they bought it as a wreck five years ago. Still very much a work in progress, it was rustic and peaceful: an oasis of leafy calm.

---

[*] Howard is the founder and owner of Submariner, a surf brand that makes and sources ethical products.

A SANCTUARY IN ÂNCORA

We spent the evening sharing stories of our adventures. We never seemed to run out of digressions, tangents and meanderings to keep the conversation going. I found it easy to be with them, as it is always easy to be with people who are interested and interesting. You could be the most fascinating person, but unless you ask questions about other people's lives too, you just turn into a bore. I liked that about Howard and Laura. They were generous with their attention. We talked until it was dark enough to make pitching the tent more difficult than it should have been.

At first light we loaded up Howard's car and set off to find some surf. At Praia da Duna do Caldeirão, the beach to the south of the river at Âncora, we found some small but fun waves. Lizzy, Rosaline, Howard, Hugo and I caught some punchy micro waves as the morning mist cleared to reveal a bright and beautiful day.

After breakfast Laura and Howard took us to their secret swimming spot. A weir, which also functions as a bridge, created a deep pool for swimming, and a culvert, diverting water to a mill, formed a jacuzzi downstream. Hugo took us to the tree where he jumps into the clear, cool water. He showed me the way to climb the tree and threw himself into the deep, cold water. I went next. Lizzy squealed as she dropped 2.4 metres into the pool.

Rosaline and Hugo played about in a small rubber dinghy and Lizzy, Howard, Laura and I sat on the granite parapet of the weir. The stone, heated by the sun, warmed my back as I lay back and fell asleep with dragonflies buzzing around my head.

I don't know if Howard and Laura realised how much we needed them at that moment. Their hospitality had a powerful effect on us, allowing us to unwind before beginning the last part of our journey. Everything they did helped in some way or other.

On the second morning we set off on a surf check in the drizzle that became a rambling tour with a quick Portugal 101 thrown in. While we checked beach after beach for waves, and didn't go in, Howard and Laura gave us basic lessons in Portuguese and explained how everything worked. Conversations in the car, like the surf check, took wild detours, flowing and swooping, sometimes ending in dead ends or stumbling over short bumpy sections, leading nowhere other than to a place that offered a comfort in sharing.

I felt much better prepared for Portugal afterwards, even though we bumped and rolled over a range of startling new surfaces in the first few miles. These included ancient flagstones and rough cobbles. They would turn out to be a feature of the riding from now on.

Our route – the Camino Portugués – followed the coast, running along wooden boardwalks, above the sand or through dunes, beside smelly piles of seaweed, through pine forest and to points where the mist-covered sea slapped against the granite.

At Viana de Castelo we gritted our teeth for the dash across the 1km-long, Gustave Eiffel-designed double-decker bridge. With trains crossing on the lower deck and cars roaring across the top deck, it was a daunting ride. We pulled out into the traffic and rode as fast as we could across the bridge in a face-stinging drizzle. No one could overtake us, because the carriageway was so narrow, so by the time we pulled off the bridge at a roundabout we had built up a healthy queue of mildly irritated Portuguese drivers.

Things didn't get any easier as the route took us into tiny villages, most of which seemed to have cobbled streets that rattled the bikes so much it felt like everything might fall apart. One set of particularly knobbly cobbles jangled us down to a wide river with a clapper bridge, made up of a dozen granite slabs supported by granite pillars, that was just wide enough for us to push the bikes carefully across.

Our first campsite, a dreary, sad place in the middle of Fão, had precious little space between the seasonal pitches, which meant we had to pitch up next to a Scout encampment. They woke us up in the night making ghostly noises and then, for some reason, got up en masse to mill about silently. It sounded like they were surrounding us.

We cycled out of Fão the next morning and on to more awful cobbled roads through farmland being worked by hand. Famers were sitting at the side of the road at stalls selling their produce. One man sat in the back of his battered pick-up tying onions into strings.

We tried out a new greeting: '*Bom dia!*'

'*Bom dia!*' came the cheery reply.

The change from Spain was immediate. The landscape was flatter and seemed a lot poorer, the people not as well dressed, the cars less modern. Some villages we passed were scruffy, with a few exceptions where modern houses had been built between the ramshackle

A SANCTUARY IN ÂNCORA

properties and ruins. When we rode into Apúlia the outskirts of the town looked downtrodden and forgotten, with untidy beach shacks and bars. A few kilometres down the road at Povoa de Varzim, a buzzing beach town with a huge harbour and beach, the contrast couldn't have been greater. There were people everywhere: in bars and restaurants, walking, cycling and exercising in the community spaces.

Just like the difference between rich and poor neighbourhoods, the bike lanes varied greatly too. Some were smooth, while some back roads, cobbled and agonising, almost shook our fillings out. In Spain everything – houses, roads, neighbourhoods – looked cared for, made to a certain standard. In Portugal the distance between rich and poor, good and bad, was stark.

There were people lining the streets as we pulled out of a dirt road on to the main drag at Praia de Aguçadoura. With accidental but immaculate timing, we had stumbled upon a cycling festival. We pulled up with seconds to spare as hundreds of cyclists riding antique bikes and wearing traditional dress streamed past us waving, smiling and ringing their bells. Men wore trousers and white shirts, with waistcoats and flat caps or felt hats and the women wore summer dresses, with headscarves or floppy hats. Some carried flowers in their front baskets. Everyone seemed to be having a great time. I wished we had been able to take part, despite having bikes that were about 100 years too new. Seeing bicycles take over the streets was refreshing. In the few encounters we had had with cars so far I was beginning to think cyclists might be second-class citizens. As it turned out, I was right.

But here, in Aguçadoura, people were looking to the past and celebrating it.

António de Oliveira Salazar was the founder of Portugal's 'Estado Novo' (New State), an authoritarian regime – dictatorship – that held Portugal back, lasting from 1932 until the Carnation Revolution* in 1974.

---

* The Carnation Revolution happened on 25 April 1974 and was so called because people gave carnations to the military who organised the coup. There were few shots fired.

During the Estado Novo political opposition could be met with a visit from the secret police. Elections were shams. Agriculture was inefficient, education and health indicators were among the poorest in Europe. In short, in recent history, Portugal was undeveloped with poor infrastructure. Many of the surfers I spoke to had described Portugal as 'third world' in the early 1970s.

Ricardo Bernado, a cyclist from Faro, explained that some generations of Portuguese still remembered a time when they were so poor the only transport they could afford was a bicycle. Now that those people, especially those in high positions, can afford big, modern cars, bikes remind them of their penniless pasts. They see cycling as retrograde, which explained why cycling infrastructure was sometimes lacking.

Ricardo said, 'Portugal is a car-making nation, with a constant pressure on the population to be productive. Bikes on the road are a hindrance to that. As a result, attitudes towards cyclists are terrible.'

The cycling festival proved that, perhaps, attitudes might be changing. Celebrating a humble past – and seeing no shame in it – meant that the country could also look to the future.

The cycle route into Porto took us along the coast, past a refinery and beaches, through tiny traditional fishing villages and into well-heeled resorts. As the coast turned eastwards and into the Douro River, we passed the lighthouse and fort at Foz do Douro and then followed the north bank in a bike lane, alongside trams and cars, that was separated from the traffic for a lot of the way. The further we got, the busier it became and the more overwhelming it was to cycle towards the maelstrom. When we ran out of cycle path and were forced on to the road into the city traffic it was terrifying. If I had become a bit testy with the drivers in Spain, Portugal was beginning to turn me into an angry but frightened cyclist, constantly on the cusp of fight-or-flight. We were seldom given enough safe space by overtaking cars, and they passed us with less than a metre of space often, even if traffic was coming in the opposite direction and even when it wasn't. That was fine when it was a small car. Not so fine

A SANCTUARY IN ÂNCORA

when it was a truck or a huge, modern 2-tonne beast.* I didn't know whether to pull off the road to let impatient drivers pass or kick their doors as they went past.

The Praça da Ribeira, a cobbled, car-free square overlooking the River Douro in the Old City, was thronged with tourists, touts, hawkers and waiters. American, French, Spanish and English voices babbled against the noise of the buskers cracking out Beatles numbers. Tourist boats ploughed up and down the river. To the east, the arched Dom Luís I Bridge, an Eiffel-inspired masterpiece that was finished in 1896 and was, at one time, the longest bridge of its type in the world, framed the river with ironwork. On the opposite bank, a cable car carried passengers to the upper span.

We pushed the bikes through the crowds and parked them next to a free table outside a restaurant in the square, so we could decompress. Between batting off people trying to sell me sunglasses – I was already wearing a pair – and avoiding the gaze of people touting for us to go on a boat trip, I looked around at the city, the half-timbered, tiled and balconied buildings, the wooden *rabelo* boats on the river and the crowds of people, and felt very proud that we had got this far – 2648km in fact – and had been able to enter the city under our own steam.

Portugal, however, felt and looked so different from anywhere we had travelled so far. It was beautiful but also a little sad. The language sounded, to us, like something from the Baltic, the traffic was terrible and the weather was, rather surprisingly, very mixed.

But at least we had got here.

---

* Have you seen the size of some modern cars? They take up so much space. Compare an original Mini with a new Mini and you can see the vast contrast between them. It's obscene.

28

The wild west

'Cycling to São Jacinto to get the ferry. People fishing, swimming, sunbathing, fish jumping. Just wanted to stop and swim – enjoy the moment. A huge artic passed by, knocking the wind out of my sails, sending me reeling and blocking the views of the estuary and all its quiet loveliness.'

DIARY ENTRY: MONDAY 22 JULY 2024

Stage 27: Days 61–62 | From: Porto | To: Figueira da Foz | Distance: 128km

We woke early to check the surf but it was small and the wind was coming from the north again, making it messy and unsurfable. We had camped at the Orbitur (a chain of campsites) site on the coast to the south of Porto at Canidelo. The long beach, rocky with a series of small, sandy coves, sat below a low cliff, a wide boulevard above with a cycle path that ran all along its length for 4km. The beachfront was backed by apartment blocks and the occasional bar or restaurant. Outdoor gyms and playparks dotted the littoral zone between the bike path and the beach.

We cruised along the coast, passing beautiful countryside, pedalling through a pine forest and a nature reserve on a dirt track and then on to a wooden walkway beside the beach that rattled in sequence as our wheels rolled over loose planks.

The surf was breaking nicely when we arrived at Espinho. A jetty of huge stone blocks provided shelter from the northerly wind so the waves were clean and about head high on the sets, the water cooler than in Spain. The crowd was small but there were a few Doras paddling around, taking waves they obviously felt were theirs. One of them paddled right in front of me to take a wave I was going for. I decided not to let it spoil my session and caught the next wave.

As one of the closest spots to Porto with good surf, Espinho has a reputation for localism, partly because it gets crowded, as much as it has a reputation for good, powerful surf. It has been the scene for a number of WSL Junior and Longboarding pro and qualifying competitions.

Espinho was the last major settlement we would see until we reached the port at Aveiro. Leaving the town on easy roads, we entered a flat, dry agricultural area, passing a few smallholdings and farms. We clickety-clacked over another long wooden walkway through a beautiful wetland reserve of reeds and willow. Cranes waded through the shallows while ducks squabbled and chattered. Afterwards there were more smallholdings where farmers tended their salad and vegetable gardens and sheep, goats and chickens in small pens.

We cycled on to the seaward side of the Aveiro Lagoon, a 75 sq km tidal wetland that ran for 25km north to south behind the dunes, ending in a narrow estuary, where we hoped to catch the ferry to Aveiro to avoid a long cycle around. The road, the N327, was mostly quiet but with occasional traffic that roared past us. All we could do was grumble and hang on tight. We stopped for a drink at Torreira, a diminutive port that was about halfway along the lagoon. It was a quiet, beautiful place. Between us and open water lay the marina, a series of floating pontoons providing a base for a small fleet of brightly coloured, hand-painted traditional fishing boats.

I googled the ferry times for the boat to Aveiro from São Jacinto. The next one, I noted, left in 45 minutes. The next one after that left three hours later. I looked up how far it was from Torreira to the port: 12km. Our average speed was about 15km/h so we'd really have to put the hammer down (as they say) if we wanted to catch the boat.

We paid up and hit the long, straight road that ran close to the water's edge. There were people fishing, swimming and sunbathing on the sandy shores. In the water, fish were jumping and shoals of sprats shimmered on the surface. As we pedalled, trying to keep the speed up to about 20km/h, we could see a small flock of flamingos – a flamboyance – wading in shallow water offshore, their beaks waving back and forth through the silt. I loved the cycling but wished we had more time so we could have stopped to swim.

We made the ferry – fully electric, ultramodern and silent – with a few minutes to spare. It took us across the estuary and on to the southern half of the lagoon, this time on a path that led us through plots of sandy farmland, sometimes separated by breezeblock walls, on the landward side, to our campsite at Praia da Vagueira. We ate chips and salad in the campsite restaurant – we had no food – while a junior disco belted out Europop for gangs of pre-teens.

In the morning we crossed over the lagoon on to the seaward side. A few miles to the south we pulled into a parking lot behind the dunes and trotted across the already boiling sand to find a small but clean wave breaking in the shelter of a jetty. The air was hot but the water was cold and I surfed for an hour on my own until the waves died a little with the tide. I made the surfer's promise while waiting, and prayed – to something – to send me a nice wave, on the understanding that I would get out afterwards. The wave, if it came, would be my last. When it did I took off, standing awkwardly on my leash before falling off. I paddled out again, instantly breaking the promise. No more waves came.

We ate lunch on a picnic bench in the shade of an alder by the lake in Mira, having completed around 35km: a good morning's ride. Dragonflies flitted between reeds and water boatmen danced across the water. It was hot and I was already tired but we were determined to get through the next section before the end of the day. The only campsite was another 30km away and it was at the other end of the Estrada Florestal, the road where we had first decided to do this trip. Having come full circle, it would be a big moment to pass the observation tower.

Our water bottles were almost empty so we looked for a tap in the nature reserve and in the grounds of a closed restaurant. There was nothing, so we set off, on a dead straight cycle path through sandy pine forest that appeared to disappear into infinity. The sun beat down and what lay ahead of us was at least 20km of undulating dunes, scrub, a few trees, and, at some point, the tower.

THE WILD WEST

We cycled on. A few hundred metres later I noticed a family filling up a trailer full of water containers from a standpipe away from the road. I jammed on the brakes and jumped off the bike. Yes! It was drinking water. Amazing. Just when we really needed it. Why did it happen like that? Whenever we got to a point where things might get difficult something always turned up to change our fortunes.

We filled our bidons to the brim and set off again.

The Estrada Florestal drifted away into the distance, a black ribbon laid upon a sea of sand and scrub. The road had been completely updated, with the tarmac re-laid and cycle lanes painted in green on the surface, making it perfect for riding: safe, smooth and flowing. I loaded up some songs on to my portable speaker and turned it up so Lizzy could hear it too. With no traffic we were able to ride side by side, boosted by music that we had chosen for our wedding party.

In that moment I was the happy cyclist riding through Portugal. I had made it this far. My knee had stood up to the hills of Spain, my back was feeling the best it had in years and I was feeling truly, madly, deeply, free. I sang along to the music.

'Do you still think I am mental?'

'Yes. Of course.'

'But we made it.'

'We did.'

A couple, looking distressed, flagged us down as we passed them, asking if we knew where they could get some water. We told them where to find the taps: only about 2km away. I didn't ask them how long they had been on the road but it must have been at least 18km, a few hours of walking without water. We offered some of ours but they refused and walked on.

The observation tower was just as I remembered: sat at the top of the tallest dune, the highest point for miles. We stopped and climbed the dune to the base of the tower but couldn't go further as someone was keeping watch on the top floor. The views of the road tapering away into the shimmering distance both to the north and south were still amazing. All around us was scrub, regenerating slowly into forest. The young pines had outgrown some of the strawberry bushes. There were insects everywhere. I watched as a yellow swallowtail butterfly fluttered from one small pink flower to the next.

We cycled until the cycle path ran out abruptly, and then cycled some more, this time on the new roadway, always travelling in a dead straight line. Then the new tarmac ran out and a barrier across the road pointed the way to a diversion, a pockmarked road leading inland. I looked at the map and figured that the diversion would add at least another 10km to our day. To continue would take us down the remainder of the Estrada Florestal – on an even rougher rough road – to a village near the campsite.

We rode around the barrier and into a section of thick, mature forest. The tarmac was uneven, with sections where the original cobbled surface showed through like open wounds. The potholes were deep and rattled the bikes and trailers each time we hit them, which was unavoidable. Eventually the tarmac covering the old cobbles ran out and we rode on the cobbles themselves. The going was slow and difficult. Avoiding the potholes meant riding on the road's verges but that meant the risk of bogging in the sand. There was no easy way through.

The forest was shady and beautiful, if remote. It buzzed with the sound of cicadas and felt wild. Between the pines, a scrub of low bushes and desert plants grew, and yellow *Verbascum*, attracting butterflies and insects, grew tall in the verges.

After 5km of cautious riding the road ended at the edge of the forest with another barrier and a collection of rusting plant and road-making machinery next to an abandoned sports centre. We rode around it and into a village where people were tending lawns and kids were splashing in round, above-ground pools. Dogs barked and a few people waved as we rode past. Down a hill to the beach and a quiet, forgotten campsite by the beach in Quiaios, a lovely town with a huge expanse of beach, a few apartment blocks and a couple of restaurants. We had completed just 52km but it felt like more. I was tired and wanted to let someone else cook: that came in the form of a small beachside restaurant. Lizzy ordered the fish special, which should have been enough for two people. She scoffed the lot.

29

The giants of Nazaré

'I knew it as a beach break which picked up loads of swell. Never really considered it as a big wave spot. Garrett had been in contact with the city hall in Nazaré. And they wanted him to come and test drive the big waves.'

ANDREW COTTON, 2024

Stage 28: Days 63–64 | From: Figueira da Foz | To: Nazaré | Distance: 80km

The hill out of Praia do Quiaios was brutal. It took us sharply up to the Serra da Boa Viagem, a small mountain range and national park between Figueira da Foz and the flat, sandy forest to the north. The road hugged the high, sometimes vertical cliffs where the mountain range met the sea, and led us up to the Farol de Cabo Mondego, a lighthouse. Separated from a deathly plunge of around 50 metres by a low crash barrier, I favoured the middle of the road, unless I was in danger of getting squashed by a car, in which case I pulled over and held on to my handlebar grips like I was dangling from a ledge.

Near the top we stopped to look at a disused factory in a quarry cut out of the cliff below us. Behind it, in a beautiful bay of golden sand, peppered with black rocks, a wave was breaking off a point. The waves wrapped around the point and then peeled into the sandy bay. It looked wonderful, even if the setting, framed by the gantries, chimneys and run-down grey buildings of the old factory, was desolate.

We watched the point for a few minutes, debating whether we could get down to it, or if we had the time to make a big diversion. While we dithered a bank of sea mist rolled in, partly obscuring the waves, until all we could see was a slice of golden sand through a gap in the gloom. We decided to give it a miss.

I hated myself. I couldn't bear that we had just ridden away from perfect, empty surf. That was the dream. That was what we were here for. Everything had conspired against us: the sea mist, the access, the fact that we knew we had a big day of riding ahead of us. And we allowed it to. We should have just stopped.

The steep descent into Figueira da Foz dropped us straight into the sea fret. It had cast a veil over the whole town and beachfront, a mile-long curve of sand and reef that we now couldn't see. We knew, from previous visits, that a series of small points that make up the curve of the bay join up to create one of the longest right points in Europe when the swell is big. Previously, we had watched, in awe, as waves of at least 15ft had broken cleanly from the tip of the bay beneath the mountains, right into the town's main beach. It was unsurfable for us but with a jet ski it might have been possible for someone with the skills. We had walked away that time too, but for different reasons: we were off to watch something even bigger – the giant waves of Nazaré.

This time we had to navigate the city, get across the Mondego River, possibly, if we couldn't get a ferry, on the vast span of the Ponte Edgar Cardoso, a 1.4km-long cable-stayed bridge that crosses the river, a couple of railway lines and a large wetland area on the south bank.

Judging by the minibus-sized ferry, the width of the access ramp and the glowering looks of people already in the queue, it didn't look likely that we would find a place on the next crossing. I doubted if they would take the trailers even if there was space.

The only other option was the bridge. We cycled along the river and then on to the town's main road system, a confusing series of roundabouts, slip roads and flyovers. Once we had taken the turn-off for the bridge there was no going back. We rode along a dual carriageway for 2km or so, hemmed in by crash barriers, and then followed a slip road towards Lisbon, a fast, single-lane road with a steep climb on to the bridge, riding as quickly as we could to avoid causing too much of a tailback. Roadworks on the bridge had reduced two lanes to one, and the cycle lane, which looked too skinny for us anyway, was closed. A big yellow sign shouted 'No Cycling'. We pulled over to let the cars go and stopped to weigh up the options: the traffic was reduced to one narrow lane and turning around would be too dangerous, so we had to carry on. Lizzy went first. A small black car pulled out to overtake her – and almost hit her – just as she was joining the bridge traffic.

I eased into the traffic and another car tried to overtake me too. The lane was too narrow for us both so I rode into the middle, blocking everything behind. Lizzy rode out in front as quickly as she could, with me following closely. As the traffic began to pull away from us and the cars behind backed up, I felt like I had a fire-spewing dragon breathing down my neck. We couldn't stop to let anything pass. There was nothing to do except keep going. For the second time that day I gripped my handlebars, as if hanging on to a precipice, and pedalled as fast as I could without sending my trailer into a high-speed wobble. The bridge seemed to go on for ever. It was like a bad dream where I was being chased by a gang of armoured clowns with chainsaws and, every time I thought I had escaped, the end of the road just kept getting further away. All told, we endured 2.4km of going like the clappers, terrifying traffic bearing down on us all the time.

The road south took us through a few villages where people sat outside bars in the sun adjacent to half-built properties and traditional tiled homes. Churches, we noted, were usually very smart, even though their neighbour might be uncared for. As the buildings thinned out, we entered the Mata Nacional do Urso, a 6,000-hectare reserve of maritime pine and scrub that was originally planted in the 14th century to protect the dunes. The wood from the pines was later used to construct the small ships – caravels – that the Portuguese used to 'conquer' the New World. A bike path ran alongside the road so the riding was easy, but it was hot and the dunes undulated like the sea after a blow. At first glance the landscape – a sandy, scrubby forest – looked desolate and seemingly empty but it was full of colour. I focused on the vegetation and was able to see the details: grasses, seed heads, flowers and young trees created subtle but lovely blues, greens, yellows, whites, purples and pinks.

We stopped at the Lagoa de Ervedeira, a small lake with a busy beach, for lunch. I sat in the meagre shade of an information sign while Lizzy stripped off and dived into the lake. At Praia da Vieira we stopped at a cafe on the seafront and glugged down a couple of cold drinks each. The young waiter, a lad of about 16, asked us if the bikes, parked outside, were ours, and if we were cycling all of Portugal. When we told him we had cycled from England and had cycled France and Spain too, he was incredulous. 'Cool!' he said. When we were leaving, we heard him tell the other staff. They waved us off.

Beyond São Pedro de Moel, where we stayed overnight, we cycled through mature forest that smelled sweet and was full of insects and butterflies. Many of the trees were being tapped for their resin, a practice that has contributed to the Portuguese economy for centuries. In many areas where there was little else, tapping provided a good income.

Outside Nazaré the cycle path ended and the forest stopped and, suddenly, we were riding through narrow streets on our way to the Largo de Nossa Senhora da Nazaré, the old square at the top of the cliff overlooking the town. It was busy in the square with restaurants spilling on to the street, souvenir shops selling surfing memorabilia and other tourist tat, and people – of all nationalities – drinking, shopping or looking at the views. One side of the square, next to the road leading down to the promontory that separates Praia do Norte from the main town of Nazaré, a low wall marked the edge of the 100 metre-high cliff. The view was incredible: an almost sheer drop down to the sea and beach below. Behind the beach was the town, and beyond the Río Alcoa and the port and beyond that, in the mist, the Serra da Pescaria, a low mountain range we would be climbing later.

We walked the bikes down the road leading to the Forte de São Miguel Arcanjo, a 16th-century fort with a low, red-capped lighthouse that sits at the end of the bluff overlooking the vast expanse of Praia do Norte. Throngs of people were walking up and down the steep hill. Looking over the beach, to the north, the statue of Veado stood 6 metres tall: an odd sight with a man's body and the head of a stag, holding a surfboard. The sculpture celebrates a local legend in which a knight, in pursuit of a stag, was blinded by a heavy fog. The stag disappeared over the cliff but the knight's horse stopped in time (at the behest of some supernatural forces), right at the spot where a lost icon of the Virgin, said to be carved by Joseph himself, had been hidden in a cave 400 years earlier by a hermit monk on the run from the Moors.

That the statue is also holding a surfboard is testament to the waves of Nazaré and what it has become, in a relatively short period of time. The story – a modern-day tale of discovery – is not unique to the surfing world but the reasons behind it are not your usual surfer-finds-wave-surfs-it-tourism-follows kind of a story.

Lizzy and I pushed the bikes down the hill to the fort. The view, of the sea beyond the bluff, was very different to the last time we were there. The wind was onshore and a few, quite big (relatively) but mushy waves were breaking on the sand. A little way up the beach a few surfers were in the water.

When we were here before, we arrived just in time for the first big day of the winter. The waves were the biggest I have ever seen – enormous. They came into Praia do Norte in thick lines and exploded under the lighthouse in huge, violent peaks. I would estimate they were anywhere between 30 and 50 feet: the height of a four-storey building. Surfers in the water looked tiny compared with the waves, especially while riding them, and the jet skis – at least 10 of them – looked like ants clambering over corrugated sheeting. The views were exceptional because the waves broke so close to the cliff.

The bluff was lined with onlookers that day. Hundreds of people, come to witness one of surfing's greatest spectacles, standing on the squat, 16th-century fort or on the cliff, watching as the world's best surfers rode giant waves. The scenario was so familiar – I had seen video footage of the lighthouse and the waves many times – that I felt as if I was on a film set. It felt equally unreal to be here with bikes too.

Our adventure felt big to us, but it was nothing like the adventure of how surfing fell in love with Nazaré.

First, it should be said that Nazaré has a bathymetry (the contours of the sea bed) that is similar to Hossegor's. A deep underwater canyon allows open ocean swell to retain its power and size so that the swell, when it hits the beach, is at its peak. These waves refract and meet waves that are travelling over the shallower seabed to the north of the canyon. When they meet, it creates huge, surfable peaks. There are lots of other factors that affect the waves, such as the swell direction, the local wind and the swell period, but that's it in a nutshell: Nazaré gets giant surf. So giant, in fact, that the Guinness World Record for the Biggest Wave Surfed was set in 2020 by Sebastian Steudtner at 86ft (26.21 metres). A PR campaign by Porsche, which employed their own 'drone technology', claimed that Steudtner may have broken it again in 2024 with a wave of 93.73ft (28.57 metres). That said, Lucas Chianca, surfing on the same day, also surfed an absolute monster of a wave that won the WSL biggest wave of the year in 2024 but has yet (at the time of writing) to be confirmed by Guinness. An HBO TV show, *100 Foot Wave*, is documenting the search for that elusive number, such is the draw of the challenge.

Maya Gabeira, four times winner of the Billabong XXL Big Wave Awards and first woman to surf Teahupo'o, is the current holder of the Guinness record for women at 73.5 feet (22.4 metres). In 2020, the year she broke the record, it was the biggest wave surfed that year by anyone.

However you look at it, waves of that magnitude belong to a completely different realm: to catch them, surfers need a jet ski to propel them on to the face. Paddling with huge boards isn't enough when the waves reach a certain size.

Nazaré's beaches have been surfed since the 1960s, albeit on smaller days. Some of the surfers I spoke to said they had gone there and surfed the main beach in the town but none of them had surfed Praia do Norte. João Luís Moraes Rocha, one of Portugal's first generation of native surfers, who started surfing in 1970, used to surf the main beach too, but, as he said, the marina, built in 1983, that now houses the workshops and gear stores for the tow teams surfing Praia do Norte, has changed the sandbanks, and so changed the quality of the waves. Another example of coastal development affecting wave quality, as at Le Barre, but in this case also providing a safe launch for the next, giant leap in surfing.

THE GIANTS OF NAZARÉ

For big wave surfers, and the wider surfing world, however, Nazaré wasn't on the radar until 2011. Praia do Norte had a reputation as a swell magnet, but, for many years it was the domain of a hardcore crew of bodyboarders. Local surfers rode it too, but only to a certain size.

The giants of Nazaré were hiding in plain sight.

Summer had always been busy in Nazaré, bringing plenty of tourist income during the season. One reason was the cliff at the northern end of the town's beach, which provided shelter from the cool Nortada wind (north wind) Portugal experiences in the summer. However, like all resorts that go dead in winter, local businesspeople were searching for something that would bring income all year round. Inspired by the success of Peniche and Ericeira, they looked to surfing.

Local bodyboarder and teacher Dino Casimiro was entranced by the size of the waves hitting Praia do Norte in the winter. With the help of the town hall, Dino invited Garrett McNamara, a Hawaiian big wave surfer, and other big wave surfers, to Nazaré to check out the size of the waves. They thought they had something, because they knew the waves could get big, but they didn't know how to go about turning it into anything that was meaningful. Garrett was the only one who replied to the emails. He flew over to look and immediately saw the potential, starting the North Beach Project in 2010.

Andrew 'Cotty' Cotton, Devon-born big wave surfer and much-respected regular, was among the first to surf Nazaré big. When he was home for a few weeks in the off season, he agreed to meet me for a coffee and a chat. We met outside Surfed Out, a surf shop in Braunton, north Devon. As we sat in the sun, Cotty explained to me how Nazaré had happened:

> They contacted Garrett and he went over. He saw how big it is and knew he couldn't do it alone so he reached out to me and Al Mennie. We were in Ireland and had started to get a reputation on a global level.
>
> We looked at Nazaré. At the time we were exploring some outer reefs in Ireland so we said we're not going to Portugal, come to Ireland! But they agreed to pay for our airfares and our accommodation if we came. And that was it.

Cotty is an interesting character. First, he's hugely likeable. Second, he's open and honest and, although careful about what he says, still manages to be candid. In 2017 he made headlines around the world for breaking his back while surfing Nazaré.* Shortly after his comeback, he injured his ACL surfing in Spain. I could relate. But there is more to him than just injuries or being the comeback kid. He is a trailblazer who would humbly suggest he was in the right place at the right time rather than say he had led the charge.

He continued:

> Basically it was a tourism project. The City Hall were looking at ways to get tourism in the winter. It was always busy in the summer but come the end of August, September, it went dead. They wanted to make Nazaré into a surf destination. So, they put a bit of money to promote it, getting Garrett there. It was all manufactured. They asked, 'What's the goal?' The answer: 'We want to get the world record.' They had a three-year plan. 'Big, Bigger, Biggest' was the motto. In three years, they hoped to get the world record for the biggest wave. Within year two, Garrett got it.
>
> The Portuguese are forward-thinking. People in the City Hall think, 'How do we increase tourism and benefit everyone?' And it comes. There are two sides to that, of course. Some of the local surfers are probably quite pissed off with it. Because now, the wave's busy and North Beach is a circus. So, if you were a local bodyboarder that loved North Beach because it was empty, and the waves are good when it's 10 feet, now when it's 10 feet, there are jet skis everywhere. People trying to tow in. Claiming it. Writing their press releases. It's nonsense! So, it has a flipside. Yes, it's great if you had a shop or an Airbnb or a hotel or a restaurant. Twelve months of the year is now busy. But if you're a local bodyboarder and you want a bit of quiet and North Beach is your sanctuary, you're pissed off!
>
> So, everything comes with for and against. As a tourism project goes, it's got to be the best ever. Not only for Nazaré. For Portugal. I think they reached out to numerous big wave surfers all over the world and I think Garrett was the only guy to reply to the email.

---

* Andrew won the WSL Big Wave Awards 'Wipeout of the Year' in 2018.

THE GIANTS OF NAZARÉ

Cotty has a place in Nazaré these days and considers it to be his second home, spending a large part of the year in Portugal. In the winter, he said, it is possible to surf waves of consequence often, unlike in other big wave spots that don't break so regularly, which is why it is so good for training.

He went on:

I enjoy the days which are big and quiet. But for me now, it's turned into something different. I'm based in Portugal because it's a good place to train. For me, as a surf athlete, the community treats us well. The facilities are set up for an athlete to train. They make it easy for you. They've supported the surfers that way because they want you to be there.

We talked about Tony Butt's explorations in Galicia.

Guys like Tony, he's a legend. And he's what big wave surfing is. It's not about the fashionable thing, it's about the next thing. Getting away from the crowd. Those guys don't get the credit for it. As soon as it gets busy, they're off to the next thing. Why did I first go to Nazaré? Because no one was there. It was amazing and it was doing something that no one had done. Working out how to do it and riding the biggest waves on the planet. But now, everyone wants to ride the biggest waves on the planet.

That's not to say that when the biggest days are in Nazaré, there's not actually many people that can surf it and I'd definitely be there. But I'm also looking. Where else? If Nazaré's on our doorstep, right there in plain sight how many more waves are there like that? Nazaré was only surfed big 13 or 14 years ago.

He then gave me a glimpse of what it's like to be a big wave surfer. And where that soul lies:

I think the core value of surfing is discovery, isn't it? That's what makes us surfers. And it's working out how to do things.

When we first went to Portugal, you couldn't get a good jet ski with a good impeller with the right set-up to tow or drive. It was tough. But now, you can rent a jet ski at the harbour, ready to tow.

You can rent a driver too. If you've got the cash, you can go. It's how much you want it.

This year we went to Cortez Bank. A mission in Morocco. A couple of missions in Ireland. The Arctic mission.* And actually, this is what surfing is. It's discovery. It's pushing the boundaries. Not going back to the same place and getting the biggest wave ever over and over again. Who's saying it's the biggest wave ever? And how do you even measure that thing?

Why did I go to Nazaré? Because I love adventure and I wanted big waves.

And if it wasn't for that tourism project, I wouldn't have been there. If I hadn't gone to Nazaré, I'd still be plumbing in North Devon. It's made my career.

There seemed to be a conflict between success and adventure but I can see the two going hand in hand. Yes, so Nazaré is an incredible story of recent discovery and its protagonists – Garrett, Cotty, Sebastian, Maya and everyone else who straps in and surfs those giant swells – are at the edge of the world every time they go out, but the surfer's paradox is at work here. You might want to discover new places, and the successes that might come with it, but is it worth it if you lose the one thing you came for in the first place? As Tony and Cotty prove, there are still places left to discover, even in latter-day Europe.

And that leads us straight back to the question that every surfer who didn't come from money has had to ask themselves: how do you pay for it? The question is always the same. The answer isn't.

Bude surfers Roger Tout and John Cutts, who like so many others were inspired to travel by the film *The Endless Summer*, discovered new waves on Gran Canaria in 1968. On the way back, while driving through Europe, they ran out of money, having survived all winter on just £100 each. Their solution was to sell their blood in Spanish hospitals. Their journey home, through Portugal, Spain and France, took them to Playa de Somo and a meeting with Jesús Fiocchi, where John filmed Jesús surfing Santa Marina Island on his Super 8

---

* At this point in the conversation Andrew showed me a picture on his phone of a huge, beautiful wave somewhere in the Arctic that he surfed with a small crew.

camera. Without those hardships there wouldn't be a priceless record from the very early days of surf travel in Europe.

Others took part in slightly less salubrious activities, the likes of which aren't uncommon in surfing.

Martin Ward, candid as always, explained:

> This shaper was notorious for making boards and putting drugs inside them. I remember driving through customs with him once and the customs man was giving us a hard time. We had seven boards on the roof and I had no idea anything was inside them, so was giving the customs guy a hard time back, being really lairy. We got through and the shaper says, 'YES! One of the boards has got 5kg in and the other has 10kg in.'
>
> I said, 'You let me do that?'
>
> 'You couldn't be better,' he replied. 'They aren't going to suspect you if you are hanging out of the window, acting like an idiot.'
>
> I didn't like authority and I didn't like being pulled over. We were just going for a surf. We would have got seven years if they'd found it.

Surfing in Nazaré has brought great – and legitimate – riches to some. The fortress on top of the cliff was used by the Portuguese coastguard until 2015, when it opened to the public as a museum charting the course of big wave surfing in Nazaré with a display of boards and photographs. As Cotty told me, in the last three years it has had over 2 million visitors. At €2 per entry that's a lot of money – and good – that goes back into the community. And that's just the tip of the tourism iceberg. Think of all the hotel stays, the lattes and the toasted almonds. Everyone benefits.

Maybe, in doing what they do, big wave surfers weren't so different from the 'beach boys' of Waikiki. Employed by hotels to entertain their guests, they did what they loved and got paid for it. From the 'beach boys' number came surfing's greatest hero, Duke Kahanamoku. The surfers putting on our sport's greatest spectacle in Nazaré deserve everything too. They put their lives on the line while the town reaps the rewards.

I looked at the waves and the people looking out to sea. The waves were small and onshore: very different to last time I was here. For those who are brought to the lighthouse by the lure of one of nature's greatest spectacles, it would have been hard for them to imagine the sign on the gantry over the road saying 'Welcome to the biggest waves in the world' was anything but hype.

Come back in a few months, I thought. When the North Atlantic unleashes its winter fury, Praia do Norte will come to life, once more, with the roar of the giants of Nazaré.

30

Island life

'I never saw myself as any sort of rebel, I was just following a fashion. We all bought surfing magazines and we saw pictures of these exotic places with lovely waves and wanted to go to them . . .'

GRAEME BUNT, 2024

Stage 29: Days 64–67 | From: Nazaré | To: Peniche | Distance: 55km

In January 1973 a 20-year-old surfer from Polzeath set off from Cornwall on a trip to explore Northern Spain and Portugal, inspired by a group of mates who had travelled to Morocco. He packed up his Morris 1000 van and caught the ferry to Spain from Portsmouth with £120 in his pocket and no idea where to go or what he'd find. With no sign of any other surfers in Spain, and no surf at any of the beaches he found, he decided to head south from Gijón, across the plain, to Portugal:

> I cut across the northern part of Spain, up into the mountains, snow, unbelievable. Down on to the Spanish plateau, freezing cold. I mean absolutely bitter. One very cold night in a van with no proper sleeping bag, just a blanket that my mother had sewn up at the bottom.

The surfer was Graeme Bunt, a well-known surfboard shaper from Cornwall who has been making boards for more than 45 years. In 1973 he hadn't yet started making surfboards and had been saving from doing odd jobs or working on building sites with his father. Today, we were sitting in Rosie's Kitchen in Bude having a coffee, laughing, as happens when you meet Graeme, watching dismal surf break on the shoreline.

> I never had rich parents. They never gave me a cent.
>
> I just wanted to surf. But my parents just didn't get it, especially my father. He was a typical hard-working Cornish man. We were building a house at Polzeath, down the end of this estate, and you couldn't quite see the sea. For probably about the 10th time I had jumped off the scaffold just to walk up to the corner to check the surf. He said, 'You won't make a living out of that!'

Sounds familiar.

Continuing the story, for Graeme is a good storyteller:

> I kept going and got into Portugal. It was borders then and they were marching around with guns. I was shitting myself. I got through and as I got into Portugal, the scenery changed and there were forests and the weather was good and I thought this is nice. Got a totally different feel . . .
>
> I was on my own and I didn't know where I was going, without word of a lie. I just started going down the coast, calling in at various places, and then I took a turning for a place called Peniche. I saw this sign that said 'bar' and I thought that meant beach, so I turned off, pulled up and parked. There was a bloke standing there with long blond hair, who looked like a surfer. I wandered over and we sort of converged. He was a South African, living there for the winter and the only surfer in town.

I sipped my tea, rapt, as the waves slapped on to the sand.

> Anyway, we struck up a bit of a friendship. He was living in a room in town. I lived in my van parked at the bar and I spent about 10 weeks there. I only had £120. Honestly, all the time we were there the only surfers we saw were a few Aussies on their way back from Morocco. One weekend four guys came up from Lisbon. They were the only other surfers we saw.

ISLAND LIFE

The fact I stumbled across Peniche was one of the luckiest things that could have happened. Because I could have just wandered around the rest of Portugal and I might have seen a few other surfers around Ericeira, I don't know.

But I guess at the time, surfing hadn't taken off in Portugal as the Portuguese people were all pretty poor. Surfboards would have been hard to get and expensive. I was very lucky I took that turn into that beach, you know.

You know the weird thing? The surf was consistent and we used to sit outside that cafe, late afternoon, after surfing, and look down the beach, and you know how when the sun gets low, any spray coming off the back of a wave gets highlighted? We used to sit there and think, 'You know there is a wave down there, isn't there?' and it always seemed to be in the same place, although it was a long way away. Never went down there, never walked down there, nothing. That was Supertubes!

The wave Graeme surfed in 1973 was Molhe Leste, a wave that breaks near the jetty, to the south side of Peniche. A little further along the beach, to the south, and the wave that Graeme and his South African friend watched for weeks is Praia de Supertubos.

Today, Supertubos is considered to be the best wave in Europe for tubes, and is often compared with Pipeline in Hawaii and Puerto Escondido in Mexico. It is hollow, heavy and unforgiving, due to an offshoot of the underwater canyon that brings huge swells to Nazaré, and a local bathymetry with a deep drop-off to the south of the beach that allows swells to converge and break, fast and hollow, close to the beach.

Supertubos, while known since the 1970s, was only really unveiled (or exposed) to the wider surf world in 2010 when the Rip Curl Search Pro rolled into town. In 2024 the World Surf League parked up its big top at Molhe Leste because local conditions meant Supertubos was blown out.

After speaking to Graeme, I wanted to find the cafe and to see the same view he had. It was remarkable that he had pitched up there by accident.

What was even more remarkable was that the four Portuguese surfers were the country's first native surfers. João Luís Moraes

Rocha was one of them. I will tell his story later, but when I met him in Guincho, he explained that he surfed with his brother and two friends, one of whom was the son of a woman who worked at the American Embassy in Lisbon and could speak English. At weekends they travelled up the coast to surf. Graeme had told me that one of the Portuguese surfers could speak English. Since they only started surfing in 1971 and there were no other native surfers at the time, it is highly likely, if not a certainty, that these were the surfers Graeme met.

Peniche was next on our destinations list, but first we had to get there from Nazaré. The climb up the Serra do Pescaria, a small mountain range south of Nazaré, was tough. The road took us away from the main road – thank goodness – in a steep climb to the ridge of the mountains through scrubby pine forest. The road, peppered with windmills, followed the ridge until it started to drop into São Martinho do Porto. At times, where the trees allowed, we could see both the sea to the west and the flat valley to the east.

São Martinho do Porto was lovely: a beach town with narrow streets and an esplanade that ran along the back of the circular bay. We left it by following a disused railway through forest before hitting the dull industrial suburbs of Caldas da Rainha. After then it got a bit weird as we travelled on dirt roads through forest and vineyards, around the Lagoa de Óbidos, a huge tidal wetland and into the Bom Sucesso gated community. Walls 1.8 metres high, which stopped us from seeing anything much behind, lined the road for a few kilometres. It was like riding in a tunnel. The walls protected those inside from the curious gaze of hoi polloi like us. Where we could catch glimpses of the riches behind the walls, we saw huge villas with perfect lawns, golf courses, equestrian facilities and tennis courts. A playground for the rich.

When the walls opened out, the road dumped us in more wild, dry scrub, on a road that was rough and difficult. Passing through young eucalyptus plantations, it gave us a few tricky miles until we reached a golf resort at Praia Piscina. Riding into the enclave, with its big cars, big houses, and women wearing capri pants and sunglasses, men in chinos and polo shirts, the contrast couldn't have been greater. I found it shocking that one moment we could be passing a smallholding with dogs barking and people bent over working in the fields and the next we were being harassed by people driving oversized black Mercs, the poverty making the wealth look offensive.

Another few miles of rough roads and scrubby farmland brought us to Baleal, a small holiday enclave outside Peniche. We had booked a room in a hostel for a couple of nights on Baleal Island, a tiny, former fishing community that is across a small sandy causeway between Baleal's north and south beaches. Our room had a terrace overlooking North Beach, where we were able to lock up the bikes and forget about them for a couple of days. We breakfasted on the terrace and watched the waves that crumbled about 30 metres away. A perfect location.

Peniche, shaped like a polyp, with narrow neck and wider head, is a fishing town that has gained fame recently because of the quality of the waves. With a wide range of surf, from board-breaking Supertubos to Baleal North Beach, a gentle, beginner-friendly wave, and the presence of a World Surf League event each year, it has become a focus for the Portuguese surfing industry. There are huge surf shops, surf schools, bars, cafes and a very mixed surf crowd. However, it has also retained its heart and soul as a fishing community, with sardine canning factories and a busy port sitting side by side with the surf schools. Churches, city walls and the fort, an infamous maximum-security prison for political prisoners, now a museum, also bring tourists.

On the south side of Peniche, a little out of town and to the south of the jetty that protects the port, Molhe Leste and Supertubos beaches sit behind protected dune systems.

The number of surfers and surfy types in Baleal and Peniche was extraordinary. Every bar or restaurant had boards to rent and offered surf lessons. The sea was awash with foamies floating about between the sets of small waves. Every car seemed to have a board on top. Despite the nearby enclaves, Baleal and Peniche appeared to have kept their heads and felt real. They had morphed into another iteration of themselves since the surfers had arrived but hadn't forgotten their roots: they hadn't shut themselves away for those who could pay.

Or maybe that was just because we felt like we were among our own kind.

We stayed put for three nights, surfing a little when the northerly winds eased or when the crowds thinned out. Lizzy swam in the morning before breakfast and I did my best to rest and recuperate. Spain had been tough but Portugal was equally difficult and I needed a few days off from cycling. The routes we took were often car-free but rough and unfinished, meaning progress was slow and difficult. My knee was beginning to hurt a little, especially on climbs and tricky, bumpy sections. Baleal was the perfect place to rest.

I had mixed feelings about leaving when our three-night mini-break came to an end.

We were about to embark on the last leg and had about 400km to cycle. I was excited that we would soon be rolling into Sagres – we had about three weeks left – but I was also very sad because I didn't want it to end. I was having such a wonderful time. All the bad bits were outweighed by the good bits. I loved cycling. I loved the surfing and I loved being with Lizzy.

But then I didn't want to leave the comfort of the room and go back to putting up tents and blowing up my bed every night. That part was tiring and, if anything was hurting my knee, it was having to kneel every time I wanted to do anything when we were camping. The cycling was just putting more pressure on.

Baleal was disappointing because the surf wasn't that great and when it was passable it was absolutely rammed with learners. I did get to enjoy a solo session on the reef in the bay – it's called Lagido – but it was only a couple of foot. I could see the potential: its fun peaks rose up quickly out of deeper water and on to the shallow reef. On the day we left it was looking amazing but, inevitably, there were 20 people surfing it. I chided myself for not going in, but didn't want to fight the crowd to get waves.

We cycled out of Baleal, into Peniche and around the port to the rough road leading to Molhe Leste, the break that Graeme had surfed more than 50 years ago. We found what we thought was the cafe and took a picture to send him. The bar had hardly changed but the area surrounding it had. Where once there were broken cobbles and weather-worn mud and sand dune, now there was a tidy car park, a low wall and a bridge across the stream leading to the beach. The surf was flat. Looking down the beach to the south towards

Supertubos there were no tails of spray coming off the back of the waves. It was flat down there too.

We cycled on, away from Supertubos, along lumpy, untarmacked roads that followed the coast between small beach towns. South of Praia da Consolação we stopped to admire a right-hand point break that was a little too small to be safe – it was breaking on a shallow ledge next to a fisherman's hut – but showed great promise. I made a mental note to return at some point in the future.

The next stop, on an unmade clifftop road with a huge drop down to the sea, was to mend a puncture on Lizzy's trailer. I noticed that the tyres, which had been brand new when we left, were wearing thin. The tread had worn off most of the tyres, making them vulnerable to sharp seeds and thorns. Annoyingly, when Eric had replaced my wheels in Soulac we had discarded the old wheels and tyres because it was a hassle to carry them.

It was turning out to be another physically tough and emotional day. The sun was hot and I was feeling tired. But, as always seemed to happen, things came right just. At Praia Areal Branca we stopped to look at the beach and check the surf. The beach was busy but there was a clean wave breaking over a very shallow sand and rock bottom that wasn't. The wind was offshore, which held up the waves nicely and made them break regularly down the side of the reef. A stand-up paddleboarder was taking the set waves and a couple of other surfers sat on the inside. It couldn't have been more different from Baleal. We locked up the bikes on the seafront and jumped in. The sea was clear and cool and the sun hot. I could see the fish swimming about on the reef below me. There was something meant to be about it: finding the beach and getting to surf it, a perfect antidote.

We sat in a bar afterwards and looked out to sea. The wind had changed and the waves, which had been great until we got out, were now ruined. We had been lucky.

It was a message: all will come good.

31

Floaters on the reef

> *'Lizzy thinks we've become haunted cyclists, perpetually tired, faraway eyes and wobbly knees. I couldn't disagree. We are always on the move, always looking to the next hill, always working out if we can go the distance.'*
>
> INSTAGRAM POST: MONDAY 29 JULY 2024

Stage 30: Days 67–68 | From: Peniche | To: Guincho (via Ericeira) | Distance: 130km

I was finding Portugal infuriating – mostly because of the traffic – but also joyful. The coast south of Peniche was all things at once too, with wild sections of unmade roads taking us along beautiful cliffs and past derelict or dilapidated houses and farms, then into well-looked-after beach towns and resorts. They were islands of neat, modern cobbles and whitewashed houses with clay-tiled roofs and glass balustrades among the agriculture and wild, open land. At times the two worlds met, with new houses sitting side by side with ports where fishermen mended nets. I found it schizophrenic and confusing but also wildly exciting and beautiful.

The route* that Komoot had plotted for us as 'cycling friendly' – and part of the EuroVelo 1 – often took us on back roads to avoid the busier roads but, inevitably, brought us back to the main

---

* We were supposed to be following the EuroVelo 1 but there was so little signage that we felt like we were on our own for most of the way.

thoroughfares when they approached villages and ports, so making the contrast seem greater.

Even when I thought I had got used to sudden changes, things would happen that would completely throw me. The steep roads in and out of Praia Porto Dinheiro, a small seaside village of fewer than a hundred houses, were busy with cars double-parked and people walking towards the beach at the bottom of the hill. More people were lining up on the road overlooking a corner of the beach that was backed by a steep cliff. We stopped to look and could see a section of the beach was blocked off with fences to make a rudimentary palisade, with the cliff making up one side and the fences taking up the other two. The only open side was the sea. Lots of people lined up around the fences, some climbing them to get better views of whatever was going on inside. A few young men and women were running around inside the palisade. A small flotilla of people on lilos, blow-up unicorns and rubber rings were floating just off shore.

It took me a while to understand what was happening – until I noticed a black and white bull in the water, facing the beach, up to its neck. The people on the lilos were kicking the water, splashing it to go back on the beach. When it did, the people on the beach were goading it, pulling its tail and pushing it. The bull, I could see, was distressed and confused. I found out later that this bull running event was part of the annual festival of the sea held on this beach each year. That it happened at all was controversial because animal cruelty groups had applied to courts in Lisbon to have it stopped. Residents had also petitioned the local council.

And yet, here it was, providing a spectacle for hundreds of spectators. We cycled away, not wanting to be any part of it, but having seen enough to understand what a pitiful and cruel form of entertainment this was. Yes, so the bull wasn't being spiked with a *puja* by a matador, but it was being taunted and treated cruelly by a baying crowd who were OK with abusing animals as entertainment. Shame on them. More of the schizophrenia: lovely people acting like savages.*

---

* I would have said the same about Spain if I had been to see a bullfight, it must be said.

There was more conflict in the next village, Praia de Porto Novo, a tiny place with a high-rise hotel on a hillside overlooking the beach, although it was probably partly due to me. We came out of another steep, rough road that had taken us through a forest of tall reeds, and straight on to the main road into the village. We got caught up behind a pony and trap that was taking tourists on a tour of the village. I started to overtake it, with plenty of room to spare, or so I thought, but when I got halfway a car came around a corner towards us. There wasn't a lot I could do because the trap was going so slowly, as was I, but the car accelerated out of the corner and, instead of slowing, as any considerate driver would have done, almost hit me as it squeezed between me and the roadside.

I shouted as the car approached me and showed no sign of slowing – 'You absolute fucker' – then as it passed – 'Wanker' – and then accelerated away – 'You pissing bellend'. Portuguese driving had made me a foul-mouthed, bad-tempered, cycling fury.

Lizzy felt the same. A steep hill took us out of another village, this time with a couple of hairpins. I was behind. At the first hairpin a car overtook me, right on the bend, almost having a head-on with another car. He pulled in between us, forcing me to brake and explete loudly, then tried to overtake Lizzy on the next hairpin. Lizzy pulled out into the middle of the road to stop him from trying it again until it was safe enough for him to overtake while I shouted at him from behind.

It wasn't a good look, I admit, but it was happening with alarming regularity and my tolerance was diminishing with every close call. I didn't feel safe. I felt the least the drivers deserved was a tirade of abuse in a foreign language.

At Santa Cruz, a little further on, the road took us up a huge hill to a viewpoint at the Miradouro do Alto da Vela. The views, looking back to the town below and out to sea, were stunning. In 2023 Santa Cruz held the European Longboard Championships. Emily Currie won the women's division, taking her first European title, while Ben Skinner took his 12th.

'Santa Cruz is a beach break,' Emily had told me, when I spoke to her before we left. 'It's not the best longboard wave, but it can be really fun. The town is lovely. It's just a really long beach and you've got different peaks. Great place to surf.'

From my current vantage point I could see white pointed tents, marquees and a music stage on the beach. We had missed the 2024 Eurosurf Juniors European Surfing Championships and the Santa Cruz Ocean Spirit Festival by a couple of days. Spain took the win, beating France into second and Portugal into third. England came fifth, with Lukas Skinner, Ben's son, missing out on a first place by fractions of a point.

'I love *pastéis de nata* in Portugal,' Emily had continued, when I pressed her about what she likes about Portugal. I couldn't disagree. 'I'm obsessed with them. I'd have one every day. Portugal is great. There is a great variety of waves. And it kind of feels a little bit more . . . like, rugged, than France or Spain, I think.'

Rugged was a good way to put it. The rutted path continued along the cliff, away from the town, dropping steeply and disappearing, looking as if it might take us straight over it. The sandstone cliffs were eroded like the Grand Canyon in weather-worn layers of different colours, from reds to oranges, brown and yellows. Below them, hundreds of feet down, yellow sand beaches met crashing waves with a few people walking or sunbathing.

The final ride into Ericeira took us along the N247, the main road. It was infuriating and terrifying in equal measure. We stopped at the top of the steep hill above Praia de Ribeira d'Ilhas, a famous right-hand point break. At the parking area and viewpoint, high above the beach, a statue of a surfer looking out to sea stood guard over the waves.* The water was busy with dots of surfers bobbing about: the waves looked good, although small and soft. They broke over a rock platform to the north side of the bay and broke in towards the beach with predictable regularity.

Praia de Ribeira d'Ilhas is one of the most famous waves in Ericeira and has been the home to surfing competitions since 1985. It is one of the many reasons the area has been designated a World Surfing Reserve (WSR). In a short stretch of coastline there are dozens of quality breaks, some of which are world-class. The idea behind World Surfing Reserves, which are designated by the Save

---

* 'The Guardian' by José Queiroz was unveiled on 25 March 2017, to celebrate the dedication of Ericeira as a World Surfing Reserve.

the Waves Coalition, is to preserve the waves, first and foremost, but also to protect the landscapes around them, promote best practice and ensure water quality remains excellent. Ericeira was designated in 2011 and was the second reserve after the spiritual home of modern surfing, Malibu, which was designated in 2010.*

I love the idea of surfing reserves. Where there are no protections in law, from marine protected areas or national parks, the reserves provide a platform from which locals and surfers can work together to protect the places they love. They add clout to environmentalism. They can also help to police the line-ups by allowing surfers to grade themselves for the types of waves available: information on the breaks is readily available, which helps to sort surfers into abilities, so stopping incompetent surfers from surfing dangerous waves. As long as it happens it is a good thing.

However, it is inevitable that becoming a WSR will bring more visitors and put more surfers in the water.

Proof, if proof were needed, came the next morning when I paddled out at Praia de Ribeira d'Ilhas for a session before breakfast. There were probably around 30 people in the water, most of whom were surfing on (I assume, rented) foamies. The waves were small but still fun, with a few bigger sets. I paddled out just to get a taste for what it was like to be in a crowd but ended up catching a lot of waves. The majority of the surfers were not really catching or trying to catch waves. The few who knew what they were doing – and who were riding big boards – caught all the best waves. I enjoyed the session immensely, more than I thought I would, and was really pleased that I had paddled out, but I did wonder why half of them had. Was it to be seen in the line-up? Or was it just about bragging rights?

Perhaps their thinking was, if you are going to surf, do it in Ericeira, at Praia de Ribeira d'Ilhas, despite Portugal having hundreds of other, more beginner-friendly places to surf.

When I was changing on the beach I noticed a guy wearing his wetsuit back to front. He was oblivious, strutting about like he was 'Da Cat' himself, the zip open like a catsuit. I guess that tells you all

---

* The 5th World Surfing Reserve is Huanchaco in Peru. It is considered to be the home of the *caballito de totora*, the first surf craft made from reeds.

you need to know. But there is such a huge chasm between learning and being able to catch and surf good waves. Some people — like me — spend their lives trying to bridge that gap.*

We cycled in to Ericeira for breakfast and sat in the Praça Republica, a cobbled square lined with pollarded plane trees for shade, watching the comings and goings of tourists, surfers and locals. It seemed to me that it was a relaxed, easy place to be. I heard lots of different accents and voices as people ordered food and chatted at the tables around us. I could have stayed longer: another lifetime maybe.

Before we left, I went into the tourist office to look at an exhibition about the surfing reserve. It seemed to me that surfing had combed its hair, put on a suit and grown up. Here in Ericeira the reserve was helping to preserve the environment, ensure people were learning responsibly and giving everyone the best chance at enjoying waves to suit their ability. How different it was from the days of struggling to learn, of making mistake after mistake and taking years to master the basics. Of having wetsuits that were too cold and stiff or boards that were too short and too difficult to ride. Of having to explore and find waves without guide books or the internet. Of being an outsider because of surfing. Of being ridiculed for being a surfer. Of being told to get a proper job. Of being told that 'you won't make a living out of that'.

I wondered if I had got it wrong, and instead of thinking the past was better — because a small number of surfers had had the waves to themselves — were the golden days of surfing happening right now? Barring the Doras and the breakdown of surfing etiquette at some places, was surfing enjoying a day in the sun where everyone could get their share if they wanted to?

Everything was laid on in Ericeira — as well as in Baleal, Zarautz, Biarritz and beyond. And was that better?

Or were the *tontons*, pioneers and forefathers the lucky ones? I was conflicted.

The distance from Ericeira to the Orbitur Campsite at Cascais was only 53km but we still managed a hefty Scafell Pike of climbing in the Parque Natural de Sintra-Cascais, a national park covering the bulbous part of Portugal to the west of Lisbon and the Tagus.

---

* That said, I did master putting my wetsuit on the right way round on day one.

After Ericeira we had been forced inland into the park and didn't see the sea again for another 35km until Azenhas do Mar, a tiny village perched on the edge of a cliff and with a small sandy bay at the bottom of a steep-sided river valley. We stopped, planning to have a swim in the sea to cool off after a tough ride.

We locked the bikes and walked down the steps to the beach. At the bottom we found an oval tidal pool, about 50 metres across, overlooked by the terrace of a restaurant with tables shaded by palm frond umbrellas. Below the tidal pool a small sandy beach was backed by high cliffs. Looking over the beach and pool, tiny whitewashed houses sat on top of each other in a hotchpotch of clay-tiled roofs, windows and balconies.

Azenhas do Mar was the kind of place that I dream of. It had all the elements of our home in Bude – restaurants, surf and a tidal pool – but it was wildly different. I imagined a twinning scheme where Lizzy and I got to spend six months here and six months at home. Great surf was close by at Ericeira and the pool would be cool on hot days.

We stripped off and swam away the stress of the close-passing cars, the climbs and the dust and dirt roads. I would have enjoyed it more but the spectre of another climb was casting shadows. We dipped and dried off and then set off again, this time with legs ready for the toughest climb in a few days, a bitch of a hill on the smooth and curly N247 through beautiful countryside with far-reaching views of the sea and some fuckwit drivers making it all a bit more miserable and terrifying than it needed to be. Interestingly, some Swiss drivers, driving bloated, overpriced cars, were among the worst offenders.

When I sat down to write up my notes that night I worked out that we had passed the 3000km mark just outside Peniche. We had survived so far. We deserved a good night's sleep.

We got one, until 3 a.m., when we were woken by terrible screaming.

32

The first waves

'It is only from this distance – now that everything has changed – that we can see the significance of these moments. They happen so frequently but are moments of great change – a meeting of cultures with a common aim.'
DIARY ENTRY: THURSDAY 1 AUGUST 2024

Stage 31: Days 69–71 | From: Guincho | To: Setúbal (via Lisbon and Costa da Caparica) | Distance: 98km

Our tent was pitched at the back of the camping area, adjacent to the toilet block at the Orbitur site at Guincho. The site was the nearest we could find to Cascais, a town on the Portuguese Riviera, a few miles to the west of Lisbon that is a tourism hotspot. It has been home to royalty and is the wealthiest area in Portugal in terms of house prices (not that we were looking) and has several winter waves when the swell gets huge to the west.

We had booked in for two nights so we could have a day out in Cascais.

Things didn't start well.

The first night was terrible. Camping often put us in close contact with other people in ways that we might not choose. They might be small irritations, like someone using an electricity point that was designated to us, but often nothing more than just annoyances. On this occasion we were confronted with something awful, and had no idea what we could do about it, if anything. In the thick, black night, surrounded by people we didn't know, it was terrifying.

THE WAY OF THE WAVES

I was woken by a child screaming and crying. It sounded like it was coming from right outside our tent. But, as sound carries on quiet campsites, it was probably about 10 metres away. I could hear a woman, whom I assume was the mother, trying to calm the child, gently at first but then becoming more demanding and threatening as the child continued to cry. She said, '*um dois três. Shhh.*' Then I heard a slap. It wasn't loud, and I wasn't sure if that was what I heard. Lizzy woke up. I whispered, 'Did you hear that?'

The child continued to cry. The mother said the same thing, '*um dois três. Shhh.*' We waited for what would come next. This time the slap was louder and harder and the child screamed.

I said loudly, 'Stop hitting your child.'

The crying continued. Another, louder slap.

I shouted it this time, if only to wake everyone up and make them aware of what was happening. 'STOP HITTING YOUR CHILD.'

'What if someone comes, for us?' whispered Lizzy.

'I can't let that happen without saying something.'

'I know. But what else do we do?'

I heard people stir and someone unzipped their tent and walked around outside. Lizzy and I lay still: hot and tense as the footsteps seemed to get closer. I was afraid. We were trapped in our hot, airless tent: it was oppressive and unpleasant. Would the violence come to us? Would anybody else do anything?

A few people got up and talked quietly outside in Portuguese, then it went quiet.

We left at first light to wash away the horror, at Praia do Guincho, a beach break down the hill from the campsite. The waves were small and punchy and it was busy: there were about 50 people in the water. The local Dora was there too. He was big-jawed and handsome and hacked at the waves with an aggressive style like he was slashing at a piece of meat with a cleaver. He paddled for everything, so, when a set came and it became clear we would both be going for it, I paddled away.

Perhaps, I thought, I should have stood up to the bullies?

The morning was beautiful and warm, with a light haze over the sea and bright sunshine breaking through. Behind the beach the hills were lush and green and dotted with villas. As always, surfing had brought a little calm and peace to us, but I doubted it could help the child. I felt terrible. What could we do? Call the Guarda? Perhaps

THE FIRST WAVES

that's what we should have done. Corporal punishment is illegal in Portugal but what good would that do in the middle of the night?

We caught the bus into Cascais and spent the day doing tourist things: eating posh pastries, walking down narrow streets, visiting ancient sites. The whole nine yards.

In the evening we arranged to meet João Luís Moraes Rocha and his daughter, Maria, at the campsite bar. João is a historian, writer and high court judge, but first and foremost a surfer. He was born in 1955 and grew up in the Estoril area, west of Lisbon, close to a lot of surfing beaches. He was quietly spoken and thoughtful.

When João was young he surfed on bellyboards and with air mattresses, using flippers to get into the waves. Bellyboarding had been practised in the area since the 1920s. João told me:

> I tried with flippers but the waves in Carcavelos are very powerful. They stand tall with a lot of power and I lost one of my flippers. My father said I will never give you another pair of flippers!

João and his brothers were excellent swimmers, which was a rare thing in Portugal at the time, and they competed for their local swimming club. When they began to surf – with boards bought from travelling British surfers – their friends from the club joined them.

> It was '71 that I started to surf with a board. That was the beginning for me and two of my brothers and a friend that lived in the same place. He speaks very good English because his mother worked in the American Embassy, here in Portugal. It was useful for us because if we speak with people, we can ask if they want to sell a board, a piece of wax, a leash. And it started from there.
>
> Our boards were from British surfers. The second board was from an American but my brother got a John Conway.

John Conway, a hugely influential figure in British surfing, was responsible for setting up *Wavelength* magazine in 1981 and for bringing professional surfing competitions to Newquay. In 1986 the Fosters competition at Fistral Beach was won by Tom Curren on his way to winning his second world title. John and João were friends for a long time, with Conway visiting Portugal each year. Conway died in 2003.

While João and his brothers were not the first surfers in Portugal – from the 1940s a few people had tried to surf there but it never went anywhere – they were the first group to take it seriously, discovering new waves and studying the conditions that made them work. They began their surfing in Carcavelos, then were joined by others in São Pedro do Estoril and then Peniche. As part of their surfing they explored their own country, travelling further to the north and surfing at Nazaré, Ericeira and Peniche.

Being a good club and competition swimmer, João was asked to work as a lifeguard at the area's more dangerous beaches during the 1970s. Until then the lifeguards weren't always great swimmers and used boats to get to swimmers in trouble. Once João and his brothers started lifeguarding, they began using boards to make rescues:

> We were very well paid. It was very good because we were lifeguards. We could surf and have money. Before, there were a lot of drownings. I went to Ericeira because the lifeguard died in the year before rescuing a family. The family died and he died. And in Costa Caparica the same thing happened. They asked me and my brother to go there because the lifeguards weren't able to rescue people.

Travelling and surfing put João into contact with other travelling surfers – Graeme Bunt, for example, in Ericeira in the winter of 1972 – but two that he remembers most clearly were Mike Doyle, an influential American surfer who surfed Malibu in the early days and, like Miki Dora, was an extra in the movie *Gidget*, and Mike Tabeling, Florida's first surfing superstar.

> Mike Doyle went to Carcavelos one day with a longboard. And Carcavelos is difficult to ride with a longboard. I was surfing and I saw him make one wave so I paddled in to be able to see how he surfed. It was the same with Mike Tabeling in Ericeira. We were surfing and I saw him take off. I had to see it so I went to the beach and I stayed there to see, to learn.

I wanted to ask João about the political situation in Portugal before and after 1974 and how it affected surfers and surfing – he would have been 19 at the time of the Carnation Revolution. I had read a fascinating piece by Alan Bleakley, a friend and colleague of John Conway and father of multiple European longboard champion Sam, in *Wavelength* magazine, about travelling to Portugal in 1970, four years before the Estado Novo was overthrown. In his piece Alan had written about being spat at and having stones thrown at him in Ericeira, just, he assumed, because he had long hair and was, therefore, a communist and enemy of the people. His surfboard, which he had had to pay freight charges for (bribes, he said) to take on the train, went missing somewhere between Madrid and Lisbon and was never seen again. João confirmed this attitude:

> Before '74 we had problems. If you wanted to carry a surfboard on a train, it was considered merchandise. We had to pay for the board by weight. It was so difficult. Before that, they said we cannot go with surfboards into the train because surfboards are merchandise and the train is only for people.
>
> People didn't understand what we were doing. It was the same with lifeguarding. It was only when we started to save lives that people changed their view.

Surfing was different from what society expected of its young people. Its acceptance depended upon proving its worth, like the surfers saving the fishermen in Mundaka. Those who had to graft each day couldn't see where its purpose lay. There was no money to be made from it. There was no industry to support it. There was nothing to it – back then – except pleasure. Life, under Salazar or Franco, wasn't about pleasure.

> One day, I was wearing a surf T-shirt. The director of my university – who had a high regard for me because I was studying in two universities at the same time – said, 'João, your T-shirt is not compatible with the people.'
>
> In '74 it changed. There were more surfers and younger people started to choose surf clothes.

With no surfing infrastructure to speak of, no surf shops and no manufacturers of surfing equipment or accessories in Portugal, or even in Spain, getting hold of surfwear or boards wasn't easy. As had happened in other places, the British surf industry was happy to oblige:

> I asked David Harewood from Freedom Surfboards in Jersey. And then Bruce Palmer in Cornwall. I went first to Jersey to speak with David Harewood, and I was there in the shaping room. He came to Portugal two or three times with a lot of surfboards. I kept most of the boards and sold them to my friends. It was the same with Bruce Palmer. I went there. We shaped one or two boards and then he came with a lot of boards.

And wetsuits?

> In the beginning wetsuits were a problem. Because the guys that came here and left them were much bigger than us. We cut the wetsuits and sewed them up but they let water in.

I asked João whether he thought the surf reserve was good or bad for surfing in Portugal. He replied:

> I think the difference was made with the schools. When the schools started, the number increased with a different speed. Differently from before. Before it increased but it increased slowly. With the schools, it exploded. It's my feeling. Now it's a show-off sport. It's important for the young people. The standard of surfing has dropped.

It made me think. With surfing made 'easier' by being more accessible to more people through surf schools, surf reserves and better equipment does the standard of surfing – and therefore its rules and unwritten constraints – drop? It seems inevitable. If it's tough, like it was for the first surfers, then it stands to reason that only the dedicated will continue to excellence.

But with more people surfing and a more democratic attitude to it, doesn't that push the standards even higher because those with natural talent – who may not have had the money or wherewithal to start in the 1970s or 1980s – can learn? In the same way that everyone having camera phones pushes up the quality of photography. Or does that just mean more shit pictures? Does privilege make you a better surfer? Or does the struggle make you better?

Meeting João was a joy. His love for surfing was infectious. But I couldn't help thinking that he was like the me of a few years ago, seeking out the quiet places and the forgotten corners because modern surfing was bringing more and more people. At the time I wanted to surf alone, with no competition or the intrusion of others, because I felt, as a surfer, an outsider. I wanted to be that again, even when surfing became mainstream. To be back there, being different, instead of following the crowd and doing something just because it was fashionable, was everything.

For about 15 years, from 1998 to 2013, I actively sought out uncrowded surf. I lived in a corner of Devon with inaccessible or difficult-to-predict waves. Getting to know them – and surfing them when they were at their best and quietest – became an obsession. I became friends with a few surfers doing the same thing. My friend and neighbour, fearless twin-fin rider, Simon, and I surfed a few waves that the wider surfing rabble knew little about or could be bothered to walk to. We started going out on boats to get to waves that took two hours to reach on foot. There were no cameras at any of these sessions and I have little record of any of the waves surfed or times had. They were great days, but always tinged with anxiety that someone else would discover us or come trotting down the coastal path, so shattering the peaceful exhilaration of surfing great waves alone.

In 2013 I moved down the coast, partly to get my kids into a better primary school. It meant I had to learn a whole new set of beaches and rules. I could still travel to surf with Simon, but lack of time, thanks to work, kids and an inevitable divorce, made me an occasional visitor to beaches I had loved.

When Lizzy and I got together I started to surf in Bude with a crew of veterans she had met. Their aims were different, with community, having a good time and mutual support more important than tubes or big waves. My attitude – which was about being secretive and selfish – shifted and I began to enjoy being in the water with lots of people I knew.

Surfing was great therapy for the vets,* although some of them, regretfully, didn't make it. We paddled out in the harbour in Bude to sit in a circle and remember them. When our friend Paul died from skin cancer about 50 of us splashed the water after his funeral, flowers between our teeth. His close friends devised a fancy-dress surfing competition to remember him.

In those moments community was everything. Everyone looked after everyone else. Lizzy began to surf with the vets because she was alone and needed a support network. I surfed with them to join in and be part of something I had lost by moving house.

Surfing became a paradox. Both selfish and giving, its soul, I decided, would have to be capable of living in two places at once. I surfed with the crowd and occasionally, when I had the time, went back to the quiet beaches.

After another tense night in the campsite, I was glad to move on. There hadn't been any obvious physical cruelty, but plenty of crying. Being there felt strained, dark and unhappy. We simply didn't know how to deal with the situation. I felt the cloying misery that comes from parental violence and menace. For the child, we knew, there was nowhere safe to go.

In the early morning we hitched up the trailers, let down the air beds, rolled up the sleeping bags and hit the road.

Being on the bike, though not resolving anything, felt like freedom and light.

Freewheeling down the steep hill to the beach at Guincho, we followed the cycle path around the bulbous headland of Cabo Raso, past the lighthouse and through a landscape that looked like it was in the process of regenerating. Low scrubby bushes filled the gaps between tall, pointed succulents on the undulating dunes of the

---

* There have been numerous studies suggesting that surfing is good for mental health as well as physical health. The rise of organisations like The Wave Project, a project for disabled and disadvantaged children, proves this beyond all doubt. Surfing increases confidence, provides dopamine and adrenaline and reduces stress, providing a close contact with nature.

landward side. On the seaward side low cliffs dropped into the sea behind dusty tracks, disused buildings and pathways. The sun was hot and it was a good day to cycle. The rushing air, created by constantly moving, kept me from overheating. As we approached Cascais the landscape gave way to resorts, hotels and villas, high-rise apartment blocks and cobbled roundabouts, the path leading us to the waterfront and a bike shop being looked after that day by José, the saint.

José, a cheerful and enthusiastic cyclist and bike mechanic, presided over a beautifully tidy and clean bike shop on Cascais's swanky Marina. The bikes on sale were expensive and light, the e-bikes state of the art, the workshop area spotless. The shops either side of it sold expensive clothes or nautical clobber for wealthy boaters.

We bought a couple of new tyres for Lizzy's trailer and fitted them while José did his best to true Lizzy's front wheel. Some of the spokes were loose and it was staring to buckle again, the result of the falls in Spain. While José worked his magic in the air-conditioned workshop we changed the tyres on the trailer, squatting in the shade down an alley at the side of the bike shop.

Cycling away, through the busy, touristy streets of Cascais, was surreal. Squinting into the brightness with sweat dripping into my eyes, I was hyper aware of the surroundings and yet I felt disconnected, as if I was riding through a film of my own life taking place somewhere far away from my own experience.

The Paseo Maritimo leaving Cascais was a dream. A green-painted path took us along the coast, past the beaches at São Pedro do Estoril and Carcavelos where Portuguese surfing had begun and flourished, despite the disapproval of the Establishment.

There was no surf and it was hot. We bought supplies in a backstreet supermarket and while I ate my lunch under the wispy shade of a tamarisk overlooking the calm, waveless water, I looked at my phone. The summer, according to Surfline, had been poor for Europe, with few swells and a lot of wind.

We weaved our way along the coast, taking back roads to avoid motorways or the railway, using cycle lanes behind the beaches when they allowed or gritting our teeth and gripping our handlebars and taking to the dual carriageways when there was no alternative. We passed the Torre de Belém, a florid, mediaeval fortress overlooking the Tagus River, and the Monument to the Discoveries, a huge concrete and stone monument celebrating the Portuguese age of discovery in the 15th and 16th centuries, set on the wide-open spaces of the regenerated quaysides busy with tourists, hawkers and stalls selling jugs of sangria. In the background, the 25 April Bridge, a huge 2km suspension bridge, framed everything.

I felt a little sad that we wouldn't be cycling the final few kilometres into Lisbon because I wanted to enjoy the feeling of having made it there. But there was a ferry at Belém that would take us across the Tagus to Trafaria and save us the trouble of having to navigate the city. That part was a relief.

The security guard looking after the gate at the ferry terminal saw us coming. He must have known we would need help because he sprang into action, checking with the captain if he could take our boards (thankfully, a yes), showing us where to buy tickets and where to get on to the boat. He opened a huge gate to make it easier for us to embark and held up the ferry while we wrangled the bikes aboard, even helping us to lift them on to the ramp. As always, I was surprised by the help we had received from the crew. We hadn't once been turned away from a ferry because our bikes were difficult. In fact, it appeared to be a matter of pride that they help us and make our crossing as easy as possible.

After the beach bars, Paseo Maritimo and smart beachfronts of Carcavelos, Cascais and Estoril, Trafaria, the place where we disembarked, was grubby and industrial, with dirty, unmade streets, a filthy-looking beach and an enormous industrial facility with huge cranes and silos on a scrappy dockside. We cycled into Costa da Caparica, a beach town on the southern side of the Tagus, and pitched up at another Orbitur campsite. This time we chose a pitch with plenty of space. Even with shade from the pines, it was sandy and hot.

We walked to the beach – Lizzy said it was like Littlehampton with sunshine – and went for a swim, then ordered a beer in a shuttered shipping container turned into a bar on the busy beachfront. The beach at Costa Caparica is 13km long, divided at regular intervals by stone jetties. Each section of beach between the jetties had a beach bar and surf school that was almost identical. A cycle path and walkway ran along the beach as far as we could see to the south. It was busy with cyclists, runners and walkers. We watched as a woman having a one-to-one surf lesson in the tiny waves paddled herself in and stood up for the first time. She was elated and whooped with joy.

While that day had been short – only 43km – the last week or so we had regularly been putting in days of 60–70km, with the longest day being 77km.* I wasn't tired with surfing – I enjoyed being able to share the woman's elation – but with the constant challenge of finding our way, putting up the tent, blowing up the bed, cooking and shopping for supplies (which we had to do almost daily). My knee had begun to hurt when I put pressure on it, particularly when climbing, although it had been almost completely flat that day. It was painful when I walked too. Perhaps, I thought, I hadn't given myself enough time to heal. The surgeon had said he'd have me on a bike in six months. I had given it 18. Surely that was plenty? Maybe the cartilages and ligaments had had enough of being abused and were fighting back. Knees are complicated things.

'Fuck's sake, Martin,' they were saying. 'Give us a break. First you twist us the way we don't want to go and some bits of us break and snap and tear, then you put us under the knife, where we get snipped and trimmed, and then you won't sit still, then you try to surf, then you make us pedal you for – what is it now? – 3200km. On top of that you make us bend down and stand up again almost every night and morning to make breakfast, blow up your stupid bed, cook your rubbish meals and crawl into your grubby sleeping bag.'

'Sorry. Just a few more days, lads.'

'We'll believe it when we see it. You should have let us stay at home and laze about on the sofa.'

'No. Not that. Anything but that.'

---

* Our longest day so far had been 80.5km, and that was on the flat, back in Nantes.

33

Climbs don't last forever

'It's been a shit day. The worst yet. We crossed the Sado on a ferry. It all went downhill from there.'
INSTAGRAM POST: FRIDAY 2 AUGUST 2024

Stage 32: Days 72–73 | From: Costa da Caparica | To: Porto Covo | Distance: 103km

Portugal was turning out to be tough. After 10 weeks of cycling and camping – almost every day – we were tired. The distances we had covered weren't particularly far in the grand scheme of ambitious, record-breaking cycling adventures, but they were still taking their toll. As we got fitter, the distances we covered became greater and the further south we travelled, the more difficult the cycling conditions seemed to get. We were also becoming acutely aware of our deadline. We had just a week or so until we were due in to Sagres. There was little time to hang about.

Finding our way in Portugal was harder than it had been in Spain or France too. We were supposed to be following the EuroVelo 1 but the signage was unreliable, which meant we had to plot our own routes and hope they would take us down roads that were passable. Away from the main roads they were rough and difficult to ride. On the main roads we felt vulnerable.

But there were, every day, moments of great beauty and joy. The colours in the scrub. The warm evenings. The beaches and the surf. The freedom I felt riding my bike. The swims on hot days. The coastal scenery. Watching road workers lay limestone cobbles with incredible artistry. Pockets of tranquil beauty in deep valleys. A welcoming smile at a campsite. Connections with people who wanted to stop and chat. Our support for each other in difficult times. And *pastéis de nata*.*

I never knew when one or more of these joys would turn up, which made them more alluring and delicious when they did. After a tough climb, a long dusty track or an unnerving encounter with a car, these small, positive things took on a greater significance. Being open-hearted and positive seemed to make them come easier too. I guess that's what you'd call PMA (positive mental attitude).

Mostly it's about understanding that climbs don't last forever.

The cycle path out of Costa da Caparica was one of those tiny gifts I was prepared to accept with grateful knees. It was smooth and easy and ran for about 5km south until it headed inland and joined a road that ran parallel to the beach for another 5km. The runners were out, rarely smiling, the walkers were walking their dogs without a care in the world and the cyclists were rolling along in the sun. There was a little surf too. The surf schools were busy with students lying on their boards in the sand, practising popping up or waiting in the shallows for the next wave.

Surfing, it seemed, was a big thing on the Costa da Caparica. Was the next world champion one of those who were taking a lesson today? It was a possibility.

Inevitably, the path fizzled out and took us over a sandstone cliff into a series of villages. They were places of great contrast, as usual, with new houses sitting side by side with derelict, fly-tipped plots where sofas and mattresses rotted away next to assorted household crap. I wondered why. Was it apathy caused by deprivation? A form of collective depression? Laziness? Snobbery? Lack of infrastructure? It was hard to know.

Our way across the Parque Metropolitano da Biodiversidade, an area of forest with tracks that should have taken us directly across the

---

* Warning: Portugal has fantastic coffee and pastry shops. They sell a vast array of cakes and pastries, many of which have yet to make their name in the outside world. There is a reason for this. On more than one occasion Lizzy's cake-loving eyes would spy 'something different' that would be inedible (but delicious to the Portuguese, no doubt). Stick with the familiar and you won't be disappointed.

peninsula to Setúbal, was blocked by a locked gate that we couldn't see a way through, under or around. This sent us off on a big detour around the forest on local roads and eventually on to a motorway junction with screaming traffic. We pulled off a busy roundabout into a half-finished side road under a flyover and tried to fathom how we were going to make our way through without taking a wrong turn on to one of the two motorways running above our heads. Whichever way we turned, it seemed, lay terror. Using our phones to navigate the detail of the complicated junction, we worked out the only way we could go was along the N738 on a section of hellish dual carriageway with slip roads to the motorways and no hard shoulder. We had little choice but to grip the bars and pedal. Of all the frightening moments, this was the worst. Huge, unforgiving articulated lorries roared past us constantly.

Eventually the junctions petered out and we came to a series of suburban villages with confusing grid systems of one-way roads. In one we came across the aftermath of an accident. From a distance I saw a few cars and something in the road, and when we got closer, we could see a smashed-up motorbike, the rider lying in the road with a woman holding an umbrella over him to shade him from the sun. A few people were standing around, their cars blocking the road, on their phones.

It was a timely reminder of our vulnerability and we rode past slowly, not wanting to rubberneck. We might get angry at drivers for passing us too closely or take risks to try to stop them from driving dangerously around us but, as we knew, it would always be us who came off worse in any physical altercation: the cyclist always dies.

A steep, quiet road took us out of the villages and into the Serra do Louro, a short and sharp mountain chain on the north banks of the Sado River. We passed farms and vineyards as the road bounced along into quiet valleys and over dry river beds. We joined the N10 for a long climb before taking a right turn towards the coast and our campsite for the night. The turn-off took us into a steep valley shaded by a glorious, riotous forest of cork oak, chestnut, strawberry trees and huge palms. This was another gift. A few moments of peaceful riding that brought us out on to the coast road between Sesimbra and Setúbal at a small inlet where a few families were eating lunch at a series of picnic tables while kids played in the shallow water.

Our campsite, an eco-park on the north side of the Sado River's mouth, looked out over the Tróia peninsula, a long, thin sandbank that forms the southern bank of the river mouth. At its tip there were a few high-rise hotels and some apartment blocks. We set up the tent and went for a swim in the bay next to the campsite. As the sun set, the buildings shimmered across the water, a Docklands in the sun, its incongruous hulks perched on the tip of the sand spit like a tax haven.

The cycle into Setúbal to catch the ferry was an easy 5km, followed by a stop at a *panadería* for breakfast at the port. The 20-minute journey took us across the mouth of the Sado to Tróia and the N253-1, the only road down the peninsula. From here we would follow the coast to the town of Sines and then into the Parque Natural do Sudoeste Alentejano e Costa Vicentina* for the final few kilometres of our journey. That was still 200km away.

The ride to Comporta, the village at the base of the peninsula, was hot and scary, with the only saving grace being the northerly wind helping to blow us along and keep us cool. And that it was flat. Everything else about it was awful: the sun was baking and the road ran almost straight, through a landscape of sand dunes with the occasional umbrella pine. On the first section we cycled past exclusive gated holiday communities and a golf resort but soon we were on our own, being terrorised by oversized saloons and growling lorries. There were no margins, only deep sand at the roadside, which meant we couldn't pull off to avoid the speeding cars. I spent a lot of the ride feeling scared.

Comporta was a pleasant surprise at the neck of the peninsula. The village centre was busy, with good-looking, well-dressed families and sun-dried locals in straw hats. Expensive-looking shops sold raffia and floaty dresses. At the Casa da Cultura, a long, whitewashed building with green doors and blue details, an art and craft market and fruit and veg stalls were attracting the crowds. This enclave was unlike anything else we had experienced in Portugal so far and had a cool, laidback, posh-Cornwall-meets-good-weather kind of vibe. I liked it and would have happily checked into the nearest Airbnb with

---

* National Park of Alentejo and Coast of Saint Vincente.

wispy white curtains and a fridge full of beer and Instagrammed the absolute hell out of it.

But no. Instead, we bought some supplies and pedalled away from the place that Forbes called 'Portugal's coolest place to holiday'* on more hot and dusty roads. We stood up to eat lunch under the shade of an umbrella palm at the side of the road, setting out a sad picnic on the top of Lizzy's strongbox. We had eaten our lunch in some odd places but this was a new low, even for us when we could have enjoyed Portugal's coolest picnic in Comporta. Heavens knows why we didn't. I guess it was feeling the pressure of needing to crack on.

It wasn't bottom for long though. The only campsite within striking distance was a Portuguese camping club site at Melides, a town another 35km further on. The 'tented area' was a dusty corridor about 3 metres wide between rows of permanent pitches. Many of the caravans, sitting under canvas sunshades on metal frames, had been there for a while and about 90 per cent of them were unoccupied. Every inch of every pitch was covered, either with a grubby canvas awning or a plastic tarpaulin, as if nature was an affront to the camping experience. Awnings were 'pegged out' with lines of breeze blocks or with 5-litre water bottles filled with water, now green with algae. The electric points, wired in like spaghetti, looked like they could explode at any moment. We had found the place where holiday dreams go to die. Mine certainly did. I looked around forlornly while pumping up my mattress, wondering where it all went wrong.

We put up the tent and went off to find the pool. It was hidden away in a corner of the site and surrounded by a high wall. Walking through the gate was like entering into a completely different world. This was where they kept the joy that had been sucked out of the rest of the campsite. The grass was spongy and the pool was cool and clean. Seeing grass, after spending so much time in sandy scrub, on hot roads lined with prickly pear cactus or on dusty tracks, was wonderful. I don't think I have ever appreciated it quite so much.

---

* I found this out later. Apparently, according to the article, Garrett McNamara, of Nazaré fame, also runs a surf school out of Comporta.

CLIMBS DON'T LAST FOREVER

I lay on my back with my head in the shade of a tree and began to read my Kindle. Before long, my eyes started to droop. Apparently, I snored my way through the rest of the afternoon, waking only when Lizzy prodded me to let me know it was time to go back to our miserable pitch.

I spent the following morning looking at dead and forgotten stuff at the side of the road while we cycled towards Porto Covo, our next night's stop on the only road south. Along with the usual cans and bottles I saw Disney sunshades (more than one) and bits of cars. These included bumpers, wheels, windscreens, trim and hubcaps. Road kill was common although I was always startled by flat snakes, and they were only trumped by the sight of a bloated wild boar taking his last snooze in the margins.

The main road turned into a dual carriageway just outside Sines. Fortunately, it had a good, wide hard shoulder so we felt safe enough even though the traffic zoomed past. We pulled off to pick up some supplies from a service station just before the dual carriageway changed into the motorway, to some confused looks from people having coffee outside. It was an odd experience cycling into a motorway service station.

The last junction before the A26, a classic motorway junction with a roundabout on a flyover, took us down a deserted road running parallel to the motorway and then through farmland and over a cutting containing huge steel pipes feeding a vast oil refinery with huge red-and-white-striped, smoke-belching chimneys.

In Sines, the home of Vasco da Gama, we found a food festival on the seafront. We ordered a huge plate of prawns and chips and sat at one of the long refectory tables to eat it.

The rest of the day we spent cycling along the top of low cliffs on a road that weaved its way around gentle contours and past small rocky coves with gorgeous sands. The wind was still blowing from the north so the surf wasn't worth getting wet for, but I could see potential around every corner. I spotted what I thought could be point breaks and quality beach breaks where aquamarine waves broke scrappily on to rocky ledges or crashed on to white sand. Every so often we passed roadside stalls selling umbrellas, chairs, windbreaks, buckets and spades and rubber rings in bright colours.

The campsite pool at Porto Covo also had the benefit of lush green grass but the site couldn't have been more different from Melides. It was well cared for, with no seasonal pitches, and a mix of clientele from all over Europe. Once we had pitched up, washed our clothes and hung them up on makeshift clothes lines around our pitch, we made a beeline for the pool. True to form, I fell asleep in the shade of a tree.

I loved Porto Covo. After watching the sun go down in a glorious blaze of colour from one of the town's coves we cycled into the old town. The main street, which led towards the sea from the large square, was busy with restaurants, shops and bars. The streets were set out on a grid system, inspired by the rebuilding of Lisbon after the 1755 earthquake that razed much of the city. A small street market had set up around the square with stalls selling jewellery, local produce, clothes and trinkets. We sat outside a whitewashed bar and watched as a street magician entertained a crowd of excited kids.

For the first time in ages I felt as if I was on holiday. The last few days had been difficult and grubby and, now that my clothes were clean and I was able to relax, I felt so much better. The wind had dropped and the evening was warm. We were surrounded by happiness. Funny how that happens sometimes.

The climbs don't go on forever.

And there was the promise of surf in the morning.

34

Locals only?

'Set off this morning after a surf on dusty roads through hot and dry farmland. After 56km, we landed at Zambujeira, where we've got a chalet so we can get some rest before the last couple of days' riding. We have just 76km to go! Can't believe we are almost there.'
INSTAGRAM POST: SUNDAY 4 AUGUST 2024

Stage 33: Day 74 | From: Porto Covo | To: Praia de Zambujeira do Mar | Distance: 56km

Lizzy and I were the first on the beach in the morning. Mind you, at 3 a.m., when the music was still blaring out from the town square, it sounded like the whole of Porto Covo had been out partying. If they had a hangover then we were the grateful beneficiaries.

The air was still and warm and the sea was dark, with a light mist hanging over it. A few fishing boats bobbed about offshore. The sun, just about rising above the cliff, lit up a line of palm-frond sunshades, creating long, pointed shadows that looked like magic mushrooms.

The waves were around head high, with the occasional set breaking a little bigger. Most of the waves were closing out but the occasional one would feel the rip and stay open, running into the middle of the beach. Despite little wind the swell was still wobbly from the night before, with the best waves breaking below the cliff at the south end of the beach occasionally breaking left into the bay. I paddled out cautiously because I didn't know anything about the beach, but I didn't want to miss the opportunity to surf before the Nortada wind got up and ruined it completely. Duck-diving the sets flushed my wetsuit with cool water and was easier than I thought. I have never been a good duck-diver and always dread it, having to remind myself it wasn't that bad after the first one goes off without a hitch.

I sat on my board just beyond the whitewater. From there I had a different view of the cliffs and beach. I could see into the next bay, where the waves were still crashing against the rocks. To the north I could just about see the red-and-white chimney of the refinery at Sines. I saw people running along the cliff path and the fiery red patches of succulents trailing over the cliff edge. The sandstone cliffs were white, yellow, grey and brown and, where the sun hit them, were lit up in deep, early-morning orange. Lizzy paddled out too, and sat on the right-hand side of the beach, looking for something to surf.

I caught a couple of good waves, making the drop and getting a couple of turns in before they shut down. I was happy. Surfing with bikes wasn't easy: always relying on pot luck to score good waves. Backtracking wasn't possible. We either surfed and were grateful for it, or we didn't surf at all.

This conflict – between keeping moving and waiting for the waves to improve – was ever-present. Most often our deadline had the upper hand and we had to keep moving. I found that frustrating sometimes, especially if I liked somewhere, like Porto Covo.

But would it have been better to stay put or keep moving? Summer had been poor for surf across Europe. The north wind had helped us but it hadn't generated any good surf. While other surfers might have been 'frothing' for bigger waves or better conditions, I was content with what I had found, even if all I saw was potential.

We caught a couple more and then headed into the village to find breakfast.

The way out of Porto Covo took us down a steep hill to the harbour, past neat rows of tiny whitewashed fishermen's cottages and stores, and to the creek running into the back of the harbour. We were about to turn back, thinking that it was leading us to another horrendous goose chase, when a car came down the steep track opposite and crossed the river. OK then! If they can get through, so can we. We cycled across the river, up the steep track and on to another long dirt track that followed the coast for a few kilometres then headed inland through plantations of pine trees, becoming rough and stony with sections of deep sand that we had to push through. A short spell on a main road – it was quiet because it was Sunday – led us into an area of back roads that felt isolated and quiet. We passed huge farms with endless polytunnels full of vegetables, squashes, beans and raspberries.

We bought food in Vila Nova de Milfontes, a surfy beach town 20km south of Porto Covo, but didn't stop to check the surf, even though it's a town with a growing reputation for surfing. There are surf lodges and surf schools and, apparently, a 'good selection of breaks for all abilities'. It seemed as if almost every car had a board on top and every person walking the streets was barefoot, with long hair, boardshorts and surfing tees. They fitted the mould perfectly.

In the distance, as we rode out of Milfontes along another long, straight road, we could see, for the first time, the green hulk of the Serra de Monchique, a small mountain range between us and the south coast of the Algarve. It was the first visible sign that we were nearing the end. I felt elated that we were close to achieving what we had set out to do, but sad that it was coming to a close.

I had mixed feelings about taking the keys for the chalet from the receptionist at Camping Villa Park Zambujeira at Praia de Zambujeira do Mar too. Part of me wanted to chill out and relax and was glad to delay the inevitable, but another part felt like I was letting myself down by choosing to check into bricks and mortar accommodation. Had we gone soft? Had we cycled all this way only to choose luxury over our lovely tented home?

Too right. It was boiling outside and the chalet – two rooms and a bathroom – was basic but cool inside, with a tiled floor and thick walls. We parked the bikes, lobbed everything inside, put on a clothes wash, lay on the bed in our pants, then dressed up in some of the clothes we hadn't worn yet, and hit the town.

Arriving in Praia de Zambujeira do Mar, initially, had felt like we had entered a forgotten frontier town. At the side of the road leading to the campsite there were tented roadside stalls selling rugs and cheap clothes. Single-storey properties, whitewashed and blue, with red-tiled roofs, sat between empty, sandy plots. There were few people around. But when we walked into the pedestrian heart of the village in search of a restaurant, I realised it was a special little place with a lovely beach at the bottom of a steep cliff and a relaxed, hippy feel about it. A bunch of bodyboarders were dropping in to a wedge-shaped left on the town's beach and having a lot of fun by the looks of it.

According to a website called Surf Atlas, Praia de Zambujeira do Mar is quiet, but has hollow, difficult waves and a crew of locals who aren't pleased to see visitors. On the page about Vila Nova de Milfontes they say, about Zambujeira, 'Try your luck, but as ever it's your cheekbone!' Great. So now there was a veiled threat of violence if you want to surf here. Is this OK? I guess it is for the locals who want to keep the waves to themselves, of course. In creating an atmosphere of menace and fear they get to surf alone. But then what happens when they want to surf somewhere else? Is it right that they should expect a warm welcome when they travel?

Is this what surfing is about? Does 'Da Cat' live on? Is that the soul of surfing? I hoped not.

The way I see it, surfing alone or with a few friends is great. You can enjoy a greater connection with nature, the surroundings and the waves if there are fewer distractions. Working hard – and by that I mean getting up early or making an effort to surf away from busy centres – can still be rewarded with empty surfs. But change is inevitable and today there are lots more people surfing. It's fact. That golden period, when our surfing elders had very little competition, is over. We should accept and embrace it. There should be no desire to go back there by creating a hostile environment.

There are undoubtedly more learners than competent surfers today than there were 10, 20 or 30 years ago. I could tell that from the boards I saw on cars in Portugal: most of them were soft tops, a type of board suitable for learning. Face up to it: surfing is no longer a niche sport.

Surfers who begrudge other surfers or who constantly feel like they have to defend their home spot must live a sad, angry existence. What joy are they getting from surfing if they must fight? Surfing is supposed to be fun. Even if waves at places like Zambujeira are for experts, then it should be up to the surf community to police them with kindness and a gentle guiding hand. Surf schools should take responsibility for ensuring their students understand etiquette* and the surf community should act as educators too. There is nothing wrong with teaching people the right way of doing things without malice.

Even if breaks have become crowded with learners – like João Luís Moraes Rocha said happened in Ericeira – or if too many surfers from outside are turning up and making life difficult for local surfers, there has to be a way of avoiding conflict rather than resorting to Dora-style tactics. Dora, and others like him, are not good role models.

I like surfing alone or with a few friends because I like to be able to have the pick of the waves. Most surfers do, I would say. But I also understand that my enjoyment of surfing doesn't have to be about wave count. It can also be about community. I enjoy seeing other people surf well and I particularly like seeing new-to-surfing surfers having good waves. Complimenting someone on a wave, showing restraint and respect or just striking up a friendly conversation isn't weakness. It could make someone's day and create good karma for later.

Lizzy and I ate local seafood at a restaurant overlooking the sea and watched the sun go down over the waves. I felt like I was on holiday again, and was revelling in the indulgence. Somewhere along the line, between the hills and the long, dusty roads, it seemed we may have forgotten that we were supposed to be on honeymoon.

---

* Years ago, I was surfing with Lizzy in Galicia. We were surfing a peak in a huge beach. A surf instructor paddled out with two Italians on a private lesson. I heard the instructor say to his clients, 'Don't worry about them. I will block for you.' Blocking is using the priority rule to block someone from dropping in so that someone else can go. It is bad form. To teach it is terrible. The Italians were lovely and chatted to us. I was happy to share waves with them. The instructor was an arsehole.

35

The last miles

'Toast. First toast since leaving home. Do not underestimate or undervalue the privilege you have and the things you take for granted. When they are gone you will notice . . . .'

INSTAGRAM POST: MONDAY 5 AUGUST 2024

Stage 34: Days 75–77 | From: Praia de Zambujeira do Mar | To: Sagres | Distance: 84km

Lizzy and I had been living in a bubble for almost three months. It was just us, the bikes, the boards and the road. We had spent precious time with people we really liked – Eugene, Nick and Abi, Ben, Howard and Laura – and they had helped us when we really needed it, but mostly it was just us. Sometimes it felt like we were under siege, with a crazy, perplexing world outside our little tent demanding our compliance or showing us life's underbelly. Sometimes we were invisible old people trying to surf among a soup of dudes: a midlife crisis on wheels. At other times we were a curiosity or object of ridicule: a rolling circus passing through. For some we were brave, and perhaps a little stupid.

Whatever we were, our legs had kept us pedalling and we had kept moving, existing in a world of campsites, badly made roads, silky-smooth bike lanes, mountains and dunes, lunch stops at beauty spots, surfing and bicycles.

Eating a slice of toast with butter, the first I had had since leaving home, made possible by staying in a chalet with a grill, on a campsite with a good grocery shop, made me realise that we were about to head back into the real world. I wasn't sure if I was ready. I had transitioned easily into the life of an international surfing cyclist and it felt natural and normal to ride my bike for four or five hours a day and to live meal-to-meal, day-to-day, hill-to-hill. I felt free and alive, if tired. What would it feel like to go home and have Marmite and toast whenever I liked, a real bed to sleep in and a fridge full of food?

My phone pinged with messages from the people staying in our house and the accountant: the hot water wasn't working and the VAT return needed signing.

I wanted the trip to change me and for those things to have a different significance. Yet I knew the bubble was about to burst. Real life was catching up.

After more toast and tea (first things first) we decided to make the most of the crisp white sheets and go back to bed. We were just about to succumb to our most intimate desires when we were caught – in flagrante delicto – by a loud knock at the door.

Pop! There goes that bubble.

'Shit. Who's that?' Lizzy whispered.

'No idea. Go and see.'

'You go.'

'Like this?'

Lizzy went to the door while I scrambled to find my shorts. I heard her laughing. Tim and Jo, the friends from home who were driving our van to Sagres so we could transport the bikes back home, had caught up with us.

'What were you two up to?' I heard Jo ask Lizzy coyly.

'Oh nothing,' replied Lizzy.

'Where's Mart?' Tim asked.

'I won't be a minute,' I shouted from the bedroom. I felt like it was my parents catching me shagging.

We weren't expecting to see Tim and Jo for a few days so it was a genuine – and very welcome – surprise to see them. They are good people to spend time with. Tim is great to surf with: he thrives off community and understands the meaning of 'blue therapy' beyond 'having a good surf'. He coaches and surfs with the veterans' group and takes time off work once a year to look after limbless vets who are learning to surf as part of their therapy. Jo also surfs, trains with the surf club and often surfs with Lizzy and their small group of women surfers. She's strong and independent, having brought up two children on her own before she and Tim got together. They live with some of their four kids near us in Bude.

Our rest day turned into a day of checking the surf (no good), beers by the campsite pool (good) and cooking dinner together (also good).

In the morning, over breakfast, we made a plan: we would meet up with Tim and Jo to catch up with a mutual friend, Mike Raven, ex pro surfer, and his wife Nicky, in Rogil, a small town inland from Arrifana, and then we would see them again at Sagres in a day's time. Lizzy wanted to have one last night of camping before everything changed. I could understand why. We were being dragged back to reality and she wanted to hang on to our existence for one more precious night.

We stayed at Camping Serrão, just outside Aljezur, for our last night under canvas. It was a huge campground with tennis courts and a pool, restaurant and bar. We pitched under mature eucalyptus trees, on a hard-packed patch of sand and stones that required us to bang our tent pegs in with a rock. I cooked an awful meal with everything we had left and, when we had struggled through it, retreated to the bar.

In the middle of the night I performed the 10-zip wriggle getting up to go to the loo. Despite never having stayed on the campsite before, I knew instinctively where to go, in the dark, without a torch, so used to being somewhere different each night that getting my bearings was instantaneous. I had developed an innate sense of direction by being a nomad. Lizzy was the same. What had become normal was nothing being the same.

The final day of cycling hit the dirt almost as soon as we had left the campsite. A deeply rutted, rocky track heading down a steep, forested hillside towards Aljezur had me off the bike and pushing before it could throw me off. It was too steep to risk riding, with loose stones and weathered ruts making it difficult to control the bike's weight. I pulled on the rear brake and followed the bike downhill as best I could, the back wheel skidding over the ruts and rocks and the trailer jangling behind. My knee ached terribly with the impact of walking downhill, each step giving me a painful jolt. I hoped it would hold out for the rest of the day. All it needed to do was another 50km.

THE LAST MILES

The road brought us out in the bottom of a river valley, where we crossed a bridge and found ourselves looking up at a steep cobbled road leading to the old village of Aljezur, a collection of whitewashed cottages built on the side of a hill, topped with a ruined 10th-century Moorish castle. Across the river, in the valley bottom, lay the new village, built after the 1755 Lisbon earthquake. The cobbled lane took us quickly upwards into the narrow streets of the old village. The layout was confusing and we messed about going up, down and sideways for some time, passing the same woman sweeping her front step a couple of times, before seeing a sign for the EuroVelo 1 – the first in days – which pointed up towards the castle and out of the village on a potholed back road. The views from the castle over the valley and to the river and white houses of the new village below were stunning. In the distance the hills of Monchique stood out against the blue sky: a wall of dark green forest.

If we had the appetite to cycle an extra 20km we could have headed towards Arrifana at this point but, having been told by Mike that it was one of Portugal's busiest surf spots, we decided to give it a miss, if only to save the riding. The wind was howling anyway. Arrifana had been home to an old friend from north Devon for a few seasons back in the early 2000s: he had slept in a cave on the beachfront, survived off fishing and surfed the right-hand point break off the harbour wall whenever it broke. I wanted to find the cave but, with Sagres in our sights, we had a deadline to meet.

After some road miles we entered a forest of young eucalyptus, following a rough track until we came out on a ridge with views all around. The further we went, the more remote it began to feel. In the valleys below us the canopy of the forest looked like a carpet of green bubbles. The road, a light yellow with dust and sand, stretched off into the distance over the spurs of rounded hills, following the contours and looking like something a child might draw. As we rode on the forest became thinner, with fewer trees. The last trees we saw, on a hillside above the road, were just burnt trunks, the result of a forest fire.

The north wind was strong and kept us cool, but when we dropped into a flat-bottomed river valley and rode into the pretty, whitewashed village of Carrapateira, where there was shelter, it was hot. We stopped for lunch at a vegan cafe, sitting in the shade and ordering tea, water and fruit juice while the sweat evaporated from our clothes. From there we rode more dirt roads, followed by a stretch on a hellish main road that took us into the last village before Sagres, Vila do Bispo.

Instead of following the main road into Sagres, a fast modern road with heavy traffic, the route took us out of Vila do Bispo on a pale-yellow dirt road up a steep hill that was exposed to the full force of the wind, which was now hitting us side-on. We had to steer into it to keep going straight. Lizzy said she was getting flashbacks of being bashed about by a constant wind when she had ridden for days on end across the Argentinian pampas. I was creating the flashbacks of the future.

The rolling landscape was stony, dry and desolate, with the odd villa or farmstead sitting at the centre of huge, hedgeless fields of dried-up grasses and finished crops. We had been riding through the heart of the Southwest Alentejo and Vicentine Coast Natural Park, one of the most isolated and wild places in Iberia, for a few days now but this was as wild as it had been at any point. Its beauty could not be denied, even though we passed ruins with roofs of broken tiles where dogs, tied up on long chains, barked at us ferociously as we went past. The last section, a dead straight with the sea shimmering at the end, took us downhill to meet the main road from Sagres to Cape Saint Vincent at a T-junction.

We turned right for the lighthouse on to a wide cycle path heading straight for the Cape. The wind slammed into us again, this time straight at us, making it difficult to keep moving. As it buffeted us relentlessly, we made slow progress along the slightly uphill, dead straight path. I almost fell off a couple of times when the wind caught the boards and pulled me sideways. The lighthouse, our point of focus for the last few kilometres, came into view and got steadily closer. To our left the ocean lay far below the vertical cliffs at the back of a couple of seemingly inaccessible coves. Wild white horses bucked and kicked offshore, the result of the wind blowing hard across the ocean.

Each turn of the pedals was tough. And each one brought a sharp pain in my knee. It had completed thousands, maybe hundreds of thousands, of revolutions over the last 77 days* and I hoped it

---

*I did a rough calculation: average cadence of 70 revolutions per minute x average four hours in the saddle each day x 72 days cycling = 1,209,600 revolutions.

wouldn't conk out at the last hurdle. It had put up with a lot beyond cycling too. I wouldn't have blamed it.

'Come on, knee, my old friend. Don't fail me now,' I said.

The wind howled and we made our way, slowly, towards the lighthouse, our eyes stinging with windborne sand and grit, our legs being exfoliated with every turn of the pedals. Sitting at the most south-westerly point of Europe, the light, when first illuminated in 1520, once marked the end of the known world. Beyond the lighthouse, which lay a few hundred metres in front of us, was the Atlantic. Beyond that, for many, until the 1500s, lay nothing.

The last vehicle before the lighthouse, blocking off most of the footpath, was our big grey camper van, parked sideways. Tim and Jo stood next to it, waving. As we approached, I saw they had rigged up a line of bunting from the bike rack to a sign post to make a finish line for us to cross. It made me laugh out loud.

Lizzy and I rolled over the line together and pulled up. We stood astride our bikes while a German family that Tim and Jo had corralled clapped.

'Oh my god!' I said to Lizzy. 'Oh my god. We did it!'

'We did!' she said.

'Well done!'

'Well done you! That was hard, but fucking amazing!'

'It was.'

'How's your knee?'

'What knee?'

Now that we had reached the end, the pain was forgotten. There was only joy. We had survived and, despite the difficulties, had had an absolute blast. I had found an inner strength that I didn't know I had and Lizzy got to remember what it's like to ride a bike for weeks on end. She did it with style, too, never flapping about distances or climbs. Her only weakness, steep descents, came from sharp, painful experience.

We had surfed and bellyboarded Europe's famous and not-so-famous waves, met some of surfing's elder statesmen and listened to stories of the golden days before surfing went mainstream. Between the surf schools and the crowds we had enjoyed some memorable sessions too, at Le Penon, Capbreton, Mundaka, Zarautz, Salinas, Playa de Merón, Praia de Ribeira d'Ilhas (albeit not always at their best).

THE WAY OF THE WAVES

It had been, without doubt, the greatest adventure of my life. Except, somehow, I didn't feel like an adventurer: we hadn't stepped off the edge of the known world, we had just got to the end of it. We may have been the first people to complete such a trip with boards and bikes but, really, I didn't care.

I was just a bloke who wanted to go surfing, was fed up with driving and furious that a doctor had tried to write him off. I had nothing and everything to prove.

The climbs, rain and sleepless nights – listening to Christina Aguilera and her mariachi band – only served as a reminder that I was capable of things I never thought possible, that the hills didn't last forever and that it was only me who could tell me when to stop.

Lizzy and I hugged, and cried, holding on to each other. We had learnt a lot about each other over the miles, had lived different lives and had loved it. Freeing ourselves from social conventions, obligations, possessions and responsibilities had been liberating and allowed us to live as our authentic selves. We answered to each other and no one else. That, for me, was wonderful – even though we didn't always see eye to eye – and showed me that kindness was everything in times of crisis. All it took sometimes was patience, especially when patience was wearing thin. No matter what the 'way of the waves' threw at us, we got through it together. We deserved, at the very least, a flipping certificate.

Lizzy wiped her eyes, laughing. There was no need to say any more. We would go over it later. We looked at each other and then turned to our friends. We hugged them, a cork was popped and, together, we downed a bottle of champagne they had brought for us.

It tasted good.

Tavistock to Sagres in numbers:

- Kilometres ridden: 3400
- Vertical metres climbed total: 29,875
- Vertical metres France: 7837

THE LAST MILES

- Vertical metres Spain: 14,800
- Vertical metres Portugal: 7238
- Days to reach Sagres: 77
- Nights under canvas: 64
- Nights in chalets: 8
- Nights in hotels: 4
- Nights in a youth hostel: 1
- Ferries: 7
- Transporter bridges: 2
- Punctures: 6
- Broken spokes: 15
- Bike shop visits: 6
- Falls: 3
- Near misses with cars: too many to count
- Zips (closed and opened): 3000 (at least)
- Revolutions of the knee: 1.2 million (roughly)

We rode into Sagres and checked into the campsite where we had booked a chalet for the four of us.

The following day we went to the beach. The wind was howling, blowing cross offshore at Tonel, one of the most popular surf spots in Sagres. The high red sandstone cliffs offered a little shelter, making it the only choice for any kind of rideable surf that we could cycle to. The waves were ragged and difficult to read, but still surfable. A couple of surf schools had claimed their territory with flags while some of their students were getting rolled around in the whitewater. Others were catching waves and standing briefly, big smiles on their faces. There were a lot of other surfers in the water, some of whom were learners, others who could surf well. Tim and I were somewhere in the middle. I caught a few waves but spent a lot of time paddling around, trying to get my position right. Lizzy and Jo paddled out too. Being in the water with them felt wonderful. I smiled to myself between rides. The waves weren't perfect, but so what? There would be other days.

Lizzy and I stripped out of our wetsuits and went back into the water with our bellyboards, where the waves were a bit smaller. The shore break was perfect for bellyboarding. The waves were punchy and fun, breaking in water that was about chest deep, with some peeling nicely into the shallows. They pushed us towards the shore with a whoosh, swirling and spitting behind us while we hooted and laughed. Our rides finished on the beach, our swimming costumes filling with sand.

This was what surfing meant to me: companionship and community, adventure and freedom, without ego or expensive equipment. We were riding waves how the *tontons* had ridden their half-boards, coffin lids,* *planckys* and *txamperos* in Biarritz, Santander, Galicia, Carcavelos, Newquay and Bude. These simple wave-riding craft had started it, for me, for Doc Sweet, João Luís Moraes Rocha and others. If we looked further back we'd get to Hawaii, and children riding prone on *papa paepo'os* made from breadfruit or *Paulownia* wood.

It all made sense. The journey had taken us on an amazing adventure to discover something we already knew: that surfing with friends is better than surfing alone, that it is something more than sport and that it doesn't matter how you do it. The learner gets as much joy, if not more, than the seasoned pro looking to find the next big thing. Surfing brings people together and people's lives become intertwined because of it. The history of surfing lies within all of us.

The 'way of the waves' gave me a new perspective on old ways and taught me that travelling in a different way can make the familiar seem unfamiliar (and saves a shitload of carbon dioxide and money), that being joyful is better than being angry and that paddling away from conflict felt better (and stronger) than staring it down.

Yes, so surfing is changing, and has changed a great deal since our surfing forefathers set off to find their surfing Shangri-Las in Europe, but the joy of riding waves will always be the same. Who are we to deny others the same pleasure? If surfing can bring people closer to nature, make them think about the impact they have on the world, or inspire them to act when it comes to the environment, then everyone should have a piece of it. It is up to us to make sure the joy doesn't wear. There is no place for localism, selfishness

---

* In Cornwall some people rode coffin lids. A local coffin maker also made bellyboards.

or violence in surfing. We are bigger than that, and the sooner we appreciate the good guys and forget the false idols, the better. They do nothing for us.

Whether it's 2 or 20 feet, surfed on a bellyboard, a longboard or a shortboard, in our own backyard or someone else's, it is up to us to make surfing whatever we want it to be.

Epilogue

Home

'As far as surfing is concerned, the late '60s to the late '80s were the golden years, no question about that. My generation is the blessed generation. We had the best waves; we had the freedom because we had nothing. As far as I am concerned, we had the best of the best and we were lucky that we could just go off and it was all new.'

INTERVIEW: MARTIN WARD, 2024

After two nights in Sagres we strapped the boards to the roof rack of our van, packed down the trailers and strongboxes and crammed them into the roof box with our panniers, and cycled 35km into the Algarve city of Lagos while Tim and Jo drove. Heading east, we entered the western Algarve, passing through Salema, Burgau and Luz. The further we got from the western coast, and away from the cool north-west wind, the hotter it got. At Salema, a beautiful village on the coast with swanky restaurants on the seafront, we stopped to swim and absorb the dying moments of the trip. It felt good to ride without the trailers but I missed creating a spectacle: they had become an extension of us and what we stood for.

In Lagos, we stayed overnight in an Airbnb and rejoined the holidaying masses, swimming at one of the beaches, eating on the street and wandering around the busy lanes of the old town. Now we had the space, I bought a shirt for the journey home and we both bought bracelets made from the links of a bike chain, to remind us that cycling and surfing had brought us as much adventure as we had ever had.

We left Tim and Jo in Lagos to get the train to Faro and headed north in the van. By this time we had used up 80 of our 90 days in the Schengen area so had a few days to revisit some of the places we loved and to find some that we had missed. We took a couple of days to surf our way up the coast of Portugal and made our way to Galicia, where we surfed some of the beaches we had bypassed. We met up with Jesús Busto and his wife Helena in Doniños and bumped into some friends from home at a tiny beach in the middle of nowhere at the end of one of Galicia's wild peninsulas.

It was easy to jump back behind the wheel but it didn't feel the same as cycling. I missed the dust and the smells and seeing everything in close-up and at a speed that enabled me to take it all in properly. We were insulated behind the windscreen as everything whizzed by in a blur. We stayed at some beaches where there were a lot of campervans and felt like we were running with the crowd. Being on the bikes had felt like we were running against it.

Of course, I also loved being in the van again. I liked being able to carry (and cool) enough food for a few days, cook with an induction hob, go to the loo whenever I wanted, sleep in a decent bed and cover ground quickly, but it still felt a little soulless.

A few days before we were due to leave Spain, Lizzy's father, who had enjoyed a long and interesting life, died suddenly at age 94 after a brief illness, with her sister and brother (and his favourite nurse) by his side. Lizzy thought about flying home but it would have made no difference so, with nothing to do other than wait for the ferry, we parked up at Playa de Frejulfe, a small beach in Asturias backed by a beautiful pine forest, while she phoned home and I had my last surf of the trip. For once, surfing felt superficial: a frivolity to use up time.

Real life was bearing down on us like a juggernaut.

We boarded the ferry with a day to spare of our 90 and settled in for the 24-hour journey home. Standing on deck as the boat eased out of Santander, we took our last looks at the city, its beaches and the mountains behind. We were happy to have completed our trip – the sense of achievement was profound – but incredibly heavy-hearted that we were leaving Europe and that we would be returning to something of a maelstrom. We stayed on deck for as long as we could, watching Spain as she disappeared into the misty, late-afternoon sunshine. We were looking forward to seeing friends

EPILOGUE

and family and our house, but, with funeral arrangements to make, the immediate future was uncertain.

Being back was difficult. Lizzy spent time contacting distant family and went back to work, picking up where she had left off three months earlier. The first week was an overwhelming, emotional whirl, and the novelty of being back soon wore thin. Dealing with the small stuff – broken dishwasher, the piles of clothes and bills – and the big stuff – family, funeral, life and death – left us wanting to set off again as soon as possible. I can see why people get on their pushbikes and never come back.

Life is hard. Cycling and surfing are simple.

This trip changed Lizzy and me, in small ways, but not so much that we would sell everything and set off around the world with nothing but bikes and boards. If anything, it taught us that time is precious. Why waste it being afraid? We planned more trips in the van, but always with ideas for bike rides we wanted to do along the way. We talked about where we wanted to cycle next. Would it be surfing and cycling around Ireland's 3000km Wild Atlantic Way? Bellyboarding around Brittany? Or California? New Zealand? Now we had done it, anything seemed possible. We planned a trip to Cape Wrath, the most north westerly point of mainland Britain, that would see us take our ebikes on a small ferry across the Kyle of Durness, overnighting on a tiny beach where the only building is a bothy.

When it came to work, and writing up this book, I tried out a 'Spanish style' work day by starting early, taking a (very) long lunch break to surf or swim, and then working later into the evening, when the tides allowed. When the weather favoured it, I cycled to work, taking the long way home along the cliffs and down quiet bridleways to wring out every drop of being on my bike. It never failed to make me smile and to think of the hard but happy miles we had put in on this trip.

We even had a go at sorting out some of our stuff. But, inevitably, real life caught up and we drifted back into routines and bad habits. I had a hernia operation – whether it appeared because I sat on my bike for days on end is hard to say, but losing weight made it obvious I should deal with it – that forced me to be inactive for weeks. Then a good friend of ours, a kindred spirit, surfer, ecologist and all-round good egg, Jeff Cherrington, died of a heart attack just before Christmas 2024. It rocked us, and made us realise that we *really* had to cherish every moment: we had to get back on our bikes.

A week later I had a panic attack that crushed me. Lizzy called the paramedics. My back, neck and chest were so tight I felt I couldn't breathe, a result of being inactive while recuperating and spending too much time internalising it. My heart was fine, of course, but it was another sign that I needed to get back on the metaphorical and physical bike. It took weeks to recover mentally, and to deal with the health anxiety that caused it. As soon as I felt like me again, Lizzy and I went for a cycle. It reminded me, when I needed it most, that riding a bike can make everything feel better.

Eventually, in the spring, we loaded up the van with boards and bikes and headed off to Scotland. It felt good to be moving again, and even better when we rode our bikes for miles along the Union Canal or in the Galloway Forest, swam in outdoor pools or surfed in new places. We found uncrowded surf on a beach in the Borders and enjoyed a rare session of beautiful, small and clean waves in freezing water. It made me think of the first-generation surfers I had interviewed and met along the way and how fortunate they were to have lived at a time when you could find empty waves almost anywhere in Europe. They had, when all is said and done, experienced a truly golden age.

But we had it good too.

Meeting those first-generation surfers, and those who had made it their life's work to live near the surf, was a privilege. There was something truly special about them; a sparkle in their eyes that betrayed the collective secret they all held in their hearts: the glide is everything, but when the swell has passed, it is nothing but a memory. Sliding down walls of water offers surfers like us moments of clarity that serve no purpose and cannot be found anywhere else, yet give meaning to our lives.

There is no doubt that being a pilgrim on the 'way of the waves' left me wanting more. I loved living outside and facing adversity, which, when I think about it, felt like a kind of freedom I had only ever experienced a few times before. A few drops of rain, putting up a tent, blowing up an air bed, climbing a steep hill and navigating traffic were simply obstacles to be overcome, not reasons to stay at home.

All we had to do was keep pedalling.

Surfing glossary

Barrel A wave that forms a tube.
Barrel-ride Riding inside the barrel of a wave.
Bottom turn A turn done at the bottom of a wave to change direction and move up it again. It is one of the most fundamental moves in surfing.
Cut back A manoeuvre to turn back towards the 'pocket' of a wave (the breaking part) to stop the surfer from outrunning the most powerful part of the wave.
Dropping in When a surfer drops into a wave. Or when a surfer drops in on a surfer who is already surfing a wave, so ruining the ride for them. It is considered very bad manners and is often the cause of conflict.
Foamie A soft-top surfboard.
Frothing Eager to get waves.
Glide Riding a wave in perfect harmony.
Green wave A wave that is unbroken.
Grom A young, keen surfer. Usually frothing.
Hitting the lip Allowing the bottom of a surfboard to hit the cresting part of a wave to use its intense power to bring the board around and to drop in to the wave again.
Hosed Beaten up by the waves.
Kook A hopeless beginner surfer.
Line-up Where surfers wait, beyond the breaking waves, for waves to ride.
Malibu board Malibu surfboards are generally considered today, to be over 2.7 metres (9ft) in length. They are named after the style of board developed at Malibu in the 1950s.

Nose rocker An upwards curve on the front (nose) of a board to stop the board from bogging or pearling.
Over the falls To go over with the breaking lip of the wave. It's not a good move – a bad mistake!
Pearling Going over the front of your board when you take off too late or when the nose of your board digs in. It is named after the act of 'pearl diving' – going straight to the bottom.
Pocket The part of a wave that is steepest, where the curl forms a tube or pocket.
Pop-out A kind of plastic surfboard that was mass produced.
Rip A current.
Rocker A curve in a board to allow it to turn or to avoid pearling.
Soft top A surfboard that has a top made from soft foam. Safer for learning.
Soup Broken waves.
Stoked Being high from the chemicals delivered to the brain and body when surfing.
Tow surfing Catching waves with the aid of a jet ski. Usually reserved for the realm of big waves that are impossible to catch by paddling.
Trimming Riding along the unbroken part of a wave perpendicular to the shore.
Tube riding Surfing in the hollowest part of the wave that creates a tube.
Washing machine Being tumbled about underwater by breaking waves, usually after falling off.
Whitewater Broken waves.
Yulex A type of natural rubber used in some wetsuits.

References

surfers have a 50 per cent bigger carbon footprint than the average person: Schultz, Tobias, C., 'The Surfboard Cradle-to-Grave Life Cycle Assessment of a Common Surfboard: Epoxy vs. UPR', [Master's thesis] University of California, Berkeley

The surf media published a piece about Tobias's work: Everard, Sophie, '10 Ways to Plan a Sustainable Surf Trip', *Wavelength*, 24 March 2023: wavelengthmag.com/10-ways-to-plan-a-sustainable-surf-trip/

in an article about the research: Meagher, Patti, 'Think globally, surf locally', UC Berkeley Engineering, 5 October 2010: engineering.berkeley.edu/news/2010/10/think-globally-surf-locally/

'the environmental costs of surfing': Ibid.

Wiliwili, an indigenous hardwood: 'Big Tree: Wiliwili', Department of Land and Natural Resources, Division of Forestry and Wildlife: Forestry Program, Hawaii.gov: dlnr.hawaii.gov/forestry/info/big-tree/wiliwili/

***Surfer* magazine said of Clark's closure**: Housman, Justin, 'Clark Foam's Demise, 10 Years Later', *Surfer*, 11 December 2015: www.surfer.com/culture/clark-foams-demise-10-years-later-grubby-clark

an interview with Viertel: Moreu, David, 'El escritor que trajo el surf a Europa', *La Vanguardia*, 3 June 2021: www.lavanguardia.com/cultura/culturas/20210306/6262895/escritor-trajo-surf-europa.html

De Rosnay had also become the 'French correspondent' for the fledgling surf magazine: *The Surfer*, Vol. 3 No 1, Spring 1962

'After surfing at Chambre D'Amour': Mansfield, Roger and Bleakley, Sam & Power Chris [eds], *The Surfing Tribe* (Orca Publications, 2011)

'In a Santa Monica beach shed': Jaggard, Ed, 'Americans, Malibus, Torpedo Buoys and Australian beach Culture', School of Communication and Arts, Edith Cowan University

'Biarritz in the Bay of Biscay has two beautiful surfing beaches': (2011). Jaggard, Ed, 'From Bondi to Bude: Allan Kennedy and the Exportation of Australian Surf Lifesaving to Britain in the 1950s', *Sport in History*, 31(1), 62–83. https://doi.org/10.1080/17460263.2011.554720

The conditions, as it were, were perfect, as Joël explained in *Surfer* **Magazine in 1962:** *The Surfer*, Vol. 3 No 1, Spring 1962

'It is a real passion. It means friendship, liberty, holidays': *Surfer*, Vol. 5, No. 5, November 1964

The 'Global Surfing Report 2024' [...] estimates, top line, that surfing in 2023 was worth €4.2 billion: Global Industry Analysts, Inc., Surfing – Global Strategic Business Report. Available at: www.researchandmarkets.com/report/surfing

Zurriola is described in 'The Surf Report' from June 1985: *The Surf Report*, Volume 66, June 1985 [updated 1991]

It was a similar story with Félix Cueto: Esparza, Daniel, 'Towards a Theory of Surfing Expansion: The Beginnings of Surfing in Spain as a Case Study', RICYDE. *Revista Internacional de Ciencias del Deporte*, vol. XII, no. 44, pp. 199–215, 2016.

According to an interview with Javier Arteche: Green, B. 'A Paipo Interview with Javier Arteche', My Paipo Boards [blog] Available at: mypaipoboards.org/interviews/JavierArteche/JavierArteche_2012-0114

'brought about by the democratic evolution of the country': Federación Española de Surfing: fesurf.es/historia-fesurfing/

is 'rarely surfed because of steep cliffs fronting the sea and dangerous ripoffs: *The Surf Report*, Volume 66, June 1985 [updated 1991]

Matt Warshaw ... describes the hard to get hold of (I have tried) Sumpter as: Warsham, Matt, 'Rob Sumpter – Surfing Royalty or Royal Scam?', Encyclopedia of Surfing, 13 June 2021: www.eos.surf/joint/sunday-joint-6-13-2021-rod-sumpter-surfing-royalty-or-royal-scam

according to Corky Carroll ... from The Encyclopedia of Surfing: Carroll, Corky, '"The dude was either really sick or really greasy" – Corky Carroll remembers Rodney Sumpter, Encyclopedia of Surfing, 12 June 2021: www.eos.surf/feature/the-dude-was-either-really-slick-or-really-greasy-corky-carroll-remembers-rodney-sumpter

at a remote farmhouse called Casa Lola: pukassurf.com/about

According to Daniel Esparza's essay: Esparza, Daniel, 'Towards a Theory of Surfing Expansion: The Beginnings of Surfing in Spain as a Case Study', RICYDE. *Revista Internacional de Ciencias del Deporte*, vol. XII, no. 44, pp. 199–215, 2016.

I had read a fascinating piece by Alan Bleakley: Bleakley, Alan, 'A Surf Trip With No Surf', *Wavelength*, 6 January 2023: wavelengthmag.com/a-surf-trip-with-no-surf/

a British-made Bilbo in Biarritz: 'HISTORIAS. Félix Cueto. El germen del surf en Galicia', desdelacroa [blog], 3 June 2010 desdelacroa.blogspot.com/2010/03/historias-felix-cueto-el-germen-del.html

'Portugal's coolest place to holiday': Villa-Clarke, Angelina, 'Is Comporta Portugal's Coolest Place To Holiday?', *Forbes*, 7 March 2024: www.forbes.com/sites/angelinavillaclarke/2024/03/07/comporta-is-this-portugals-coolest-place-to-holiday/

'good selection of breaks': Francis, Joseph Richard, 'The Ultimate Guide to Vila Nova de Milfontes Surf', *The Surf Atlas*, 9 October 2023: thesurfatlas.com/surfing-portugal/vila-nova-de-milfontes-surf/

'Try your luck, but as ever it's your cheekbone!': Ibid.

Resources

Films and TV programmes
The Endless Summer (Dir. Bruce Brown, 1966) – A film about chasing the sun that inspired a generation
Gidget (Dir. Paul Wendkos, 1959) – The movie that brought surf culture to the masses in the USA
The Big Sea Documentary (Dirs. Lewis Arnold and Chris Nelson, 2023) – A film about cancer and neoprene thebigsea.org/
100 Foot Wave (HBO 2021)

Books
All For a Few Perfect Waves: The Audacious Life and Legend of Rebel Surfer Miki Dora, Davind Rensin, (Yellow Jersey, 2017)
Los orígeness del surf en Galicia, Jesús Busto, (Libros del Océano, 2023)
The Islander: Further Adventures of Lom Lombard, Surfing Super-Stud, Bez Newton (HarperCollins, 1978)
The Natural, Bez Newton (HarperCollins, 1978)
The Surfing Tribe, Roger Mansfield and Sam Bleakley (Orca Publications, 2011)
The Stormrider Guide: Europe www.stormrider.surf/

Websites
La Vélodyssée: www.cycling-lavelodyssee.com/
Camino de Santiago: http://caminoways.com/camino-de-santiago

Apps
Buen Camino – App with details of all the caminos, available on Apple and Android.
Komoot – Cycling app for wayfinding, available on Apple and Android.

Acknowledgements

Lizzy, for being my cycling buddy and the love of my life.

Tim Bates and everyone at Peters Fraser + Dunlop, my agent, for believing in this project.

Charlotte Croft, Megan Jones, Lucy Doncaster and all at Bloomsbury, for also believing.

Sam Chivers, for the cover that makes me want to set off all over again.

Ana and Teresa at The Caravan and Motorhome Club, for helping us with campsite bookings.

Nikki Nichol, for setting us up with insurance and encouragement.

Leigh at Ride It Bude, for the bikes, spare spokes and advice.

Andy, for getting our gear home safely.

Nick and Abi, Howard and Laura, and their families, for putting us up.

Tim and Jo, for the driving.